Assess for Success

Assessment, Evaluation and Reporting for Successful Learning

A Resource Booklet
Published by
the Educational Services Committee 1993

Authors

Dale Midwood
Frontenac Secondary School
District 20, Kingston

Ken O'Connor
Program Department, Scarborough Board of Education
District 16, Scarborough

Marilyn Simpson
Sir Frederick Banting Secondary School
District 4, London

Editor and Director — Resource Booklets

Kevin Crouse
Ancaster High and Vocational School
District 36, Ancaster

Cover Design

Gail Smith
Central Technical School
District 15, Toronto

Desktop Publishing

Claire McMillen
Newtonbrook Secondary School
District 13, North York

I.S.B.N. # 0–920930–60–3
Ontario Secondary School Teachers' Federation
60 Mobile Drive
Toronto, Ontario M4A 2P3

Revised: July 1994

Written *by* educators *for* educators

Sponsored by

OSSTF's Educational Services Committee

EDUCATIONAL SERVICES
OSSTF/FEESO

Companion Volumes

Assess for Success is the companion volume to King and Peart's research report *The Numbers Game*. In *Assess for Success* the authors have tried to address the issues raised by the research and provide practical strategies for teachers. Educators interested in the references to the research in this resource book and in the research base should refer to *The Numbers Game, OSSTF (1994)*.

Table of Contents

Acknowledgments

Dale Midwood would like to acknowledge the support of

- the staff and students of the Frontenac County Board of Education, especially the staff of Frontenac Secondary School, Kingston, Ontario (District 20)
- Judy, Sydney-Leigh, Katharine and Jonathan
- Frank and Mary; Dave and Maureen

Ken O'Connor would like to acknowledge

- the support of the staff of the Scarborough Board of Education, especially the Program Department
- the influence on his thinking about assessment provided by Lorna Earl and Rick Stiggins
- the encouragement and support provided by his family — Marilyn, Jeremy and Bronwyn, and by Peter Lipman

Marilyn Simpson would like to thank

- Gary and Maya for their continued support and encouragement,
- the staff at OSSTF (60 Mobile Drive) for their ongoing assistance during the month of July, and
- the educators of Ontario who continue to strive to provide high quality learning environments in their schools and classrooms

Preface — To the Teacher

> "evaluation is the most difficult part of my job ...; it requires more thought and energy than anything else because I really want to make sure that I am doing it (assessment/evaluation) to the best of my ability and that they (the students) are deserving of the evaluation they receive."
>
> *(Teacher quote in King and Peart, **The Numbers Game**, Chapter 3.)*

> "Success occurs when opportunity meets preparation."
>
> *(Schurr, **The ABC's of Evaluation**, 1992, p. 10.)*

These two quotations provide an excellent summary of the authors' beliefs about assessment and evaluation — it is very complex, but, carried out with care and quality, assessment can — and should — **promote learning and student success**.

This book is meant to be useful to the classroom teacher; it should make assessment better, and, eventually, easier and faster. The latter two won't occur immediately, but should happen in time as teachers apply the principles and use the practices outlined in the book. Don't try to do it all at once — start with one or two new approaches. Don't try to do it alone — work collaboratively with other teachers who are trying to "Assess for Success".

There is a huge quantity of information available about student assessment. This book is not the "be all and end all" — it contains the ideas on what is important in student assessment that three teachers were able to compile in the summer of 1993. The objective of the book is to provide helpful (philosophical and practical) information in the hope that teachers will become reflective practitioners in the area of student assessment. Please start — or continue — this journey; it will lead to greater success for students and greater personal and professional satisfaction.

Dale Midwood, Ken O'Connor, Marilyn Simpson

The Power of Assessment

If you wish to appear accountable, test your schools.

If you wish to improve schools, teach teachers to assess their students.

If you wish to maximize learning, teach students to assess themselves.

(Stiggins, Workshop presentation, May 1993.)

Introduction

This book is the fourth produced or sponsored by OSSTF on the subject of student assessment and evaluation in a period of just over 20 years. An examination of the content of each of these four books provides insight into how thinking about assessment has evolved over those twenty-plus years.

Objective Testing was published in 1971. It is a slim volume of 40 pages which was apparently written to help teachers fill the gap left by the end of the Grade 13 examinations in Ontario. It contains brief sections on Principles and Types of Tests but over fifty per cent of the book is about measurement — how to interpret and manipulate the numbers that come from testing.

Student Evaluation ... The Bottom Line was published in 1981. It is a larger book of some 75 pages. Many aspects of assessment and evaluation were covered in the book but none were examined in great depth. While a broad view of assessment and evaluation is put forward, and a considerable variety of approaches are mentioned, the emphasis appears to be on meeting Ministry requirements and establishing and following policies. About twenty per cent of the book deals with the statistical aspects of assessment.

Making the Grade — Evaluating Student Progress was first published by the Etobicoke Board of Education in 1985 and then, with the sponsorship of OSSTF, was republished by Prentice Hall in 1987. It is a large book consisting of some 272 pages. This book was very successful and had a major impact on assessment practices in Ontario. The authors described the relationship between educational objectives and the evaluation of student progress but the main feature of the book was the focus on assessment approaches used in the classroom. Most of the assessment techniques described in detail were paper and pencil procedures — tests, examinations and projects and the modifications that could be made to these procedures for exceptional students and for different levels of ability.

Assess for Success continues the changing emphasis seen in the first three books. As is evident from the title, the focus of this book is that assessment should be used to improve student success. This was stressed in *The Bottom Line* and *Making the Grade* but the emphasis is much greater here. The distinguishing characteristics of this book are

- the emphasis on a set of guiding principles,
- detailed descriptions of a broad range of assessment techniques, emphasizing performance assessment, personal communication and self-assessment,
- significant information on grading and reporting practices, and
- many ideas about organizing students for success.

This book is based on the beliefs that assessment is an integral part of teaching and that good teaching is good teaching regardless of grade, ability or level of instruction. There are sections of the book on specific subjects and special needs students, but for the most part the principles and practices described in the book apply to all subjects in secondary schools. (It is perhaps worth noting that while this book is primarily designed for teachers of Grade 9 to OAC (Ontario Academic Credits), the principles and practices can be applied from kindergarten to university.)

The major responsibility of teachers is to encourage and develop successful learners, but King and Peart's research *(The Numbers Game)* shows that to meet this responsibility there is a need for some changes in instructional and assessment practices.

The experience in other provinces in Canada, especially Alberta and British Columbia, and in the U.S.A. with the emphasis on external examinations and/or standardized testing demonstrates clearly why teachers in Ontario must strive to do a better job of assessment and evaluation — to keep the focus of student assessment where it should be — in the hands of the classroom teacher. This book should help teachers to do this.

The 'clients' of the school system want to know

- what is being done in school classrooms,
- why it is being done, and
- how well it is done.

In general, schools do a fairly good job of answering the first question; with the increasing emphasis on outcomes, better answers are being given to the second question; improved assessment and evaluation practices will lead to better answers to the third question. This book should help teachers to provide those better answers about student learning.

"Assess for Success"

(Source unknown.)

Chapter 1
Context

Context

To be able to make worthwhile suggestions about how assessment should be carried out in schools, it is essential to examine the characteristics of the society and the education system within which one operates. This contextual setting includes the changes which are or will likely be occurring in society, changes in our knowledge about learning and the strengths of the education system and challenges it faces. These three factors are leading to an educational "paradigm shift" which has significant implications for instruction and assessment.

Change

The one constant that most futurists talk about is change. It is widely acknowledged that continuing change will be the norm well into the next century. Changes are occurring at a rapid pace in every aspect of life; we have moved from a so-called "industrial age" to an "information age". We have also moved from a world of separate nations with some super-national groups to a true "global village".

The labour market for unskilled students continues to decline and so there is no longer a clear continuum along which students can be sorted — some to the unskilled labour market, some graduating from high school directly to work and some going to post-secondary institutions. Now, many more students must graduate and be able to be competent contributors to (a radically changing) society.

This globalization has been accompanied by an emphasis on the ideals of quality and continuous improvement. *(See Holt, 1993.)* A very significant result of this emphasis has been a broadening of the skills which the business community says are needed in employees. (The Conference Board of Canada Employability Skills Profile provides an excellent example of what the business community believes about needed skills (see page 12)). This profile can also be seen as a life-skills profile. Associated with the emphasis on quality has been a demand for accountability, especially of public institutions and governments. Another part of the change mixture has been a demand for equity, i.e. fair (or fairer) treatment for all regardless of socio-economic status, ethnicity, religion, age or gender.

Knowledge about Learning

There have been many developments in knowledge about learning over the last few decades. "Educators and researchers have become knowledgeable about, and have demonstrated the importance of, such things as learning styles, brain theories, developmental stages, and multiple intelligences. This knowledge contributes to the continual reshaping of what and how educators teach."

*(Scarborough, **Guiding Principles: Student Evaluation**, 1992, p.9.)*

Employability Skills Profile: The Critical Skills Required of the Canadian Workforce (Business Point of View)

Academic Skills	Personal Management Skills	Teamwork Skills
Those skills which provide the basic foundation to get, keep and progress on a job and to achieve the best results	The combination of skills, attitudes and behaviours required to get, keep and progress on a job and to achieve the best results	Those skills needed to work with others on a job and to achieve the best results
Canadian employers need a person who can:	Canadian employers need a person who can demonstrate:	Canadian employers need a person who can:

Academic Skills

Communicate
- Understand and speak the languages in which business is conducted
- Listen to, understand and learn
- Read, comprehend and use written materials, including graphs, charts and displays
- Write effectively in the languages in which business is conducted

Think
- Think critically and act logically to evaluate situations, solve problems and make decisions
- Understand and solve problems involving mathematics and use the results
- Use technology, instruments, tools and information systems effectively
- Access and apply specialized knowledge from various fields (e.g., skilled trades, technology, physical sciences, arts and social sciences)

Learn
- Continue to learn for life

Personal Management Skills

Positive Attitudes and Behaviours
- Self-esteem and confidence
- Honesty, integrity and personal ethics
- A positive attitude toward learning, growth and personal health
- Initiative, energy and persistence to get the job done

Responsibility
- The ability to set goals and priorities in work and personal life
- The ability to plan and manage time, money and other resources to achieve goals
- Accountability for actions taken

Adaptability
- A positive attitude toward change
- Recognition of and respect for people's diversity and individual differences
- The ability to identify and suggest new ideas to get the job done — creativity

Teamwork Skills

Work with Others
- Understand and contribute to the organization's goals
- Understand and work within the culture of the group
- Plan and make decisions with others and support the outcomes
- Respect the thoughts and opinions of others in the group
- Exercise "give and take" to achieve group results
- Seek a team approach as appropriate
- Lead when appropriate, mobilizing the group for high performance

(This document was developed by the Corporate Council on Education, a program of the National Business and Education Centre The Conference Board of Canada, 255 Smyth Road, Ottawa Ontario K1H 8M7 Telephone: (613) 526–3280 Facsimile: (613) 526–4857.)

Two areas of knowledge about learning are particularly worthy of attention as we look toward implications for assessment — the theory of multiple intelligences and ideas about metacognition.

Multiple Intelligences

This concept has been developed by Harvard University psychologist, Howard Gardner. He believes that all normal individuals are capable of at least seven different and independent forms of intellectual accomplishment. In other words, according to Gardner, humans don't have one overall intelligence, but at least seven distinct ones: linguistic, logical-mathematical, spatial, musical, bodily-kinesthetic, interpersonal, and intrapersonal. We each possess all seven, though one or more may be stronger than others. This tendency toward greater strengths in certain intelligences over others makes a difference in many areas of our lives, from the things that interest us both in school and out and to our career choices.

Spotting the Seven Intelligences

Linguistic Intelligence involves ease in producing language and sensitivity to the nuances, order, and rhythm of words. Students who exhibit linguistic intelligence love to read books, write and tell stories. They have good memories for names, places, dates, and trivia.

Logical-Mathematical Intelligence relates to the ability to reason deductively or inductively and to recognize and manipulate abstract patterns and relationships. Students who excel at math, have strong problem-solving and reasoning skills, and ask questions in a logical manner exhibit this intelligence.

Spatial Intelligence is the ability to create visual-spatial representations of the world and to transfer those representations mentally or concretely. Students who exhibit spatial intelligence need a mental or physical picture to best understand new information; do well with maps, charts, and diagrams; and like mazes and puzzles. They can design, draw, and create things.

Musical Intelligence includes sensitivity to the pitch, timbre, and rhythm of sounds, and responsiveness to the emotional implications of these elements. Students who remember melodies or notice pitch and rhythm exhibit musical intelligence. They tend to be aware of surrounding sounds.

Bodily-Kinesthetic Intelligence involves using the body to solve problems, create products, and convey ideas and emotions. Students who exhibit bodily-kinesthetic intelligence are good at physical activities and have a tendency to move around, touch things, and gesture.

Interpersonal Intelligence refers to the ability to work effectively with other people; to understand them; and to notice their goals, motivations, and intentions. Students who thrive on co-operative work, have strong leadership skills, and are skilled at organizing, communicating, mediating, and negotiating exhibit this intelligence.

Intrapersonal Intelligence entails the ability to understand one's own emotions, goals, and intentions. Students who exhibit this intelligence have a strong sense of self, are confident, and often prefer working alone. They also have good instincts about their strengths and abilities.

*(**Instructor**, July/August, 1992, pp 48–49.)*

According to the Multiple Intelligence theory, children who are not strong in certain domains can improve — they just need to use their "best" intelligences first. This is important because Gardner says that intelligences almost never operate in isolation. The implication for instruction is that teachers need to broaden the strategies they use to fit the intelligences (needs) of a wider range of students. This means that teachers need to collaborate across departments. It also means that **assessments must be developed to gather information about all of the intelligences not just the linguistic and logical-mathematical intelligences which are usually the focus of school assessment**.

Monitoring Multiple Intelligence Strategies

Date: _____   Name/Class: _____

Record each time you practice or I teach using a different intelligence. Let's try to give examples.

Linguistic: _____

Visual: _____

Logical/Mathematical: _____

Body/Kinesthetic: _____

Musical/Rhythmical: _____

Interpersonal: _____

Intrapersonal: _____

* Did you have a preference for any intelligence or any combination?

* Were you surprised by any aspect of this record?

* What is your plan to expand your thinking?

(Costa et al, 1992, p. 29.)

Metacognition

Knowledge about, awareness of, and control over one's own mind and thinking is referred to as metacognition. Research in reading, in particular, has clearly indicated that being able to monitor our own learning is critical to being able to learn, e.g. to learn to read the learner has to be able to identify what the problem is, and what to do about it if reading skill is going to improve. This is equally true for mathematical and physical skills. The Elements and Levels of Metacognition are set out in the figures below.

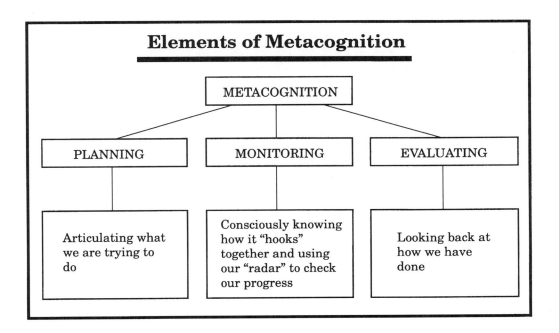

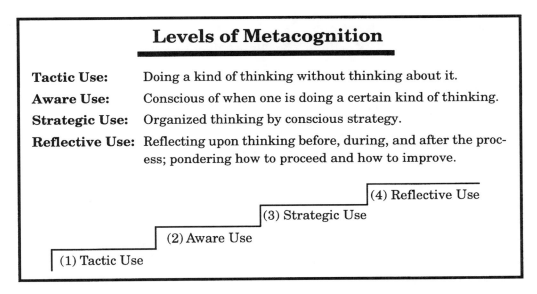

(Costal et al, 1992, p. 11. (based on Swartz & Perkins))

The result of this knowledge about metacognition is that there must be much greater emphasis on self-assessment; only by helping students to evaluate their own learning will students be able to become truly successful learners. This is well illustrated in a surprising source — an Ann Landers column *(**Toronto Star,** June 20, 1993.)*

> **A Lesson From My Crazy Dad**
>
> It's raining, it's pouring
> My homework is boring, and
> In walks my father from a
> Hard day's work.
> "Dad, I don't understand my math."
> "Wait," he says —
> He takes off his jacket.
> "Let me take a look," he says —
> He does it wrong, and in many
> Painstaking steps.
> "No, dad, not like that," I say —
> After about an hour of theoretical
> Explaining and arguing and
> Frustration
> With his ignorance, I realize —
> I really like my father — and I know
> My math much better than I thought.

Teachers should teach students (and parents) to ask questions like "What are you doing?", "Why are you doing it?", and "What would you do differently next time?".

For further ideas about self-assessment see *The Mathematics Teacher*, Vol. 85 No. 8, November 1992, pp. 636–637 and National Council of Teachers of Mathematics, *Assessment in the Mathematics Classroom, 1993 Yearbook*, pp. 230–236.

Significant Aspects of Ontario Education

There are many aspects of Ontario's education system which need to be noted when directions in assessment are being considered. King and Peart's research *(The Numbers Game)* provides a comprehensive picture of the state of assessment and evaluation in Ontario.

Ontario's education system has a number of strong features such as

- *inclusivity:*   duration of formal education and the percentage of the population who attend university are among the highest in the world.

- *equality of opportunity:*   there is great emphasis on the provision of ESL and Special Education programs.

- *gender equality:*   unlike many other countries, more females than males are now completing secondary school and attending universities.

- *broad range of electives:* choice is provided for students so that the emphasis is on educating the whole child. Schools have also taken on the responsibility for awareness education in a broad range of social issues, e.g. drugs, AIDS, environmental concerns, etc.

- *extensive extra-curricular programs:* drama, music, sports and a huge variety of clubs are an important part of the school experience. (It is worth noting that all these activities are led by teachers who volunteer and are not paid for this extra activity); and

- *internal evaluation:* since the elimination of the "departmentals" or Grade 13 examinations in 1968, assessment and evaluation in Ontario schools has been done almost entirely by classroom teachers. These assessments have been supplemented by Board and Ministry program evaluations such as OAC T.I.P. and Provincial Reviews.

There are also a number of major challenges facing Ontario education; some of the most significant are as follows:

- *lack of curriculum focus:* OS:IS was introduced in 1984, but before it has been fully implemented and evaluated, significant changes have been imposed with the destreaming of Grade 9 and the introduction of The Common Curriculum.

- *heterogeneous student population:* there is a wide variety of student backgrounds in Ontario; schools have done a good job of absorbing large numbers of people from different cultures but the degree of heterogeneity is, and will continue to be, a challenge.

- *staff development:* in the face of massive changes in society and in education very few resources (time or money) are provided for staff development. At the very time when more and better staff development is needed, the Ministry and school boards are drastically cutting the people, time and money for practitioner education; and

- *structural aspects:* little opportunity has been provided for meaningful communication between elementary schools and secondary schools and between secondary schools and post-secondary institutions. Organization by departments in secondary schools and by division in elementary schools has also hindered communication.

The "Paradigm Shift" in Education

The societal changes, the development in knowledge about learning and the "state" of education in Ontario means that the "rules" have changed. This sort of drastic change is often referred to as a "paradigm shift". The paradigm shift in education has been characterized in a number of ways; J.J. Bonstingl in *Total Quality Measurement*, pp. 83–85, describes it as from "Teaching and Testing" to "Teaching for Continuous Learning and Improvement"; Rick Stiggins talks about the old era of "sort and select" and the new era of "competency" *(Reinventing Assessment, workshop presentation, 1993)*; Dean Fink, former Superintendent, Halton Board of Education, refers to it as the change in focus from Intelligence to Mind. He lists the characteristics of the two views in this way:

Knowledge is a function of:	
Intelligence *(Old View)*	**Mind** *(New View)*
1. distributed on normal curve	1. capacity for thoughtfulness is widespread
2. immutable	2. ability can be modulated by experience and instruction
3. association between levels of intellect and group membership	3. multiple intelligences
4. some knowledge culturally more important	4. applied learning
5. learning is sequential	5. learning is uneven as we develop qualitative understanding
6. individual activity	6. thinking and learning are social activities
7. artisans use tools; thinkers use their intelligence **(learning to know)**	7. thinking occurs in conjunction with resources **(learning to do)**

These new ways of looking at the purposes of education have profound implications for school cohesion, curriculum, teaching/learning strategies, assessment and evaluation, student support services, school organization and partnerships (school/board/Ministry/business).

One of the most important issues involved in this paradigm shift is that of **standards**. As a society we (profess to) care a great deal about standards but we show very little understanding of them. Standards (e.g., those provided by external examinations) are generally perceived to be "good" and some (e.g., those provided by internal examinations) are perceived to be "not so good" while in fact the opposite may be true.

For example,

    (i) where norm-referenced standards are used the performance of all students might be poor but those who did the best will receive high marks even though their performance was poor;

(ii) 50% is generally considered a pass mark but for some critical outcomes it is insufficient; and

(iii) hitting the ball successfully three times out of ten is considered very good in professional baseball (four times out of ten is exceptional) but scores like that on a test in school are considered failures even though some learning, and maybe even considerable learning, has occurred.

In the new paradigm criterion-referenced standards must be emphasized because our concern is competency, not lining students up on a continuum. Wiggins stated the issue very clearly in his article "Standards, Not Standardization: Evoking Quality Student Work" in the February 1991 edition of *Educational Leadership*:

"a standard offers an objective ideal, serving as a worthy and tangible goal for everyone — even if, at this point in time, for whatever reason, some cannot (yet!) reach it." *p. 21*

"our schools must no longer accept token efforts judged by variable criteria. We must expect quality from every student based on models of outstanding performance." *p. 18*

"A school has high standards when it has high and consistent expectations for **all** learners in **all** courses." *p. 24*

The clear messages in these ideas are

(1) that the criteria for student performance must be clearly stated and available to all, and

(2) that students must be provided with models or examples of high standards. As Stiggins says, "students can hit any target that they can see clearly and which stands still for them."

In order to have high standards and the clearly articulated criteria which make the standards meaningful, we must have a very clear vision of what we want students to be able to do. It is this need for clarity of focus which has led to the emphasis on outcomes. In the past we have emphasized objectives and these tended to focus on what teachers would do rather than on what students actually can do.

Outcomes can be described as the observable results of the knowledge, skills and values that students have acquired. Outcomes describe what students should know, should be able to do and should value as a result of their learning experiences. Vital to an understanding of outcomes is the idea that students have to **demonstrate** their learning. This idea has been further developed by Theodore Sizer in his fascinating book *Horace's School* where the whole curriculum is built around exhibitions.

One major problem with the focus on outcomes is deciding what the **critical outcomes** are or should be. Lorna Earl suggests that "there is no absolute, immutable list of educational outcomes. The educational outcomes that are valued are inevitably the best judgments of the people in the society, and different people have different visions about what those outcomes should look like."

*(Earl, L., **Research Speaks to Teachers**, Scarborough, February 1993.)*

The diagram below provides one helpful way of identifying what the critical outcomes are. It is clear that there is a future focus in each of the four areas and that the critical outcomes should be where the areas overlap.

What are "Critical Learning Outcomes"?

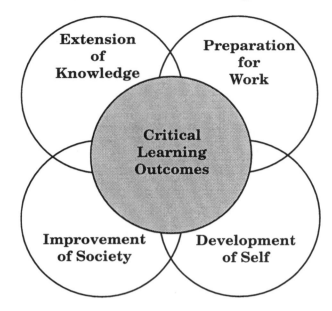

(Gail Rappolt and Burle Summers, Workshop presentation, Sept. 9, 1992.)

It is also clear that the development of the outcomes for a province, board or school must be done collaboratively; input is required from the community as well as from administrators, teachers and students. One example of a set of outcomes which have been developed with considerable community involvement is the outcomes statement for the Waterloo County Board of Education (see page 21).

It can be readily seen how these outcomes can provide a clear focus for all activities within the board or school be they administrative, technical or instructional; all one has to ask is "will it contribute in a meaningful way to one (or more) of the outcomes?"

A potential confusion that needs to be addressed is the confusion between outcomes and "outcome-based education" (OBE), the approach being proposed by the educational sociologist, Bill Spady. Outcomes as described and defined above can be used in almost any educational setting but "outcomes-based education" as formulated by Spady has very clear characteristics and principles.

Spady calls the three main trends in outcome-based design and delivery models traditional OBE, transitional OBE and transformational OBE and believes that they represent the evolution in thinking about outcomes from the micro to the macro level. The distinctions are important because how we structure curriculum, assessment and instruction will be a direct result of which one of these models we support.

Traditional OBE: In this model, outcomes are defined as micro-level instructional objectives derived from existing curriculum. Their focus is usually mastery of subject-based content and specific course-level skills and applications, and the context for traditional outcomes is the individual classroom or course. The proponents of traditional outcomes know that different students will take more or less time

Learning Outcomes for Students of
The Waterloo County Board of Education

Global

An informed and caring world citizen who:

- evaluates and responds to social, economic and political issues in an ever-changing world
- appreciates and respects individual, cultural and political differences among all peoples
- acquires the knowledge and acts responsibly to improve the global environment
- analyzes and adapts to technological change in an interdependent world

Relationships

A sensitive, caring person who:

- interacts from a positive perspective in all roles and relationships
- displays respect, trust, loyalty, honesty and dependability in relationships with all others
- employs all forms of communication in an open, active and effective manner
- supports and co-operates with others as a partner, friend, team-member and colleague
- promotes the growth, development and pursuit of excellence in self and others

Work

A quality conscious, productive worker who:

- adapts to change in positive, innovative ways
- works productively in both collaborative and independent ways
- works in a responsible and ethical manner
- exhibits a work ethic that includes pride and satisfaction in the quality of work
- values the diversity and dignity of all work

Learning

A life-long, self-directed learner who:

- initiates and sustains learning based upon goals, trends, values and interests
- acquires, analyzes, synthesizes and communicates information individually and collectively to solve problems and achieve life goals
- applies knowledge, skills and attitudes to achieve one's personal best

Citizenship

An informed and involved citizen who:

- embodies ethical, moral and law-abiding behaviours
- identifies and evaluates the issues and needs of the community and responds in a co-operative, caring manner
- undertakes actions which balance the rights of self and others
- volunteers service and resources for the benefit of the community

Culture

An active participant in the culture of Canada who:

- understands our national heritage
- respects the diverse multicultural nature of our country
- takes responsibility for our emerging culture
- pursues the arts, recreation and leisure activities to enrich all aspects of life

Personal

A happy, wise and caring individual who:

- applies critical, flexible and creative thinking
- uses ethical values throughout one's life
- takes responsibility for one's personal well-being
- sets realistic goals and strives to achieve one's personal best

Mission Statement — Empowering life-long learners who strive for excellence in a changing world.

to reach the outcomes; hence, flexibility is built into instruction so that students have more than one chance to improve their performance. Even with this flexibility, the curriculum and the students' actual accomplishment is constrained by the traditional school organization and timetable. Traditional OBE is not very different from current practice.

Transitional OBE: Transitional OBE is different from traditional OBE largely in scope and purpose. Those who support transitional OBE are talking about a fundamentally different kind of outcome — they identify outcomes that reflect generic, higher order competencies that cut across subjects — things like critical thinking, problem-solving and effective communication skills. Subject content becomes the vehicle to assist in the cultivation of these higher order competencies. With this conception, the whole curriculum is available for students to acquire the skills and there is much more flexibility in how and when students reach the outcomes. All programs and/or subject areas address the same underlying competencies and these are the outcomes of significance for students in school, to be taught and to be assessed.

Transformational OBE: Spady's third model, the one that he has developed most recently, he calls transformational OBE. This is the one that could dramatically change the face of education as we know it. Transformational OBE steps outside all of the given structures of schooling and asks some very basic questions about the purpose of the educational system and how it should operate. It is premised on three questions:

> What are the conditions that our students will face in the future when they are assuming various roles in their adult lives?
>
> What skills, knowledge, strategies and attitudes will they have to have to be successful in those future contexts?
>
> What learning experiences will facilitate their accomplishment?

None of the prevalent features, programs or structures of schooling are assumed to be inherently appropriate or useful and, if they don't support the crystal ball outcomes, they are abandoned and replaced. Schools won't necessarily be the place where learning occurs, credits will be tied to learning not time, subjects may be unnecessary, the school day and the school year become meaningless organizers and assessment will be demonstrations of these outcomes of significance in real life settings. This kind of outcomes-based education is revolutionary."

*(Earl, L., **Research Speaks to Teachers**, Scarborough, Feb. 1993.)*

There is considerable confusion about outcomes and outcomes-based education but it would appear that outcomes offer the probability of providing a useful focus for schools which will serve our students well. It is necessary, therefore, that we begin to design the curriculum, instruction and assessment requirements of this focus whichever of its formulations we choose to follow. To this end, the following models and planning sheet should be helpful. The Instructional Model focuses on alignment between outcomes, instruction and assessment and the necessity of linking information from assessment back to instruction and outcomes. The Teaching Model provides one way that schools and teachers could put the broader model into practice, while the Unit Planning sheet brings the process to the classroom level.

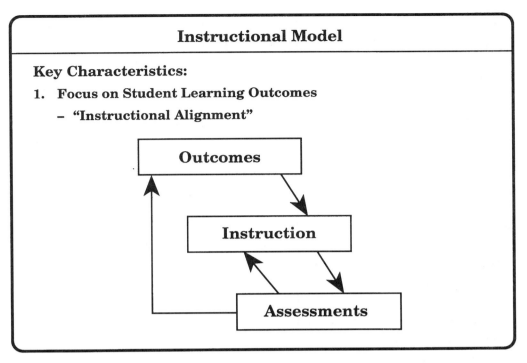

(Fitzpatrick, Kathleen, Workshop presentation, May 1993.)

The Teaching Model For Each Unit

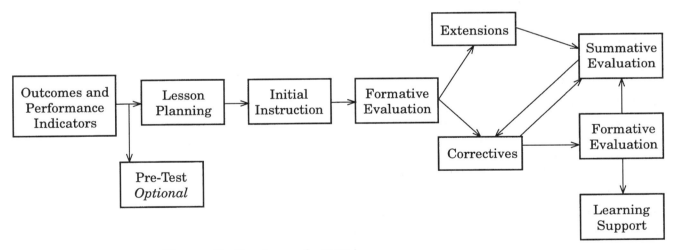

(Baxter, G., Scarborough, 1993.)

Implications for Assessment

Changes in our society, in our knowledge about learning and in our concepts of what education is and how it is or should be organized and focused have profound implications for assessment and evaluation. These implications are well summarized in the following charts; the first two are general in nature while the third concentrates on what aspects of assessment in mathematics need increased and decreased attention.

Unit Planning Sheet

Page ___

UNIT TITLE: _____

Outcomes: 1.

2.

3.

Indicators	Assessment/Evaluation	Instructional Strategies	Resources
1.1			
1.2			
1.3			
2.1			
2.2			
2.3			
3.1		Remediation Strategies	Enrichment Strategies
3.2			
3.3			

(Gerrard, D., Scarborough, 1993.)

Assess for Success

School-Based Curriculum Planning
Shifting Paradigms
Assessment and Evaluation Approaches

THEN	NOW
Student is assessed on the ability to recall detailed facts	Student is assessed on the application of skills, the demonstration of broad understandings and values, and critical thinking
Standardized tests	Assessing to standards
Measurement	Assessment and evaluation
What is correctly recalled	What is done well, understood conceptually and is of value
Ranking	Accomplishment
Norm-referenced	Criterion-referenced
Quantity and rank	Quality and progress
Learning growth seen as a comparison among students with grades and marks to rank	Learning growth seen as a comparison to learning outcomes
IQ number	Multiple intelligences

Woodall, Dave, School-based Curriculum Planning Paradigms, Workshop Presentation Notes, 1993

Shifting Paradigms in Mathematics Assessment

Increased Attention	Decreased Attention
✧ Assessing what students know and how they think about mathematics	✧ Assessing what students do not know
✧ Having assessment be an integral part of teaching	✧ Having assessment be simply counting correct answers on tests for the sole purpose of assigning grades
✧ Focusing on a broad range of mathematical tasks and taking a holistic view of mathematics	✧ Focusing on a large number of specific and isolated skills organized by a content-behaviour matrix
✧ Developing problem situations that require the applications of a number of mathematical ideas	✧ Using exercises or word problems requiring only one or two skills
✧ Using multiple assessment techniques, including written, oral, and demonstration formats	✧ Using only written tests
✧ Using calculators, computers, and manipulatives in assessment	✧ Excluding calculators, computers, and manipulatives from the assessment process
✧ Evaluating the program by systematically collecting information on outcomes, curriculum, and instruction	✧ Evaluating the program only on the basis of test scores
✧ Using standardized achievement tests as only one of many indicators of program outcomes	✧ Using standardized achievement tests as the only indicator of program outcomes

(National Council of Teachers of Mathematics, 1989, p. 191.)

Many of the ideas on the right side of these charts have been addressed in some detail above or later in this book but in summary it would appear that the main implications for assessment are:

- the focus of assessment should be on what students are able to do directly. Many of the outcomes that we now recognize as vital cannot be effectively assessed by paper-and-pencil tests (see chart below from Gronlund and Linn); so, we must increase the use of demonstrations of student achievement. These demonstrations or performances should also reflect as much as possible, real life situations, i.e. they should be "authentic";

- students must be provided with second chances that provide them with the real opportunity to demonstrate that they have achieved an outcome after receiving feedback and reteaching following a first effort that was less than satisfactory;

- assessment must be seen as an integral part of the teaching/learning process. It must be seen as a collaborative venture with students to improve their learning and to help them demonstrate what they have achieved.

Outcomes Requiring Evaluation Procedures Beyond the Typical Paper-and-Pencil Test

Outcome	Representative Behaviours
Skills	Speaking, writing, listening, oral reading, performing laboratory experiments, drawing, playing a musical instrument, dancing, gymnastics, work skills, study skills, and social skills.
Work habits	Effectiveness in planning, use of time, use of equipment, use of resources, demonstration of such traits as initiative, creativity, persistence, dependability.
Social attitudes	Concern for the welfare of others, respect for laws, respect for the property of others, sensitivity to social issues, concern for social institutions, desire to work toward social improvement.
Scientific attitudes	Open-mindedness, willingness to suspend judgment, sensitivity to cause-effect relations, an inquiring mind.
Interests	Expressed feelings toward various educational, mechanical, aesthetic, scientific, social, recreational, vocational activities.
Appreciations	Feeling of satisfaction and enjoyment expressed toward nature, music, art, literature, physical skill, outstanding social contributions.
Adjustments	Relationship to peers, reaction to praise and criticism, reaction to authority, emotional stability, social adaptability.

(Reprinted with permission. Gronlund and Linn, 1990, p. 176.)

References

Barker, Joel A., <u>Future Edge, Discovering the New Paradigms of Success</u>, 1992, Morrow, New York.

Bonstingl., John J., <u>Schools of Quality, An Introduction to Total Quality in Education</u>, 1992, ASCD, Alexandria, VA.

Costa, A., Bellanca, J. and Fogarty, Robin, <u>If Minds Matter, Volume II</u>, 1992, Skylight: Palatine, IL.

<u>Educational Leadership</u>, November 1992, Improving School Quality.

Gronlund, N. and Linn, R., <u>Measurement and Evaluation in Teaching</u>, 1990, Macmillan: New York.

Holt, Maurice, "The Educational Consequences of W. Edwards Deming", <u>Phi Delta Kappan</u>, January 1993, pp. 382–388.

<u>Instructor</u>, July/August, 1992, pp. 48–49.

<u>Mathematics Teacher</u>, Vol. 85 No. 8, November 1992, pp. 636–637.

National Council for Teachers of Mathematics, <u>Assessment in the Mathematics Classroom, 1993 Yearbook</u>, 1993, Reston, VA.

National Council for Teachers of Mathematics, <u>Curriculum and Evaluation Standards for School Mathematics</u>, 1989, Reston, VA.

Sizer, Theodore R., <u>Horace's School; Redesigning the American High School</u>, 1992, Boston, Houghton Mifflin.

Stiggins, Richard J., "Assessment Literacy", <u>Phi Delta Kappan</u>, March 1991, pp. 534–539.

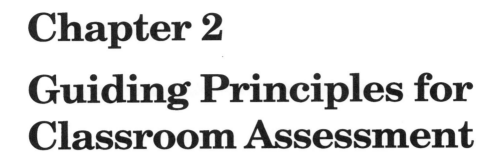

Chapter 2
Guiding Principles for Classroom Assessment

Guiding Principles for Classroom Assessment

Assessment should be an integral part of teaching and learning. Teaching for successful learning cannot occur without high quality student assessment. In order to obtain quality assessment it is desirable that boards and schools have a set of "Guiding Principles" which provide the assessment and evaluation expectations which educators should follow. These Principles should encourage the use of appropriate techniques and make practices more consistent.

It is important to note that the emphasis here is being placed on **principles not policy**. Principles incorporate parameters which should be adhered to, but within such parameters considerable flexibility should be allowed for variability in teacher practice. Policies, on the other hand, are usually much more rigid and allow for little flexibility. Since assessment is a complex interpersonal activity and not a clinical scientific process, some flexibility is desirable.

Principles

The Principles which follow draw heavily on *Principles for Fair Student Assessment Practices for Education in Canada,* 1993, Edmonton Joint Advisory Committee and Scarborough Board of Education, *Student Evaluation: Guiding Principles*, 1992. They are also consistent with the comprehensive evaluation standards developed by the National Council of Teachers of Mathematics — see NCTM, Commission on Standards for School Mathematics, *Curriculum and Evaluation Standards for School Mathematics*, 1989, pp. 189–248, especially pp. 193–204.

A. General

1. Student assessment should be humane.

Pratt, 1991, p. 86 states that "the first order of priority should be humanity. He suggests that assessors should consider these questions: "Does it help the learners to thrive and grow as persons? Does it develop learners as social beings? Does it avoid causing unnecessary anxiety, pain, humiliation, or self-doubt?" He concludes that "regardless of how valid and reliable an assessment may be, **if it is inhumane it is inappropriate for use with human beings**."

Some considerations that relate to humanity — and fairness — are

- the condition in which assessment is taking place (e.g. light, temperature, noise, workspace, time, fire drill, etc.);
- the number of characteristics being observed (these should be limited so that observation can be made accurately and so that students have an adequate opportunity to demonstrate the outcome(s) being assessed); and

- the directions provided to students should be clear, complete and appropriate for the ability, age and grade level of the students.

B. Responsibility (Who?)

2. Student assessment should be the responsibility of classroom teachers.

Teachers who work with students should be responsible for developing, in collaboration with students, the assessments that really matter to students. This responsibility should not be given to external assessment(s) which may not measure the actual learning that has occurred (in a given classroom/school). As Stiggins stated so clearly in a 1991 workshop presentation,

> "the assessments that count in terms of student learning and academic self-concept are the assessments that teachers develop or select and conduct in classrooms on a day-to-day basis. ... those are not the assessments that get all the publicity and are reported in the newspapers and to the school board, ... (but) they are the 99.5% of assessments that really make a difference."

C. Standards (How Good?)

3. The standards used for interpreting student assessment results should be consistent with the purposes of the evaluation.

Standards are just reference points for judgments about how well (or how poorly) a student has performed. Teachers use three different kinds of standards — criterion-referenced, norm-referenced and self-referenced. (For more information on these standards see Chapter 8.) These standards can be used by teachers independently or in combination, but their use must fit the purpose. For example, if we are trying to assess how successfully a group of students has achieved a critical learning outcome then a criterion-referenced standard should be used; on the other hand, if we are selecting students, say for post-secondary education, some sort of norm-referencing would be more appropriate.

D. Purposes (Why?)

4. Student assessment should be used for a number of purposes.

"Evaluation is not an end in itself; it is rather a part of the learning/teaching process for both the student and the teacher."
(OS:IS, revised 1989, 7.2.)

Traditionally student assessment has focused on the sorting and selection or ranking of students to place, promote and/or certify. This is still an important function but assessment must also be used to provide feedback to students and parents, to develop self-evaluating individuals, to diagnose specific student needs and to motivate students. Students are and should always be the most important users of evaluation.

5. The purposes of student assessment should be understood by teachers and students.

Teachers should have a very clear understanding of why assessment is taking place when they design, administer and score any assessment procedure. Students should be told why assessment information is being collected and how the information will be used. Students should be involved in the development and application of criteria so that they clearly understand what is being assessed and what constitutes satisfactory/unsatisfactory performance.

E. Evaluating What We Value (What?)

6. Assessment practices should reflect all the valid outcomes (of a unit, course, school or board).

Schools are now expected to provide wide-ranging programs and experiences for students so that they develop not only knowledge but also skills and values which will help them to lead productive and enjoyable lives. It is no longer sufficient to say that we value skills and attitudes but only evaluate knowledge. Everything that is important enough to be included in the curriculum is important enough to assess. "The outcomes schools evaluate and the way schools evaluate them are the ultimate statements about what teachers value in the classroom."

*(Scarborough Board of Education, **Student Evaluation Guiding Principles**, 1992, p. 9.)*

7. Assessment techniques should measure the learning that they are intended to assess, i.e. they should be valid.

Assessment is usually defined as valid if it measures what it purports to measure. The more directly and completely an assessment technique measures the knowledge, skill or attitude being assessed the more valuable it will be in helping teachers make correct and useful inferences about student learning.

It is important to recognize that many assessment techniques measure intended learnings indirectly and by sampling. Knowing this, it is essential that the intended outcomes be assessed as directly as possible; e.g. students' ability to work collaboratively should be assessed, not by a paper-and-pencil test, but by direct observation of their class and group work. Currently the term authentic assessment is often used for assessment methodologies which directly assess the intended outcome.

F. Variety (How?)

8. Student assessment procedures should be varied and consistent with the purpose(s) of the assessment(s).

> "Multiple observations of the child throughout the school year should provide the teacher with an understanding of the whole child."
>
> *(Scarborough Board of Education, **The Primary Log**, 1991, p. 2.)*

Although the above quotation is from a primary education source, it is applicable at all levels of education. The broad range of outcomes that we want students to demonstrate requires that a variety of assessment practices be used in a purposeful manner. It is important that the methods used assess both process and product and achievement in knowledge, skills and values. Teachers have available a wide range of assessment techniques to do this and they should be skilled in developing and using varied assessment methods.

9. **More than one assessment method should be used to ensure comprehensive and consistent indicators of student performance, i.e. to enhance reliability.**

The issues here are consistency and generalizability. If only one assessment method is used, it is quite likely that the result will not be an accurate record of a student's achievement. Pratt states that "there is a law of measurement that reliability increases as a function of the number of observations." *(1991, p. 88)* This increase in reliability occurs because "Use of more than one method will also help minimize inconsistency brought about by different sources of measurement error (for example, poor performance because of an 'off-day'; lack of agreement among items included in a test, rating scale, or questionnaire; lack of agreement among observers; instability across time)."

(Principles for Fair Student Assessment Practices for Education in Canada, 1993, p. 4.)

10. **Assessment methods should take into account the backgrounds and prior experience of students.**

Assessment methods should be free from bias brought about by student factors extraneous to the purpose of the assessment. Possible factors to consider include culture, developmental stage, ethnicity, gender, socio economic background, language, special interests, and special needs. Students' success in answering questions on a test or in an oral quiz, for example, should not be dependent upon prior cultural knowledge, such as understanding an allusion to a cultural tradition or value, unless such knowledge falls within the content domain being assessed. All students should be given the same opportunity to display their strengths.

Content and language that would generally be viewed as sensitive, sexist, or offensive should be avoided. The vocabulary and problem situation in each test item or performance task should not favour or discriminate against any group of students. Steps should be taken to ensure that stereotyping is not condoned. Language that might be offensive to particular groups of students should be avoided. A judicious use of different roles for males and females and for minorities and the careful use of language should contribute to more effective and, therefore, fairer assessments.

(Principles for Fair Student Assessment Practices for Education in Canada, 1993, p. 4.)

G. Frequency (When?)

11. **Evaluation should occur throughout the teaching/learning process.**

Frequent small assessments (diagnostic or formative or summative) are more effective than widely spaced major assessments (e.g. examinations). Many opportunities to demonstrate performance and practice skills contribute to greater success in student learning. They also provide opportunities for feedback to students and parents and information for program adjustments.

H. Modifications

12. Alternate assessment procedures should be used for students with special needs.

Modifications need to be made for some students to ensure the greatest possible understanding of student performance. Modifications may include:

- oral instead of written format;
- individual rather than group administered;
- translation into first language;
- providing additional time; and/or
- permitting the use of a word processor.

I. Communication (Grading and Reporting)

13. Procedures for "scoring" student performance should be appropriate for the assessment method used and be consistently applied and monitored.

Appropriate and consistently applied "scoring" procedures are necessary so that we have accurate, fair and complete records of student performance. Procedures which should be followed include:

- marking schemes or scoring guides should be prepared before an assessment method is used; and
- students should be told how their performance will be scored before an assessment method is used.

14. Procedures for summarizing and interpreting assessment results (i.e. grades and reports) should provide accurate and informative representations of student performance.

Regardless of the appropriateness of the assessment methods used, student performance will not be accurately evaluated if appropriate grading practices and informative reporting practices are not used. Procedures should be developed to ensure that:

- the purposes of student evaluation and the way(s) in which summary comments and grades are developed are understood by parents/guardians and students;

- the meaning of comments and grades are clear to parents/guardians, students, employers and post-secondary institutions. To this end grades should reflect achievement; other student characteristics, such as effort, attitude and participation should be reported separately;

- the results used to produce summary comments and grades should be combined in a way that ensures that each result receives its intended weight or emphasis; and

- interpretation of assessment results are made with due regard to the inherent limitations of the assessment methods used and the collecting and scoring of these methods.

15. Reports should be clear, accurate and informative for the recipients of such documents.

Reports should be part of a communication system which includes meetings, correspondence and telephone calls. Communication with parents and guardians and students provides the opportunity for teachers to provide information on the performance of individual students in achieving the intended learning outcomes and how they could improve their performance. Reports should contain:

- descriptions of the learning outcomes, and
- complete descriptions of the strengths of students and suggestions for improvement.

Practical Approaches to Applying Such Principles to a School or Board

1. A **rating scale** could be used as a diagnostic tool to see where a school, department or a teacher stands in terms of student evaluation and the learning process. The descriptors could be adapted to include any number of Principles.
2. A **checklist** for teachers to discover how their assessment practices fit with the Principles. Again the descriptors could/should be changed to include the most critical Principles in a specific school/department.
3. A **sample** of the assessment and evaluation guidelines and principles adopted for Grade 9 students in 1993–94 by one school in Frontenac County. This statement could be used as a starting point for other schools.

Other useful checklists for reflecting on principles of assessment and current practice can be found in *Saskatchewan Education*, 1991, pp. 38–39 and *Making the Grade*, 1987, pp. 7–8 and pp. 232–234.

Established Evaluation Practices						*Recommended Evaluation Practices*
Infrequent — lengthy periods of teaching are followed by major tests or exams	1	2	3	4	5	Continuous and non-disruptive
Teacher-designed strategies	1	2	3	4	5	Students involved in designing strategies
Teacher as sole evaluator	1	2	3	4	5	Teacher, peer and self-evaluation
Evaluation used to measure student success	1	2	3	4	5	Evaluation used to change curriculum objectives and/or teaching approach, as well as to measure student success
Limited use of evaluation techniques, mainly tests and exams	1	2	3	4	5	Use of a wide variety of evaluation techniques, including observation and checklists
Use of common, group evaluation procedures	1	2	3	4	5	Use of evaluation procedures tailored to individuals as well as to groups
Evaluation criteria not specified and teacher controlled	1	2	3	4	5	Evaluation criteria explicit and collaboratively determined

*(Original developed by Neil Graham; Metropolitan Toronto School Board, **Does This Count**, 1990, p. 4.)*

Teacher Responsibilities Checklist

Assessment	Current Practice			Necessary Action	Review Date	Fully Impl.
	Seldom	Some-times	Often			
Assessment is continuous, co-operative, and comprehensive.						
Students are aware of assessment techniques and criteria before beginning a task.						
The following methods are used in the assessment of student achievement. • checklists • conferences • rating scales • group work • projects • portfolios • independent study • tests • examinations						
Self-assessment is employed.						
Peer-assessment is employed.						
Assessment measures both process and product.						

*(Adapted from **Pro File: An Implementation Planning Guide for English: Intermediate and Senior Divisions**, OME, 1987.)*

Sample Grade 9 Assessment, Evaluation and Reporting Policy

Guidelines for Grade Nine Assessment, Evaluation and Reporting

The reasons for a unique set of guidelines for students in the grade nine program are:

(a) there will be no ability groupings and an 8 credit equivalency will be assigned for successful completion of the complete grade 9 program. The fact that there are no ability groupings demands a fundamental change in evaluation practices.

(b) assessment will reflect that students acquire and demonstrate learning in a variety of different ways.

(c) emphasis will be on continuous assessment. There will be more emphasis on day to day learning and less on final summative evaluation.

(d) a variety of assessment tools and evaluation techniques must be used in order to provide a holistic profile of the student learner.

(e) there will be emphasis on both process and resulting outcomes.

(f) there will be more emphasis on following sound problem-solving skills in developing an answer and less on the "right" answer.

(g) the focus in education is changing to outcome or performance based evaluation.

(h) there will be a common foundation skills component.

(i) a recommendation regarding selection of appropriate year two courses will be made by the teacher on a subject by subject basis by the end of the semester.

As a result of the above considerations, the following principles have been developed for **Assessment and Evaluation of Students in Grade 9 courses**.

1. Evaluation is used to communicate the following:
   a. pre-instructional knowledge, skills, and attitudes
   b. learning in progress
   c. achievement profile
   d. program effectiveness

2. Each student will complete the foundation skills component.

3. Student achievement will be measured against grade nine learning outcomes.

4. A variety of assessment and evaluation techniques will be used in each course. Teachers will inform students of the criteria used in all types of evaluation and, where practical, supply a sample of checklists, marking schemes, test/quiz outlines, etc.

5. Students will show their learning in a variety of ways. Examples include: reports, projects, performances, essays, publications, dem-

onstrations, displays, presentations, tests, examinations (oral, written, practical).

6. Assessment and evaluation will recognize the various abilities of students and, when necessary, help teachers direct students to appropriate remedial or enrichment learning situations.

7. Assessment and evaluation will occur frequently and will emphasize daily participation and progress (process of learning) as well as end-products. Information concerning progress will be reported to the student on a regular basis.

Reporting

1. The overall purpose of reporting is to present an accurate profile of the student as a developing learner. Detailed information will help not only with decisions concerning specific areas that require attention, but also with decisions regarding appropriate future course and program selections.

2. The first indication of student performance below, at, or above stated outcomes will be reported to parents early in the semester and not later than the mid-semester report.

3. Evaluation will be classified according to knowledge, skills, application, and learning behaviours.

4. Anecdotal reporting will play a significant role in student assessment and evaluation.

5. Reporting will focus on student knowledge, skills, attitude, and effort in each subject so that a clear learner profile can be presented. The report will indicate effort and achievement relative to the individual learner profile. Indication as to whether the student is below, at, or above grade nine learning outcomes, and progress related to peers will also be included where appropriate.

6. Reports will be constructed so that each department can fit its information on one 8.5 x 11 sheet.

7. Each successive report will display the evaluation on the preceding report.

8. Reports will be issued three times per semester — early report (week 5), mid-semester report, and final report.

9. Report cards will have a guide that explains the reporting system to parents and students.

*(Adapted from **Staff Handbook**, Frontenac Secondary School, 1993, Section 8.1.)*

References

Metropolitan Toronto School Board, <u>Does This Count</u>, 1990.

Ministry of Education (Ontario), <u>Pro-File: An Implementation Planning Guide for English: Intermediate and Senior Divisions</u>, 1987.

<u>Principles for Fair Student Assessment Practices for Education in Canada</u>, 1993. Edmonton, Alberta, Joint Advisory Committee (Centre for Research in Applied Measurement and Evaluation, 3–104 Education Building North, University of Alberta, Edmonton, Alberta, T6G 2G5).

Scarborough Board of Education, <u>Student Evaluation Guiding Principles</u>, 1992, Scarborough.

Chapter 3
Organizing for Successful Learning

Organizing for Successful Learning

> "The truly educated person is the one who has learned how to learn and how to change."
> *Carl Rogers (1969)*

Study Skills

Success in learning is too frequently gauged (only) by success in evaluation. Other than the influence of the teacher, students' success in evaluation is very closely related to their attitudes, their methods of learning, and their study skills. For many students, success in learning and in evaluation depends particularly upon how they study. Because studying is such an important skill for success in learning, it must be taught and practiced and re-taught. Teachers should not assume that study skills have been taught in previous years or in other subjects.

*(**Making the Grade**, 1987, p. 44.)*

The relationship between self-esteem and how well a student does in school is a strong one (for more information see *The Numbers Game*, King and Peart, Chapter 5). The fact that a strong study skills program can not only help a student learn more successfully but can also raise his/her self-esteem are two very strong arguments for the inclusion of study skills in the curriculum.

The research on study skills quite clearly shows that there are a number of considerations that need to be addressed to provide a successful study skills program.

1. Teachers who believe in study skills should be the people to begin study skills in a school.

2. Study skills should be incorporated into the core curriculum.

3. Base teachers (teachers experienced in study skills) should train other teachers through in-servicing.

4. Study skills should be introduced as early as possible and continue throughout the grades.

5. Teachers need to become aware that retention is related to feelings of success and satisfaction — study skills can help students achieve greater success and satisfaction.

6. The most critical study skills to be taught at the high school level are:
   - Time management
   - Listening skills
   - Taking notes
   - Organizational strategies

*(M. Simpson, K. Hiebert, S. Buchner, K. Stapleford, **Summary of Research Findings on Study Skills**, May 1992, unpublished paper.)*

Study Skills of Incoming Grade Nine Students

A Case Study

Kevin Crouse, Principal of Mount Albion Public School and Ancaster High School, discovered that Intermediate Division students were particularly deficient in test-taking, learning from texts and note-taking skills. He gleaned this information from assessing 120 Grade 7 and 8 students and 255 Grade 9 students by using the *hm Study Skills Inventory*. In both schools, students experienced similar difficulties. This inventory, which is self-scoring, allows students to construct graphs of their strengths and weaknesses in the Study Skills area. Once students became aware of their deficiencies, they were much more receptive to instruction in this area. By concentrating on students' weak areas in a year-long instructional program, Kevin secured a 25% increase in literacy skills and a 43% increase in numeracy skills at the Grade 8 level. Literacy skills were determined by the number of "S's" on interim reports. Numeracy skills were assessed by using the "All students will …" column of the Grade 9 Ontario Benchmark program.

Values Underlying the hm Study Skills Program

1. Study skills are problem solving methods.
2. Study skills are learned by doing.
3. Study skills instruction must allow for trial and error experiences.
4. Study skills instruction must be integrated into the regular curriculum.
5. Study skills development involves learning about one's own learning style.
6. Study skills offer the potential for transfer of learning.
7. Study skills must be developmentally appropriate for learners.

Ancaster High and Vocational School

Grade 9 Cohort
October 1993

Student Skills Inventory Results
Sample (255)

Skill	Aggregate Score	Average Score	
		Raw	*Percent*
(1) Test-taking	4074	16.0	64%
(2) Reading from Textbooks	4097	16.1	64.4
(3) Note-taking	4223	16.6	66.4
(4) Memory	4434	17.4	69.6
(5) Listening	4454	17.5	70.0
(6) Organization	4563	17.9	71.6
(7) Vocabulary	4585	18.0	72.0
(8) Motivation	4611	18.1	72.4
(9) Problem Solving	4633	18.2	72.8
TOTAL	**39674**	**17.3**	**69.2**

hm Study Skills materials can be purchased through:

> Paul Ruta
> hm Study Skills Consultant
> c/o 320 Sherbrook Street
> Winnipeg, Manitoba
> R3B 2W6
> 1–204–784–1268.

Materials were developed by the NASSP and the NAESP.

Study skills are methods for solving learning problems. These skills for learning are as basic as any skills teachers can teach. Students learn study skills best by applying these skills. Instruction in study skills must involve the student in an organized curricular program, one that allows for the necessary trial and error experience of learning any new skill. Students need to learn more about their own learning style and learn more about exercising their own choice and judgment during the learning process. Study skills need to be integrated into the curriculum in as many ways as possible and in every subject area. This allows the skills learned to be transferred to other learning situations.

Student activities described in this chapter are only the entry point to further activities and practice in a particular area depending on student needs. It is important that teachers reinforce these skills in all subject areas to ensure that students have learned them and can demonstrate their application.

Study Skills

Foundation Skills

Where Do You Start?

Begin by having students establish their current level of competence. Several examples of helpful checklists have been included on the following pages.

Getting Organized

Students need to understand the importance of coming to class prepared. For each class they should bring the following:

> binder or notebook
> textbook for the class
> pens (more than one colour), pencil, eraser, ruler
> planner (often available from individual schools
>   which includes a calendar, school events, etc.)
> other learning materials necessary for specific classes

Students also need to understand the importance of coming to class on time and attending regularly to benefit the most from the classroom environment and ultimately to learn successfully.

Teachers may wish periodically to evaluate the extent to which students come prepared to class. This may be done as part of the reporting that takes place in the classroom.

Study Environment

Students need to select one study location with good lighting, a firm chair, and a flat writing surface. Any reference materials, including a dictionary and thesaurus, and stationery supplies need to be kept close by. They should try to eliminate as much as possible any distractions and interruptions such as telephones, radios, and TV sets, and try to study in the same place and preferably at the same time every day.

Time Management

One method that many people use to organize their time is a **schedule**. A **schedule** is a plan that a person creates to determine how he/she wants to spend available time.

Provide students with a variety of schedules that they can experiment with in terms of time management. Many students have a complex day that includes not only school work, but a part-time job, family responsibilities, and, of course, social time with their peers. Students need help to balance their time and to provide quality time for school work and study.

Practical Worksheets

1. Study Skills — Personal Work Habit Inventory

Read each sentence and decide how it applies to your work habits. Place a checkmark in the column that best describes your work habits. You need not share this inventory with your teacher or friends unless you wish.

Date: _____

	Very Seldom	Usually	Always
1. I plan my study time …			
2. I know exactly what the assignment is …			
3. I can find a good place to study …			
4. I keep my homework up to date …			
5. I keep my mind on my work …			
6. I keep my study equipment in order (pen, paper, notebook, etc.) …			
7. I listen attentively in the classroom …			
8. I can follow directions …			
9. I get my assignments in on time …			
10. I take part in class discussions …			
11. I ask questions when I am not sure of something …			
12. I review class notes as soon as possible after class …			
13. I begin preparing for a test several days in advance …			
14. I review lessons previously taught …			
15. I try to make the best grades I can …			

In order to improve your schoolwork, start working on the points you checked in the *Very Seldom* and *Usually* columns. Keep this inventory and re-do it at least once each term or semester.

(***Making the Grade***, 1987, p. 45.)

2. Study Skills — Personal Study Inventory

Read each sentence and decide how it applies to your work habits. Place a checkmark in the column that best describes your study habits. You need not share this inventory with your teacher or friends unless you wish.

SECTION A: CLASSROOM WORK

Date: _____

	Very Seldom	Usually	Always
1. I listen carefully to the teacher and to other students' response ...			
2. I read ahead in the text ...			
3. I make mental notes of important points ...			
4. I check blackboard work against the text ...			
5. I use the dictionary and reference material ...			
6. I ask the teacher for clarification of difficulties ...			
7. I check the timetable so that I am sure to bring the required materials to the lesson ...			
8. I discuss with classmates what has been taught ...			
9. I relate what has been taught to other subjects and to everyday experience ...			
10. I make notes of key points ...			

SECTION B: STUDYING AND HOMEWORK

Date: _____

	Very Seldom	Usually	Always
1. I work in a quiet, well-lit study room whenever possible ...			
2. I turn off or down distracting TV ...			
3. I assemble required materials before I start ...			
4. I work from a timetable to make sure that I will have time to study all subjects ...			
5. I check the wording of each assignment carefully ...			
6. I maintain a systematic review ...			
7. I provide for short vocabulary drills in appropriate subjects ...			
8. I set aside a regular study time each day ...			

SECTION C: READING AND STUDYING A TEXTBOOK   Date: _____

	Very Seldom	Usually	Always
1. I first skim quickly through the headings and subheadings to get an overall sense of the chapter ...			
2. I divide the chapter into sections and read them carefully ...			
3. I use appropriate reading techniques for each section of the chapter, such as first skimming and then reading for detail ...			
4. I look for relationships, connections, and important points ...			
5. I ask myself questions about the content I have finished reading and try to answer them without reference to the text. Then I re-read the text as a check ...			
6. I make a written outline or summary for each chapter ...			
7. I re-read the whole chapter or section rapidly ...			
8. I summarize the main points ...			
9. I use a dictionary or glossary to understand essential words ...			
10. I use the table of contents and index when searching for topics or answers to questions ...			

*(**Making the Grade**, 1987, pp. 46–47.)*

Study Skills: Adult Learners

Returning to School — Some Special Considerations

School Work

Back in the Classroom

1. Resume Your Studying Gradually
2. Set Realistic Educational Goals for Yourself
3. Establish a Pattern of Learning Success for Yourself
4. Expect Gaps in Your Knowledge

Study Skills

1. Determine Your Most Effective Learning Style
2. Exercise, Sleep and Eat Sensibly
3. Increase Your Concentration Span
4. Look for Important Clues
5. Get the Additional Study Help You Need

Time Management

1. Analyze Your Time Honestly
2. Determine Your Priorities
3. Eliminate or Postpone Some of Your Optional or Discretionary Time Uses to Make Time for School

(Sparling, 1985, p. 43.)

(Further information on adult learners can be found in Chapter 7 — Adult Learners.)

Working with Schedules

Have students write down on a weekly schedule everything that they do during the course of **one average week**. Also, write down the time of day of each activity, and how much time it took; then have students use the actual week's activities to **plan** their time.

They should:

- enter "fixed" activities first, e.g. band practice, classes
- then schedule "flexible" ones (including fun activities)
- schedule study time on a daily basis, choosing a time that they are the most alert because we learn much more efficiently when we're alert
- include time to review **all** of the work covered at the end of each day and week

Using Your Schedule: What Happened?

You now have a schedule that you've created for yourself. The next step is up to you. Try to follow your schedule for a week.

At the end of the week, take a few minutes to answer the questions below about how well your schedule worked for you.

1. How much did you follow your schedule? Circle the word or words below that best describe how much you followed your schedule.

   completely   mostly   some   a little   not at all

2. If you followed all or most of your schedule, how did you feel about using it?

3. If you didn't follow much of your schedule, what got in the way of your using it?

4. How useful did you find your schedule?

5. Do you think you will try creating another schedule? Why or why not?

6. Identify your major "time wasters". What can you do about them?

*(Adapted from **hm Study Skills Program**, National Association of Secondary School Principals.)*

Listening and Speaking

Listening and speaking skills are skills through which you communicate and learn with others.

The checklist below describes several good listening and speaking skills. Check each statement which is true for you. Try to improve in the areas you did not check.

Listening and Speaking Checklist

I listen and speak to others the way I would like others to listen and speak to me. ❏

I look at the person with whom I am speaking. ❏

I think about the reason for what I am about to say or what is being said. ❏

I listen to all of what a person is saying before starting to respond to it. ❏

I try to understand what is being said, ask questions, and give my ideas about what is being said. ❏

I ask the speaker to explain information I do not understand and volunteer to explain information which others do not understand. ❏

I take part in the group discussion. ❏

I find out if I should take notes on what is being said by my teacher or group members. ❏

After the discussion, I go over the main points of what was said, if necessary. ❏

---

*(Scarborough, **Scarborough Student Skillsbook, Level 1**, 1989, p. 13.)*

Improving Memory Skills

Students Retain

10% of what they hear

20% of what they see

50% of what they read

90% of what they do

Memory can be categorized as sensory memory (sight, hearing, touch, smell etc.), short-term memory (active, immediate memory system), and long-term memory.

There are a number of ways to improve our ability to remember:

1. *Grouping:* grouping means to organize information so that details are brought together under the main idea or category that connects them.

2. *Visualizing:* visualizing means to see an image or picture in your mind's eye.

3. *Repeating:* repeat information that you want to learn. Be sure to say it in your own words. Even though you've already learned something, go over it one more time. If you say the information aloud, not only are you repeating it, you are also hearing it.

4. *Choosing to remember:* the more you want to learn and know, the more you'll be able to remember what you have learned.

5. Be sure you understand any material you wish to remember.

6. Learn to outline or organize the facts.

7. Select or create key words to represent the facts to be remembered.

8. Take advantage of your memory type, e.g. visual, auditory, verbal, etc.

9. Memorize by using the method most appropriate for the materials to be memorized.

10. Use short practice periods.

11. Use a flash card system.

*(Adapted from **The Reading Edge**, OSSTF, 1987.)*

Mnemonics

Mnemonics is the art of remembering. Mnemonic methods are ways of remembering more efficiently. Three useful mnemonic methods are:

1. **The link method**

   Link each word in a list with the one following it by creating a picture or image in your mind's eye in which you see objects or events representing both words.

2. **Acronym**

   An acronym is a word that is made by taking the first letter from each word that you want to remember and making a new word from all of those letters. Use the letters of the words that are part of your long-term memory to help you recall lists that you are trying to get into your memory.

   Example: **H** uron

   O ntario

   M ichigan

   E rie

   S uperior

3. **Acrostic**

   An acrostic is a sentence that is made by taking the first letter from each word or symbol that you want to remember and inserting another word beginning with that same letter. Construct a sentence that uses familiar words. The initial letter of each word in this "acrostic" should correspond to a word you are attempting to memorize.

   Example: Classifications in biology

King	**K**ingdom
Phillip	**P**hylum
Came	**C**lass
Over	**O**rder
For	**F**amily
Green	**G**enus
Stamps	**S**pecies

   or **K**ing **P**hilip **C**an't **O**perate **O**n **F**rog **G**uts **S**uccessfully.

Memory and Forgetting

Recall after a learning period initially *rises*, and only then declines, following a steeply falling concave curve that levels off.

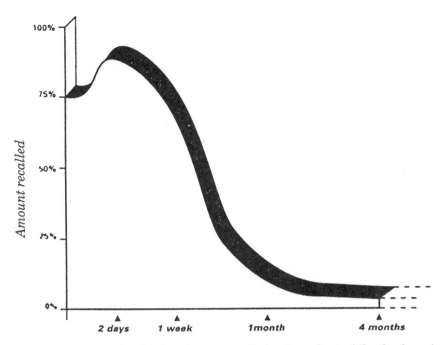

Graph showing how human recall rises for a short while after learning, and then falls steeply (80% of detail forgotten within 24 hours).

*(NASSP, **Hm Study Skills**.)*

Once it is realized that the brief rise does take place, the reason for it can be understood: at the very moment when a learning period is finished, the brain has not had enough time to integrate the new information it has assimilated, especially the last items. It needs a few minutes to complete and link firmly all the interconnections within the new material — to let it 'sink in'.

The decline that takes place after the small rise is a steep one. Within 24 hours of a one-hour learning period, at least 80 per cent of detailed information is lost. This enormous drop must be prevented and can be by proper review techniques.

If review is organised properly, the graph shown can be changed to keep recall at the high point reached shortly after learning has been completed. In order to accomplish this, a programmed pattern of review must take place, each review being done at the time just before recall is about to drop. For example, the first review should take place about ten minutes after a one-hour learning period and should itself take ten minutes. This will keep the recall high for approximately one day, when the next review should take place, this time for a period of two to four minutes. After this, recall will probably be retained for approximately a week, when another two minutes review can be completed followed by a further review after about one month. After this time the knowledge will be lodged in long-term memory. This means it will be familiar in the way a personal telephone number is familiar, needing only the most occasional nudge to maintain it.

(Buzan, 1989, pages 63–64.)

Learning Styles

> "Perhaps, for educators, the major outcome of (this) study is a greater understanding of the need for young people to be treated as individuals by teachers and administrators alike. This means a willingness on the part of educators, in and out of classes, to recognize and accept the differences between young people."
>
> *(King, A., **The Adolescent Experience**, OSSTF, 1986.)*

A great deal has been written about learning styles. OSSTF has published several resource booklets that teachers may wish to use. (See *Learning Styles: 4 Mat Ontario — English, Family Studies, Science, and Business and Technical Studies*.)

The most obvious and necessary benefit of teaching through learning styles is that it increases academic achievement. Numerous studies have shown that students learn more, students learn more easily and students even remember better, when taught through preferred learning styles. Studies also indicate that student attitudes toward schools, teachers, and learning improve when they are taught with their unique characteristics in mind.

*(**Teaching and Learning Styles: Celebrating Differences**, OSSTF, 1986, p. 5.)*

Teachers need to evaluate using a variety of assessment techniques to address the different learning styles of students in the classroom. As students learn more about their own learning styles, they can appreciate more their own strengths and weaknesses around the whole area of assessment and evaluation.

Student Preferences

The Concrete/Sequential learning style prefers:

- field trips organized step-by-step, with a goal
- structured, hands-on materials such as models
- structured demonstration lessons
- simulations that follow the rules
- using step-by-step directions to complete a task
- using concrete materials and following directions

The Concrete/Global learning style prefers:

- optional assignments involving real things
- problem-solving simulations
- open-ended, discovery-type field trips
- learning through trial and error and using real objects
- committee work on real projects
- discovery learning

The Abstract/Sequential learning style prefers:

- lectures, with question and answers in a step-by-step sequence
- audio and/or video tapes in a step-by-step sequence
- almost all textbooks
- presenting logical thought and constructions
- explaining theories through deductive reasoning
- getting the main idea through sequential presentation

The Abstract/Global learning style prefers:

- open-ended think sessions
- group discussions
- allowing think time for reflection before beginning a project or assignment
- allowing students to make intuitive leaps
- using the synthesis process to allow the students to get an "Aha!"
- optional reading assignments

(Hasenstab, 1982.) ***(Celebrating Differences, 1986, p. 56.)***

Learning Styles and Student Evaluation

A schematic representation of some evaluation techniques suitable for the 4MAT system learners:

1. **4MAT Preferences**

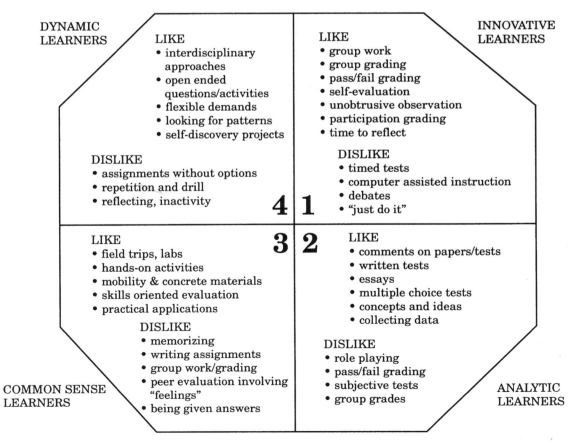

DYNAMIC LEARNERS

LIKE
- interdisciplinary approaches
- open ended questions/activities
- flexible demands
- looking for patterns
- self-discovery projects

DISLIKE
- assignments without options
- repetition and drill
- reflecting, inactivity

INNOVATIVE LEARNERS

LIKE
- group work
- group grading
- pass/fail grading
- self-evaluation
- unobtrusive observation
- participation grading
- time to reflect

DISLIKE
- timed tests
- computer assisted instruction
- debates
- "just do it"

4 1

3 2

LIKE
- field trips, labs
- hands-on activities
- mobility & concrete materials
- skills oriented evaluation
- practical applications

DISLIKE
- memorizing
- writing assignments
- group work/grading
- peer evaluation involving "feelings"
- being given answers

COMMON SENSE LEARNERS

LIKE
- comments on papers/tests
- written tests
- essays
- multiple choice tests
- concepts and ideas
- collecting data

DISLIKE
- role playing
- pass/fail grading
- subjective tests
- group grades

ANALYTIC LEARNERS

*(**Celebrating Differences**, OSSTF, p.68.)*

2. Anthony Gregorc and Kathleen Butler provide some useful evaluation and instruction strategies for the Energic styles approach.

Evaluation Techniques for Gregorc's Energic Styles Model

Concrete Sequential
- workbooks
- handbooks
- lab manuals
- field trips
- ditto sheets
- assembly techniques
- drill
- direct application problems
- work study
- hands-on evaluation

Concrete Random
- independent study
- computers
- games
- simulations
- open-ended problem-solving
- mini-lecture and exploration
- reading assignments

Abstract Sequential
- lectures
- audio tapes
- textbooks/exercises
- supplemental readings
- syllabus
- viewing and answering questions

Abstract Random
- view and respond
- T.V., video, movies
- guided imagery
- assignments with reflection time
- group planning/discussion
- short lecture with question and answer

When the full potential of learning styles theory is realized, it could drastically alter the way we evaluate and report our students' achievement.

(*Celebrating Differences*, OSSTF, 1986, pp. 68–69.)

Practical Worksheets

Classroom Application
A Checklist for Teachers
Affective Learning Styles

Directions: Observable behaviour is a reliable indication of learning style. Observation helps to confirm data from student self-evaluation and/or other diagnostic measures. Remember that many young teens tend to be quite energetic. A kinesthetic style of learning for them may be an adolescent phase, valid for the present. It may be less a part of their style as they move into adulthood.

Students do not have to exhibit all of the traits in one pattern to exemplify that style. A preponderance of traits, or a few that are intense, may be enough to signify learning strength.

Checklist for observing learning styles in students

Auditory Student

____ enjoys listening, but cannot wait to talk

____ is easily distracted by sound

____ reads aloud or subvocalizes

____ talks problems out

____ remembers stories and directions after hearing them

____ hums, talks to self or others

____ enjoys music more than visual arts

____ expressed displeasure by "blowing off steam" but calms down quickly

____ remembers by auditory repetition and saying it

____ may perform rote memory tasks well if "sung" to a tune

Visual Student

____ thinks in pictures, visualizes details

____ is distracted by clutter or movement

____ can plan in advance; writes thoughts down

____ stares or doodles or finds something to look at when inactive

____ is often unaware of sounds

____ remembers by writing things down

____ likes order in appearance, notebook, locker, desk

____ may repress emotion, cry easily, or show emotion through facial expression

____ tends to be a good speller

____ learns by reading or watching demonstrations

Kinesthetic Student

____ drums fingers, taps toes, or asks to leave room frequently

____ gestures when speaking

____ is not attentive to visual or auditory presentations

____ tends to be impulsive

____ selects options with the greatest physical activity

____ reflects emotion through body: stamps, pounds, jumps, hits, hugs

____ pushes hard on pencil, breaks point easily

____ learns by trying things out: touches and manipulates

____ tends to have disheveled appearance because of activity

____ likes sports and games with movement

Left-Brain Learner

____ responds well to verbal information and explanations

____ prefers to talk or write

____ is interested in reward

____ tends to be reflective, analytical

____ likes ordered information: logical, sequential, systematic

____ relies on language in thinking and remembering

____ likes multiple choice items on tests

____ solves problems by logical analysis and systematic solutions

____ is conscious of time, likes schedules

____ can logically explain answers to math (or other) problems

Right-Brain Learner

____ likes open-ended information

____ responds well to demonstrations or symbolic instruction

____ relies on images in thinking and remembering

____ has difficulty with simultaneous number and word concepts

____ likes to draw or manipulate objects

____ has little sense of time; dislikes schedules

____ prefers essay questions

____ solves problems with intuition, playing hunches

____ looks at the whole, rather than details

____ often knows an answer but may not be able to explain why

(Schurr, 1992, pages 146–147.)

Learning

People learn best in different ways. Discover how you learn best.

On the chart below, check, in pencil, the ways in which you learn best. Your teachers will help you.

Strengthen your learning by practising learning in the ways you checked and in the other ways, too.

I learn best by ...	
seeing what I must learn	☐
hearing what I must learn	☐
working with materials	☐
working with other people	☐
experiencing a situation	☐
having to solve a real problem	☐
being creative	☐
having information explained to me	☐
asking questions about a subject	☐
writing information down	☐
reading on my own	☐
looking for answers on my own	☐
discussing with others	☐
discussing with one other person	☐
following instructions	☐
thinking about what I have heard or read	☐
learning from my mistakes	☐

*(Scarborough, **Scarborough Student Skillsbook, Level 1**, 1989, page 3.)*

How Do I Learn Best?

Student Exercise: Basic Learning Style Inventory

Jeffrey Barsch, Ed.D.

Name   _____

School   _____

Grade or Year _____   Date _____

Counsellor/Teacher/Examiner _____

To gain a better understanding of yourself as a learner you need to evaluate the way you prefer to learn. We all should develop a style which will enhance our learning potential. The following evaluation is a short, quick way of assessing your learning style.

This is not a timed test. Try to do as much as you can by yourself. You surely may, however, ask for assistance when and where you feel you need it. Answer each question as honestly as you can. There are twenty-four questions.

When you have finished, transfer each number to its proper place on the scoring sheet. Then, total each of the three columns on that page. You will then see, very quickly, what your best channel of learning is. At that point you will know whether you are a visual, auditory, or tactile (Kinesthetic) learner. By this we mean that you learn best through seeing things, hearing them or through the sense of touch (writing).

For example:

- *If you are a visual learner*, that is, you have a high visual score, then by all means be sure you see all study materials. Use charts, maps, filmstrips, notes, and flashcards. Practice visualizing or picturing spelling words, for example, in your head. Write out everything for frequent and quick visual review.

- *If you are an auditory learner*, that is, have a high auditory score, then be sure to use tapes. Sit in the lecture hall or classroom where you can hear lectures so that you can review them frequently, tape them frequently. Tape your class or lecture notes. After you have read something, summarize it on tape. Verbally review spelling words and lectures with a friend.

- *If you are a tactile (Kinesthetic) learner*, that is, have a high tactile score, trace words, for example, as you are saying them. Facts that must be learned should be written several times. Keep a supply of scratch paper just for this purpose. Taking and keeping lecture notes will be very important.

Discuss the results of this test with your teacher or counsellor. You will develop, through conversation, other helpful ways to study and learn more efficiently. Good luck for a more intelligent study pattern.

Place a check on the appropriate line after each statement.

	Often	Sometimes	Seldom
1. Can remember more about a subject through listening than reading.	_____	_____	_____
2. Follow written directions better than spoken directions.	_____	_____	_____
3. Like to write things down or take notes for visual review.	_____	_____	_____

       Assess for Success

	Often	Sometimes	Seldom
4. Bear down extremely hard with pen or pencil when writing.	_____	_____	_____
5. Require explanations of diagrams, graphs, or visual directions.	_____	_____	_____
6. Enjoy working with tools.	_____	_____	_____
7. Am skillful with and enjoy developing and making graphs and charts.	_____	_____	_____
8. Can tell if sounds match when presented with pairs of sounds.	_____	_____	_____
9. Remember best by writing things down several times.	_____	_____	_____
10. Can understand and follow directions on maps.	_____	_____	_____
11. Do better at academic subjects by listening to lectures and tapes.	_____	_____	_____
12. Play with coins or keys.	_____	_____	_____
13. Learn to spell better by repeating the letters out loud than by writing the word on paper.	_____	_____	_____
14. Can better understand a news article by reading about it in the paper than by listening to the radio.	_____	_____	_____
15. Chew gum, smoke, or snack during studies.	_____	_____	_____
16. Feel the best way to remember is to picture it in your head.	_____	_____	_____
17. Learn spelling by "finger spelling" or writing out the words.	_____	_____	_____
18. Would rather listen to a good lecture or speech than read about the same material in a textbook.	_____	_____	_____
19. Am good at working and solving jigsaw puzzles and mazes.	_____	_____	_____
20. Grip objects in hands during learning period.	_____	_____	_____
21. Prefer listening to the news on the radio rather than reading about it in a newspaper.	_____	_____	_____
22. Obtain information on an interesting subject by reading relevant materials.	_____	_____	_____
23. Feel very comfortable touching others, hugging, handshaking, etc.	_____	_____	_____
24. Follow spoken directions better than written ones.	_____	_____	_____

*(**Barsch Learning Style Inventory**, 1980, Academic Therapy Publications, 20 Commercial Boulevard, Novato, CA 94947.)*

Scoring Procedures

Often = 5 points

Sometimes = 3 points

Seldom = 1 point

Place the point value on the line next to its corresponding item number. Next, add the points to obtain the preference scores under each heading.

Visual		Auditory		Tactile (Kinesthetic)	
No.	*Pts.*	*No.*	*Pts.*	*No.*	*Pts.*
2	_____	1	_____	4	_____
3	_____	5	_____	6	_____
7	_____	8	_____	9	_____
10	_____	11	_____	12	_____
14	_____	13	_____	15	_____
16	_____	18	_____	17	_____
20	_____	21	_____	19	_____
22	_____	24	_____	23	_____
VPS =	_____	APS =	_____	TPS =	_____

VPS = Visual Preference Score

APS = Auditory Preference Score

TPS = Tactile Preference Score

My dominant learning style is _____. Therefore, I learn best by

_____.

How to Use This Information

This form is to be used in conjunction with other diagnostic tools to help you determine some of the ways you are best able to learn. Discuss your scores with someone who is qualified to interpret them in order to make the best use of the time and effort you have invested.

The ideal in terms of overall learning is a score of **32 or greater** in all three learning styles (eclectic method).

- most students tend to show a dominant and a "weak" learning style

- scores **below 24** are considered low and indicate a strong need for the student to foster and develop a learning mode affecting his/her style ... you **can** improve on learning methods through conscious efforts!

Reading Techniques

> Little by little, does the trick.
> *Aesop*

1. Look for organizational points.
   "On the other hand" — the other side of the argument.
2. Summarize paragraphs in your own words.
3. Ask yourself questions and answer them.
4. When you don't understand, go for help.
5. Recite aloud and in your own words.
6. Review.
7. Reflection.
8. Textbooks study method — SQ4R

understanding	**S** Survey	=	look over, glance through
	Q Question	=	ask yourself questions about the chapter
	R Read	=	read carefully to understand
memory	**R** Record	=	highlight and/or make marginal or summary notes
	R Recite	=	recall from memory points that are important
	R Review	=	check through the chapter immediately after reading it, and periodically after that. Devise ways to self-test. Use a study guide if possible.

*(Adapted from **The Reading Edge**, OSSTF, 1987.)*

How to Get More from Your Textbook

1. Begin with a purpose.
   Decide what you want to get out of your textbook.
2. Give yourself assignments.
   Set a goal for yourself above and beyond what the teacher sets.
3. Preview, read, and review.
4. Read, write, and remember.
5. Anatomy of a textbook.
   Title page, copyright page, table of contents, preface, units, chapters, sections, appendix, glossary, bibliography, index.
6. Search for clues in the table of contents.
7. Find things fast in the index.
8. Do a section inspection.
   For new chapters, read the title, skim the whole section.
9. Read first things first.
   Read the first sentence of each paragraph for an introduction of ideas that are to follow.
10. Follow the headings.
11. Investigate words.
    Write them down and learn what they mean.
12. Check lists and outlines.
13. See what's in the boxes.
14. Look at the pictures.
15. Read maps and graphs, charts and tables.
16. Study summaries.
17. Answer the questions.
    Assign yourself the questions at the end of the chapter/section.
18. Look at sources and resources.
    Bibliography, sources, suggested readings.
19. Examine the appendix.
20. Come to terms with the glossary.

*(Adapted from **The Reading Edge**, OSSTF, 1987.)*

Methods of Note-Taking

Notes should always be written in your own words. It is possible to write down word-for-word what is being said or what is in the textbook without being able to recall anything of value. Try to rephrase in your own words so that you are sure that you have thought through what you write.

Assess for Success

A. Outlining

Outlining involves deciding what is the main idea or the theme of the lesson, discussion or reading selection, First, write down, in your own words, the main idea and then follow it with a list of the important details.

Activity 1

Read paragraph 1 and take notes in the outline form in the space provided.

Paragraph 1

> From the 17th century when tobacco was first introduced into Europe, up until the early 1960's smoking was thought of as a harmless activity. However 25 years ago the Surgeon General in the U.S. published a report on smoking that clearly indicated its harmful effects. From that time until the present there has been a growing movement in much of the world to limit the use of tobacco. Smoking is now seen as being the cause of heart disease, cancer and other health problems. Second hand smoke has also been recognized as a problem for non-smokers. This concern has led to the establishment of non-smoking areas in restaurants and the work place.

1. (Main Idea) _____

   A. _____

   B. _____

   C. _____

B. Mapping

This is another good way of organizing information and ideas. This is a particularly valuable technique for students whose learning style is essentially visual. If you have found the outlining method awkward or difficult to use you may find that mapping can help you. Read paragraph 2 and study the map that is shown below.

How to Map

1. Read and study the whole section, chapter or paragraph for which you are taking the notes.

2. Decide on the main point and then write it in the centre of the page — draw an oval around that point or idea.

3. Identify the important, supporting details and write them on lines that connect to the oval you have drawn.

4. Include sub-details as shown in example given. These should be connected to the appropriate supporting detail lines.

Note: You draw the map and make the connecting lines in such a way as to make sense to you. It is your map for your use. If you do this well you will have all the necessary notes ready for your future use.

Activity 2

Read paragraph 2 and take notes in the mapping form in the space provided below.

Paragraph 2

> The air over most modern cities is polluted. It usually contains particles and gases from automobiles, trucks, buses, smoke stacks, and other industrial sources. As many of these pollutants are poisonous, the air we breathe in cities is harmful to our health, in addition to being unpleasant to breathe. On bad days when pollution levels are high, people cough, choke and occasionally faint. Over a period of time polluted air can cause serious respiratory problems, particularly for the elderly and very young. It has been found that this air can also cause allergies, cancer and various lung diseases. Air which is polluted in this way can also hurt plants and reduce the yield from fruit trees and vegetable crops.

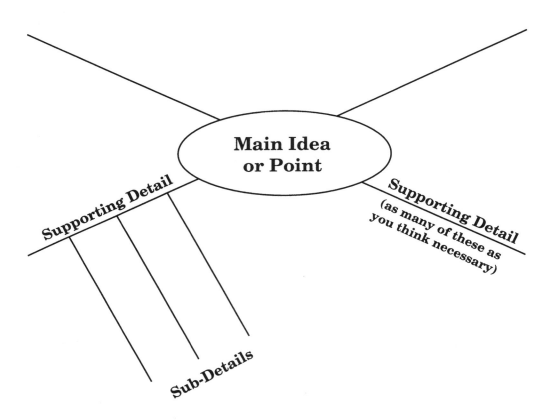

Main Idea or Point

Supporting Detail

Supporting Detail (as many of these as you think necessary)

Sub-Details

*(OSSTF, **The Reading Edge**, 1987, p. 106.)*

C. The Herringbone Method

This method of note-taking makes use of the fact that many ideas or blocks of information can be understood by asking six very basic questions. They are: who? why? where? when? what? and how?

How to Use the Herringbone Method

1. Read through the material you are studying.

2. As you are reading ask yourself the following questions:

   (a) Who was involved? (the answer should provide the name of one or more persons or groups)

   (b) What did this group or person do?

   (c) When was this done? (refer to event discovered in (b))

   (d) Where was it done?

   (e) Why did it happen?

   (f) How was it accomplished?

3. Along the "spine", or centre line, of the herringbone write in the **Main Idea**.

4. Enter the answers to questions (a) to (f) on the "bones" that angle out of the herringbone's "spine".

Note: If it helps to identify more than one answer to questions (a) to (f) then add extra "bones" as necessary. There is no limit to the number of these.

Remember: Your purpose is to make notes that help you to learn.

Activity 3

Read paragraph 3 and make notes on the paragraph using the Herringbone Method.

Paragraph 3

> Millions of years ago, dinosaurs may have walked right through the area where your home is now situated. These huge creatures roamed over most of what is now North America and also other parts of the world. The word "dinosaur" means terrible lizard but they were not lizards and many of them were not terrible. No person ever saw a live dinosaur, because they had died out long before there were people on earth. However, the world of today contains a great deal of evidence that they did exist. In Alberta and many other places their fossils have been found and in California, among other places, their traces have been left in ancient tar pits and rock layers.

(**hm Study Skills Program**, *National Association of Secondary School Principals.*)

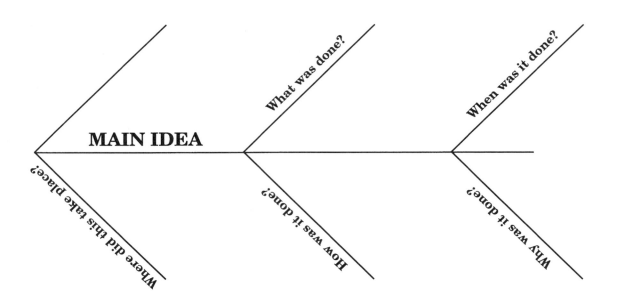

MAIN IDEA

What was done?

When was it done?

Where did this take place?

How was it done?

Why was it done?

Using Abbreviations and Symbols in Note-Taking

One good way to save time when you're taking notes is to use **abbreviations** and **symbols** whenever you can. You can use abbreviations and symbols that are generally accepted, and you can develop your own as well.

An **abbreviation** is several letters taken from a word that are used to stand for that word.

Examples of abbreviations:

word	abbreviation
continued	cont
United States of America	USA
mathematics	math
government	govt

A **symbol** is a letter or marking that is used to stand for a word or words.

Examples of symbols:

word	symbol
with	w
and	&
without	w/o

Student Exercise

Directions: Create a symbol or abbreviation for each of the following words.

1. Canada _____
2. equals _____
3. department _____
4. against _____
5. therefore _____

6. individual _____
7. because _____
8. biology _____
9. information _____
10. that is _____

*(Reprinted with permission. Danyluk, J., **Learning Strategies and Examination Preparation**, Guidance Centre, Toronto.)*

Assess for Success

What to Look for in Note-Taking Skills
Grade 9 English Learning Strands in Note-Taking Skills

Check Where Applicable

Students should be able to

take point-form notes

use orderly, logical short forms

transcribe correctly from board notes

use headings

add missing information to homework notes

correct quizzes/tests

bring notebook to class daily

Check Where Applicable

Students should be able to

generate notes with less teacher direction (teacher may provide headings, guide questions)

make point-form notes from group discussion and brainstorming sessions

summarize information

use key words

re-state key ideas in their own words

Check Where Applicable

Students should be able to

demonstrate independence of skills identified in minimal and medial competence

experiment with the form that best suits the individual learning style

| 5 | 6 | | 7 | 8 | | 9 | 10 |

Numerical Score

Name: _____

Date: _____

(Lester B. Pearson C.I.: An Ontario Transition Years Pilot School, 1992.)

Self Check: How Are You Doing?

The following questions help you survey how you generally approach reading, note-taking and the recall of information. They are intended to increase your awareness of the strengths and weaknesses of your present approach.

	Yes	No	Sometimes
1. Do I read fast enough?	___	___	___
2. Do I preview what I am going to read?	___	___	___
3. Do I ask myself questions as I read?	___	___	___
4. Do I know the difference between important and unimportant information?	___	___	___
5. Do I have a purpose in mind when I read?	___	___	___
6. Do I remember what I read?	___	___	___
7. Do I look and listen for clues regarding what is important in a lecture?	___	___	___
8. Do I have a method for taking notes?	___	___	___
9. Are my notes useful for review?	___	___	___
10. Can I remember details?	___	___	___
11. Do I have a method for memorizing that works?	___	___	___
12. Do I review on a regular basis to retain information I have learned?			

If you answered "no" or "sometimes" to:

- **questions 1–6**, refer to the section on reading
- **questions 7–9**, refer to the section on note-taking
- **questions 10–12**, refer to the section on memory

Writing a Lab Report

This section will help you with writing a lab report.

Follow your teacher's instructions for writing a lab report. The following method may be recommended.

Purpose:

a short statement of why the experiment was done or what problem you were trying to solve.

Apparatus and Materials:

a list of the equipment and materials needed to complete the experiment.

Method (What you did):

a description of the steps followed in doing the experiment. It should be written in sentence form, like this, "The test tube was held over the flame." Personal pronouns ("I" and "We") should never be used. It should be clear enough so that others could copy the method to do the experiment.

Observations and/or Calculations (What you saw):

Facts should be presented in tabular or graphic form, whenever possible. All measurements should include the units used. All calculations should be shown.

Conclusion:

a short statement summarizing the results of your experiment.

Discussion (What you learned):

Try to answer these questions:

- do the results help answer the purpose?
- did this experiment help accomplish the purpose of the experiment?
- are the results different from results reported by others or found in books? If not, how can you discover why? What may have gone wrong with experiment, and why? What caused the error?
- what did you learn from the experiment?
- how might your results be checked by others?
- how can the results be useful to people in their daily lives?

*(Scarborough, **Scarborough Student Skillsbook, Level 1**, 1989, p. 38–39.)*

Orientation to the Library

Station 1: The Card Catalogue

Look up your own last name in the author file.

Do we have a book written by someone with your surname?   Yes: ___   No: ___

If yes: Title of Book _____

Copyright Date: _____

If no, look up the name *Mowat, Farley* and write down the title of one book written by Mowat.

Title: _____

Copyright Date: _____

Look up the **subject** English Literature.

Title of *One* Book on This Subject: _____

Call Number: _____

Station 2: The catalogue of the Public Library is on microfiche.

1. What is a microfiche?

2. What disadvantage does this type of catalogue have when compared with the card catalogue?

3. Look up a subject in which you are interested in the microfiche catalogue of the Public Library. Write down the complete entry for one book.

Station 3: Encyclopedias and Reference

1. Jot down the names of two **general** encyclopedias which we have in the resource centre.

2. Jot down the names of two **specialized** encyclopedias.

3. What other **types** of books are found in the reference section (at least three)?

Assess for Success

Station 4: Magazine or Periodical Section

Browse through two magazines which appeal to you.

1. _____   _____
   Title of Magazine   Date of Issue

2. _____   _____
   Title of Magazine   Date of Issue

Where would you write if you wished to subscribe to one of the above magazines?

Find the Periodical Indexes and see if the magazine is indexed.

Yes _____   No _____   _____
                                         Title of Index

Station 5: Vertical files

Browse through the files to find one which interests you.

_____
Name of File

Remove the file and look through it. Briefly describe the type of information found there (i.e. newspaper clippings etc.)

Station 6: Non-Fiction

Scan the 150 section. Subject covered?

Scan the 400 section. Subject covered?

Scan the 800 section. Subject covered?

Scan the 971 section. Subject covered?

Station 7: Fiction

Go to the fiction section. How are the books in the fiction section arranged?

(G.A. Wheable Centre for Adult Education, London Board of Education.)

Basic Research Strategy

SELECT A TOPIC	**WHAT DO I KNOW NOW?**	• initial experience • exploring situations, experiences • collecting and mulling over ideas • reading • brainstorming • identifying significant characteristics of an object or event • abstracting ideas from an experience
SELECT AND NARROW A TOPIC	**WHAT DO I WANT TO KNOW?**	• differentiating between known and unknown • formulating a research question or hypothesis
PLAN SCOPE AND DIRECTION OF RESEARCH	**IN WHAT WAY COULD I FIND ANSWERS?**	• suggesting a range of reasonable alternatives to answer the question • developing subtopics
LOCATE POSSIBLE SOURCES	**WHERE COULD I LOOK?**	• recognizing direction to be taken in collecting data (libraries, organizations, resource people, computers)
LOCATE INFORMATION	**HOW DO I GET INFORMATION?**	• library research skills, reading, viewing, listening • interviewing skills
IDENTIFY AND RECORD INFORMATION	**WHAT SHOULD I RECORD AND HOW?**	• recognizing relevant ideas • recognizing intent, authority, currency, bias • notemaking
SYNTHESIZE AND DRAW CONCLUSION	**DO I HAVE THE INFORMATION I NEED?**	• analyzing data • assessing which data best answers research question(s) • assessing whether conclusion adequately answers research question
EXPRESS CONCLUSION	**HOW SHALL I PRESENT IT?**	• organizing • writing, speaking, audio-visual presentation skills
EVALUATE RESEARCH	**WHAT HAVE I LEARNED?**	• assessing growth in knowledge, skills and personal development

Essay Organization — Do You Need An Outline?

(A) INTRODUCTION

GENERAL TOPIC

SPECIFY TOPIC (THEME STATEMENT)

(B) SUB-TOPICS

(C) DETAIL

(D) ORDER: AFTER LISTING SUBTOPICS AND DETAILS, ARRANGE THEM IN ORDER BY NUMBERING THEM! (PUT A NUMBER IN EACH CIRCLE)

(E) CONCLUSION: REFER TO THE THEME STATEMENT AGAIN AND STATE WHAT YOU HAVE PROVED

Making a Class Presentation

A class presentation is usually a demonstration or short talk. You may be required to make a class presentation alone or with a partner or a group.

Good preparation is the key to success in what you say (content) and how you say it **(delivery)**.

These tips will help you give great class presentations.

Preparation:

Make copies of the checklist on this page and use a copy of the checklist as you prepare.

1. These questions should be answered in the assignment or by your teacher so that you know what is expected of you and/or you and your group.
   - *How long* should the presentation be?
   - *When* is the presentation to be given?
   - May notes be used?
   - Will an outline, a survey, or questionnaire for the class to read or complete be useful?
   - Will books, pictures, slides, tapes, overheads, maps, charts, posters, films, videotapes, filmstrips, blackboard, artifacts, displays, computer hardware and software, music, mime, poetry be helpful? Your teacher will help you decide.
   - Should class members take notes?
   - Should an assignment be given to the class?
   - How is the presentation being marked?
   - Should a written copy be handed in?
   - How should the work and responsibilities be divided up among partners or group members?

2. **Gather information** by following the chart on page 76. Your teacher and teacher-librarian will help.

3. **Select** the main ideas which you wish to present.

4. **Organize** the points which go with the main ideas.

5. **Write down** what you plan to say.

6. **Prepare handouts** and organize audio and visual materials.

7. **Write** a clear, neat copy of your presentation for your teacher, if a written copy is required.

8. **Rehearse** and time your presentation in advance. Make any necessary changes.

9. **Have** two or three **questions prepared** for the class and **be ready** to answer questions from the class.

Preparation Checklist

1. The assignment is understood. ❏
2. Information has been gathered. ❏
3. Main ideas have been selected. ❏
4. Main points have been organized. ❏
5. Points to be made have been written down. ❏
6. Handouts and other materials have been prepared. ❏
7. A clear and neat written copy has been prepared, if required. ❏
8. The presentation has been rehearsed. ❏
9. Questions for the class have been prepared and the group is ready to answer questions. ❏

Presentation:

If you are well prepared, you will be confident and your presentation will go well. Remember to

- work with your partner or group members throughout the presentation.
- have your notes handy to trigger your ideas.
- use posture, gestures, and facial expressions to make your presentation more effective.
- speak loudly and clearly.
- speak at a moderate pace.
- avoid reading to your audience.
- make eye contact with your audience.
- use good English.
- use your audio and visual materials.
- pause once in a while to see if there are questions from the class and give some time for discussion.

*(Scarborough, **Scarborough Student Skillsbook, Level 1**, 1989, pp. 35–37.)*

Studying

Suggestions for Creating a Good Study Environment

1. Choose a place at home for studying where you feel comfortable, and study in that place. If you have your own room, that's probably the best place. If not, choose a place to work where you will be interrupted by other people as little as possible.

2. When you study, try to remove things that will catch your attention and distract you. TV is very distracting and will take your attention away from what you're trying to learn. So will windows if you sit in front of one. The less distractions that you can see, the more effective your learning will probably be.

3. Noise is also a powerful distraction. Try to make your study place as quiet as possible. Ask people not to talk to you when you're studying. If you usually study with music on, try working without it for a week. You may discover that you can learn better without it.

4. If it's hard for you to find a place at home where you can study, ask your family to help you. Tell them that you're trying to study and that you need to reduce the distractions around you as much as possible. Ask them to help you create a good study environment for the time you need to do your work.

5. Some people can study even if they are surrounded by distractions. These people have learned to concentrate on what they are doing and ignore everything else. Find out how well you can do this. Can you do some of your work in school during study halls? Can you study on the bus? Sitting outside in the sun? Early in the morning before breakfast? Discover where and when you can study effectively!

(hm Study Skills Program, p. 52.)

Magic Dozen Study Hints

1. **Keep up with your work** so that you do not have to catch up.

2. Doing homework is a way of studying. **Read class notes before doing homework** in any subject. Some important ideas are always forgotten between class and the time you do the homework.

3. When doing homework, do not waste time trying to answer a question you find impossible. If after five to ten minutes you cannot answer the question, **check your notes or text**. If you are still unable to answer the question, **go on to the next one** and return later — you may be able to answer it this time.

4. Remember your daily planner? Build in **regular study time** and follow your planner.

5. Be kind to yourself. **Break your studying up into small chunks.**

6. **Divide your study time** among different subjects.

7. **Read over your notes** before you start studying new work.

8. Begin your studying by getting a **"bird's eye view"** of the work you are about to study. Make a list of the major topics. This will be your study outline.

9. When studying topics on your outline, try to **finish one major task** before you take a break.

10. Take a five to ten minute **break** after about twenty minutes of studying. Do not forget to come back!

11. **List your subjects from strongest to weakest.** Give more time and attention to the weakest.

12. **Write down the topics** as you learn them. Compare this list with the list of major topics on your study outline. You will quickly see what you have left to study.

(Scarborough, **Scarborough Student Skillsbook, Level 1,** *1989, p. 16.)*

Preparing for Writing Tests and Exams

Before tests and exams, go over the following checklist with students to help them prepare for the upcoming more formal evaluations.

Writing Tests and Exams:

Before writing tests and exams,

1. **Organize your study** and review.
   - (a) Review each week.
   - (b) Review several times one week before your exam.
   - (c) Organize your review — list all material to be studied and divide it into several sessions.
   - (d) Set the night before for a final, complete review.

2. **Record** the date, time, and location of each test and exam on your planners.

3. Plan a **study schedule** as soon as you find out the date of a test or exam.

4. **Ask your teachers for information** about tests and exams; for example, information on style, format, types of questions and mark values, material to be covered.

5. For practical subjects, review the equipment you will be using and how to use it. **Practise using the equipment** under the guidance of your teacher(s). Learn problem areas and safety items.

6. Pay careful **attention to class review**.

7. **Attend class before exam**. The teacher may give a brief overview of the test material or last minute study suggestions.

8. Consider **studying with others**. This forces you to become actively involved as you discuss content and explain points to each other.

9. Decide **what to study**.
   - (a) Textbook
   - (b) Notes
   - (c) Previous exams and notes
   - (d) Teacher handouts
   - (e) Out-of-class assignments
   - (f) Talk to others

10. **Organize information**. Get a perspective on the information you have; see how it interrelates; decide what is important.

11. Make **summary notes** in point form. Underline, circle, or highlight important information.

12. Do **practice questions** given to you by your teacher, made up by your group, or taken from your notes or text.

13. **Share quizzing** of the material with someone.

14. **Draw diagrams or pictures** to help you remember information.

15. **Learn** and **memorize**. Use the style best for you.

16. Get a **good night's sleep**.

17. **Be prepared** with pens, pencils, erasers, calculators, math tools, and so on.

18. **Arrive** at the test or exam location **early**. Do not try to study anything new. You may want to read over your own summary sheets or just relax.

Make copies of the checklist below.

Use the checklist to test your readiness to write a test or exam. On one copy, check, in pencil, those tasks which you have completed. Complete all tasks before each test or exam.

Use other copies of the checklist for other tests and exams.

Skillsbook Steps to Test and Exam Success

1. I have recorded the date, time, and location of the test or exam. ❏
2. I have planned a study schedule. ❏
3. I have received information from my teachers about the test or exam. ❏
4. I am prepared for practical exams. ❏
5. I am paying attention to class review. ❏
6. I have made summary notes. ❏
7. I have worked on practice questions. ❏
8. I have shared quizzing of the material. ❏
9. I have made diagrams and pictures to help me remember information. ❏
10. I am well rested and prepared with the necessary materials. ❏

---

*(Scarborough, **Scarborough Student Skillsbook, Level 1**, 1989, pp. 17–18.)*

Easing Fear of Tests — Adult Learners

Adult learners have special needs when testing takes place. The suggestions for teachers listed below may be helpful not only for adult learners but adolescents as well.

How to Test Adults Who Fear Tests

Most adults fear and dislike tests. Many have memories of unpleasant test experiences in the past, and they bring these memories with them into your classroom. For that reason, one of your major jobs in testing adult students is to figure out ways to ease their fears. Some teachers use the device of disguising their tests — presenting tests as something else. Others avoid using the word test. Others break big tests into small tests, giving them to the class a bite at a time.

Bite-Size Tests Go Down Well

Adults are particularly intimidated by a long list of test questions. They wonder whether they'll be able to answer them all correctly. And they are reminded of similar long tests in their early school days. To get around this problem, try preparing a series of tests which could include short quizzes, word lists, essay questions, multiple-choice questions. Then, instead of giving them to the group in one indigestible lump, place one question a day on the chalkboard. Or type the questions on a sheet of paper, cut the questions apart, and put them in a bowl or basket and let your students draw one question out each day.

Students Can Prepare Their Own Tests

It takes a lot of the terror out of testing when students are allowed to build their own tests. And they usually do it well. "I have had generally successful experiences in having the students construct their own tests, either for themselves or for their fellow students, individually or in learning teams," says Malcolm S. Knowles in his recent book *The Modern Practice of Adult Education — Andragogy Versus Pedagogy*.

Students Should Let It All Hang Out

Each student probably thinks he or she is the only one in the group who is afraid of taking tests. They want to hide that fear, like an unsightly wart. It is both healthy and helpful for them to get their fears out into the open. They'll soon realize that they are not alone, that test phobia is a common ailment. Airing their feelings in a friendly, accepting atmosphere is of great help.

After students have admitted their fears, they can start talking about how to get rid of them. For example, they can focus on the kinds of tests or test questions they are most afraid of. They might want to discuss the idea of taking practice tests before they take the real thing and explore the idea of why tests are given, which kinds are most helpful to the students themselves and who should score the tests.

Practice Tests Ease Student Fears

If you make the mechanics of test-taking familiar and routine to your students, they will be much more relaxed about the whole procedure. The best way to familiarize them with test-taking is to give them practice tests.

One of the most tension-making aspects of tests is the pressure of time. So, when you give practice tests, time the students in ten-minute blocks. After the answers are checked, have a relaxed and untimed discussion of how it felt to be timed, whether further practice with a stop-watch would help, etc. Given the chance to experience being timed, knowing the test is not for real, students can work out for themselves a balance of speed and accuracy.

The next step is to time them while they do the actual number of questions appearing on the final test. (They should have some experience answering the various types of questions before trying a full test.) Pre-practice sessions can be shortened by timing half the test and doubling the score.

*(**The Journey**, OSSTF, p. 94–96.)*

Tips for Students Before Tests

Score

- To SCORE well on tests:
  - **S** — SCHEDULE your time.
  - **C** — Use CLUE words.
  - **O** — OMIT difficult questions.
  - **R** — READ carefully.
  - **E** — ESTIMATE your answer.

- **Schedule time:**
  1. Find the total marks for the test/examination.
  2. Calculate the time available for each question.
  3. When you reach the end of the allotted time without finishing a question, leave some space and go on to the next question.

- **Clue words:**
  1. When reading the questions on a test, jot key words, (clue words), and phrases in the margin, around the question, on a scrap paper or on the answer paper.
  2. Write further clue words or idea words as they come to you.
  3. Use the clue words to develop your answers, whether for objective-type answers or for essay-type answers.

- **Omit questions:**
  1. If you think a question will be difficult for you, omit it until you have completed the easier questions.
  2. Limit yourself to the time you have scheduled for each question. If you have finished the easier questions quickly, you may be able to give more time to the difficult ones.

- **Read carefully:**
  1. When you have finished each question, read it carefully to check for accuracy, omissions, idea flow, details and completeness.
  2. Make sure that you have answered each question as it was asked.
  3. When you have finished the test/exam, read the whole paper again to make final additions and corrections.

- **Estimate answers:**
  1. Try to estimate the mark you should receive for each of your answers; this will help you to put the accuracy of your answers in focus.
  2. When you get your marked answer paper back, compare your estimate of each answer's value with what you receive from the test marker. Use this information to improve future answers.

(Elliot-Faust, South Secondary School, London Board.)

Tips for Taking Essay Examinations

1. **Read the Directions:** Be sure you understand exactly what is being asked. Underline important words.

2. **Read the Entire Test:** This will enable you to budget your time. Notice point count and organize timetable. Answer the easy questions first so you are sure of those marks.

3. **Make Sure You Understand the Question:** Read the question carefully and look for key words/limiting words/clues to organization.

4. **Make an Outline:** Make list of main points that you can support with details and examples.

5. **Do Not Begin Answer with Repetition of Question:** Show your knowledge. Begin with your thesis statement.

6. **Answer the Question in Correct Paragraph Form:** Include thesis statement at the beginning, put each new point and its support in separate paragraphs and write conclusion.

7. **Avoid Opinions and Judgments:** These should be included *only* when asked for.

8. **Avoid Padding:** Show your knowledge again. Do not mistake quantity for quality. Highest grades are given to those answers that contain the most relevant information.

9. **Write Simply and Carefully:** Your writing should be clear, concise and organized.

10. **Make Answers Readable:** Write legibly. Use ink. Write on one side only. Number pages and put name on each sheet. Do not scratch out errors — draw a single line through incorrect answer.

11. **Pace Yourself:** Watch your time and work according to your timetable.

12. **Leave Some Space Between Answers:** This will enable you to fill in ideas as they occur.

13. **Finish with a Brief Summary:** Make sure all your answers are concluded with a summary to end your discussion.

14. **Avoid Cramming:** Use proper reviewing techniques. The memory value of cramming is minimal. Cramming also increases tension and anxiety.

15. **Proofread Your Paper:** Check for proper spelling, grammar and punctuation, legibility and completeness.

Note: If time runs out and you haven't answered a question, answer it in outline form. You may receive partial credit and you are demonstrating that you knew the answer.

*(Adapted from **The Reading Edge**, OSSTF, 1987.)*

Assess for Success

Studying for Specific Subjects

1. Studying Foreign Languages

Math, science and languages all build on themselves. That is, each new fact is based on a previously learned fact. Therefore, learning them is simply a process of going back to the basics and knowing each step, each rule and each formula before proceeding.

Foreign languages are easy to learn. (After all, millions of children in foreign lands are learning a language every day, so why not you?)

First of all, use as many of your senses as possible. Review out loud, use a tape recorder and listen to yourself. You can learn a language almost twice as fast if you *read*, *recite*, and *listen* instead of memorize, memorize, memorize.

A language can be broken down into two main parts — grammar and vocabulary. Make up some flash cards of the rules and terms. Carry them around with you. Label the items around your room. And review in many short sessions instead of long one or two hour periods.

Write the language. Get a pen pal in a foreign country. Watch travelogues about the country. Subscribe to a foreign magazine. Collect artifacts, coins, stamps. Save up for a trip there.

Read, write and listen to your foreign language.

Keep flash cards handy for quick reviews.

Use pen pals, magazines, travelogues, to help you understand your language.

2. Studying Math and Science

Math can be interesting if we give it half a chance. Knowing math is essential to getting through each day — in school and in life.

Study by taking examples of math problems from your text. Write them out — out of sequence. Now try solving them. (They probably won't show up in order on the exam). And have a pencil in hand when you review anything.

Study 125% for that first test. This will build confidence and lower your stress to a manageable level. During the test, read an entire problem before trying to solve it. Estimate answers. Double check for misplaced decimal points. Beware of careless mistakes — 0's that look like 6's, or 1's that look like 7's. Check, check, and recheck.

Remember, math is hard for those who don't know how it works. For those who do, it's easy.

Give 125% on that first test.

Practice using math every day.

Science, like math is primarily a left brain subject — requiring a logical, analytical approach. You can increase the use of your left brain by using the opposite side of your head. For instance, if you are on the telephone with a friend sorting out science or math problems, listen with your right ear instead of your left. If you are using a tape recorder with an earphone, use your right ear.

Break down a science review into basic types of test questions: definition of terms, relation of terms to each other, formulas, drawings, and applications. And remember the basic rules and formulas for science. They never change.

Learn the basic steps, rules and formulas.

*(Olney, **Where There's a Will, There's an A**.)*

Teacher Self Check #1

Questions to Ask Oneself About Giving the Test

- ✧ Have I checked to see whether the same students have other tests scheduled for the same day?
- ✧ Have I avoided scheduling the test at inappropriate times during the week?
- ✧ Have the students been given sufficient advance notice in order to prepare adequately for the test?
- ✧ Have the students been informed about.
  - ➤ the date of the test?
  - ➤ what is to be covered by the test?
  - ➤ the length of the test?
  - ➤ kinds of questions to be used (for example, objective or essay-style, or both, or open-book)?
- ✧ Have the students been taught how to answer the type of question to be used on the test? (The test experience should never be the first experience of any type of question.)
- ✧ Have the students been taught how to study for a particular type of question?
- ✧ Have students been taught how to deal with key directing words and phrases in questions. such as compare, *identify*, *state the importance of*?
- ✧ Have I ensured that the students know the meaning of all the words used to ask the questions?
- ✧ Have I considered appropriate modifications for students with exceptionalities?
- ✧ Have I allowed time for students to ask me clarifying questions during the day or so leading up to the test?
- ✧ Have I informed the students of the materials, instruments or printed matter they will need to bring with them to the test? Are the students aware of the routines (e.g., consequences or procedures) which will likely follow if they fail to bring the appropriate materials to the test?
- ✧ Is all the material I need for conducting the test present in the classroom?
- ✧ Is the room in which the test is to be given suitable?

*(**Making the Grade**, 1987, p. 116.)*

Teacher Self Check #2

Questions to Ask Oneself While Marking and After Marking the Test

- ✧ Were the questions or problems clearly stated?

- ✧ Is there evidence that a number of students, including the exceptional students, had inadequate time to complete satisfactorily particular questions or the whole test?

- ✧ Is there evidence that a number of students were ill-prepared to answer a particular question?

    - ➤ Was the lack of preparation the result of inadequate study on the part of the students?

    - ➤ Was the material taught too abstract for the intellectual development of the students?

    - ➤ Was the method of presenting the material in class clear and sufficiently extensive?

    - ➤ Was the method of presenting the material in class appropriate to the level of student ability?

    - ➤ Was sufficient time devoted to follow-up activities after presenting the material in class and prior to the test?

    - ➤ Were the questions appropriate to the specific level of ability of the students?

- ✧ Is there evidence that I should adjust my marking scheme and re-score tests already marked?

- ✧ Am I alert to unexpected, acceptable responses which differ from those listed in the marking scheme?

- ✧ If the number of students obtaining a low mark or a high mark is above expectations, how am I going to use the marks?

- ✧ If the level of achievement on the test was very low, what changes should I make in my methods of classroom presentation and follow-up?

- ✧ If the results of other teachers' classes using the same test differ greatly from mine, what could be the cause of this discrepancy?

- ✧ What other methods of evaluation might have been more useful?

- ✧ Did the test results adequately reflect the provisions I made for students with exceptionalities when I prepared the test?

- ✧ Were the questions which required higher level thinking too easy, adequate or too difficult?

- ✧ Should I use this test again?

(Making the Grade, 1987, p. 117.)

Managing Anxiety

There are many situations when students may become anxious — participating in an important sports event, a school play, dealing with a difficult interpersonal situation or completing an educational assessment. The techniques or strategies presented below should be practised on a regular basis to help students manage anxiety in a variety of situations. To focus these strategies only on assessment activities may heighten the importance of these activities and create undue stress.

There are four main strategies to help reduce stress and/or anxiety — Deep Breathing, Visualization, Muscle Relaxation, and Self-talk.

1. **Abdominal or Deep Breathing:** Practice taking a deep breath in and then slowly breathing out. Count 1–2–3 in, and 1–2–3 out. Repeat several times.

2. **Visualization:** As you do deep breathing, visualize a number of different scenes, e.g., see yourself becoming a rag-doll; see yourself climbing to the top of a slide and see yourself sliding down, etc.

3. **Muscle Relaxation:** Tense up the muscles in the neck and arms as tight as possible and hold for five seconds, and then slowly let them relax. Repeat the same procedure for arms, legs, abdomen, whole body.

4. **Self-Talk:** Replace all negative self-statements with positive ones — e.g., "This is hard" becomes "This isn't too hard" or "I can do this, just relax and take it slowly."

It should be noted that it will be very helpful when preparing students for assessment activities to keep the atmosphere as normal as possible. These activities should not be seen as a very special event, but part of the normal program to help students see their strengths, and find the areas that require more work.

(Psychological Services, London Board of Education.)

The Road to Success

I	Never	Seldom	Sometimes	Usually	Always
1. come prepared to class with all needed equipment					
2. listen attentively to all					
3. try to participate fully in class and group discussions					
4. keep a proper notebook					
5. use all class time effectively					
6. get clarification and help when needed both from the teacher and peers					
7. complete all homework, assignments, and projects					
8. make sure if away all notes are caught up					
9. prepare thoroughly for tests					
10. have a peer check and review previously taken work with me					

*(London, **Regional Geography — Travel and Tourism**, 1992, p. 14–8.)*

Assess for Success

References

Buzan, Tony. Use your head. London: BBC Books, 1989.

Cornfield et al. Making the Grade. Prentice Hall, 1987.

Elliot-Faust, D. "Strategic Learning Skills Training Manual". South Secondary School, London Board of Education.

Huff, P., Snider, R. & Stephenson, S. Teaching and Learning Styles: Celebrating Differences. Toronto: Ontario Secondary School Teachers' Federation, 1986.

National Association of Secondary School Principals. Study Skills Program Level II (revised edition). Reston, Virginia: National Association of Secondary School Principals, 1986.

Olney, Claude. "Where there's a will there's an A". no date.

OSSTF. The Journey. 1988.

OSSTF. The Reading Edge. 1987.

OSSTF. Study Survival Tips. Pamphlet available free from OSSTF office, Toronto.

Scarborough Board of Education. Scarborough Student Skillsbook, Level 1. Program Department, 1989.

Scarborough Board of Education. Scarborough Student Skillsbook, Level 2. Program Department, 1988.

Schurr, S. The ABC's of Evaluation. NMSA, 1992.

Chapter 4
Methods of Organizing Student Assessment

Methods of Organizing Student Assessment

Overview of Chapters 4–7

The purpose of this book is to help the classroom teacher to develop and *maintain* a positive, constructive assessment environment. To attain this goal, the classroom teacher will need to employ a variety of assessment techniques. To facilitate the acquisition of expertise with respect to the purposes of assessment and the range of combinations and techniques, the following chapters have been designed for ease of use for specific applications.

Chapter 4   presents methods of organizing student assessment.

Chapter 5:   presents types of student assessments.

Chapter 6:   presents subject specific suggestions for dealing with assessment concerns.

Chapter 7:   presents additional considerations for exceptional students, ESL students, and adult learners.

Methods of Organizing Student Assessment

Whether assessing students during their ongoing activities or in a quiz or test situation, there are broader organizational decisions to be made. The match between the most appropriate organizational method and the type of student information to be gathered needs to be determined. Organizational methods are listed below.

1. Individual assessments
2. Group assessments
3. Contracts
4. Self-assessments
5. Peer-assessments
6. Portfolios
7. Independent study

1. Individual Assessments

Individual assessments focus on individual student progress. Assessment activities constructed by the teacher are completed individually by the students.

Teachers may wish to have students work individually on written assignments, presentations, or performance assessment tasks in order to assess individual progress.

2. Group Assessments

Group assessments focus on the progress a group of students has made by cooperating and collaborating to complete assessment activities organized by the teacher.

In order to assess social skills and cooperative learning processes, teachers may decide to have students complete written assignments, presentations, or perform skills and processes in groups.

3. Contracts

A contract refers to an agreement between a student, or a group of students, and a teacher regarding what activity will be undertaken, who will do it, how it will be done, when it will be completed, and how it will be evaluated according to the criteria established.

Contracts can be organized on an individual or a group basis and may involve written assignments, presentations, or performance of skills and processes as part of the structure. Students may partially fulfill the requirements of their contracts by self-assessment of their work.

4. Self-Assessments

Self-assessment refers to the students' own assessment of their progress in knowledge, skills, processes, or attitudes.

5. Peer-Assessments

Peer-assessment refers to student assessment of other students. Peer-assessments can be conducted either individually or collaboratively in groups.

Note: Students may be involved in a variety of self- and peer-assessment activities using their individual efforts, their participatory efforts in a group, their own end products of written assignments and presentations, or their performance of skills and processes. Students may also be involved in assessing their efforts on quizzes and tests. Contracts frequently have a self- or peer-assessment component.

6. Portfolios

A portfolio is a collection of student work that assists the student and teacher to make judgments about student learning progress. Samples of work to be included may be selected by the student, by the teacher, or by the student and teacher in consultation.

Copies of assignments, contracts, assessments of presentations, assessments of the performance of skills and processes, quizzes, and tests are all examples of items that may be included in portfolios. In addition, samples of students' day-to-day work may become part of the portfolio.

Samples of work completed on an individual basis may be included along with work completed by groups. Copies of self-assessment instruments and peer-assessment instruments may also become part of the portfolio.

(Saskatchewan Education, 1991, p. 46.)

7. Independent Study

"Independent study is a teaching/learning process that develops student autonomy in the acquisition and application of skills and knowledge."

*(OSSTF, **Independent Learning**, 1989, p. 7.)*

It may involve a variety of assessment methodologies such as written assignments, projects, demonstrations, etc.

1. Individual Assessments

Description

Individual assessments involve techniques used to assess individual student progress toward learning outcomes.

Evaluation Context

When using individual assessments, teachers must have a clear understanding of whether evaluation is formative, diagnostic or summative and whether progress will be self-criterion or norm-referenced. All assessments must be related to clearly defined learning outcomes.

Using Technique to Best Advantage

Individual progress can be monitored and encouraged most effectively using self- and criterion-referenced standards; when ranking students is absolutely essential, criterion-referenced results can also be effectively used for this purpose.

Guidelines for Use

Students must be **fully informed** as to how their learning will be assessed and evaluated.

A variety of assessment techniques should be used so that as complete a "picture" as possible of a student's learning profile is obtained.

Information from individual assessments should be used only for the purpose for which it was intended.

Using the Information for Student Evaluation

Individual assessments form the basis of most schools' grading and reporting systems.

Limitations

Overemphasis on individual assessments may lead to an overly competitive environment which will restrict learning opportunities for some students.

Individual assessment cannot be used for some important learning outcomes, e.g. co-operative work and social interaction outcomes.

2. Group Assessments

Description

Group assessment is a technique for gathering assessment information on students working in learning groups.

Evaluation Context

Teachers and students should take active roles in formative and summative evaluation of academic and social learning in groups.

Using Technique to Best Advantage

Group assessment nurtures co-operative learning and can lead to improved communication and social skills, and higher achievement. Greater student responsibility for learning is fostered and greater breadth and depth of learning outcomes can be attained.

Guidelines for Use

Teachers must match the most appropriate group strategies to the specific classroom situation and to the desired learning outcomes. The effect of the evaluation scheme on the outcomes of the group activities should be monitored closely. As groups become more comfortable with co-operative learning, evaluation approaches may be adjusted. The evaluation technique, specific criteria, and teacher expectations should be communicated clearly to the students.

Using the Information for Student Evaluation

Group work can be evaluated by:
- anecdotal records/rating scales/checklists
- awarding the same mark to all members of the group
- assessing individual student progress within the group structure
- awarding both group and individual marks

The type of evaluation and the time it takes will depend on the length of the collaborative activity. For a relatively short collaborative activity, observer feedback, individual and group processing and reflection are appropriate; no grade or mark need be given.

When groups work together over a longer period of time, however, the evaluation should include both the learning processes and the desired skills and knowledge. Therefore, a variety of skills should be evaluated: problem-solving skills, organizational skills, collaborative skills, and self- and peer-evaluation skills. As in other learning methods, evaluation activities may take many forms (quizzes, tests, assignments, presentations, group discussions, group checklists, reports and observation), but should be related to the outcomes for the lesson.

(Growing Collaboratively, 1993, p. 81.)

Assess for Success

Rationale for Small Group Learning and Group Assessment

Small group teaching is an approach to classroom organization, encouraging a wide variety of techniques for structuring the relationships of students and teachers. It changes the way in which students and teachers behave when engaged in learning and teaching, and the kinds of roles they fill. Students who participate in co-operative groups tend to view their studies as work and see their teacher as a coach.

> "Fundamental to **all subject areas** is the need to extend students' thinking abilities and the capacity for initiative, self-discipline and co-operation through small group activities. ... The key to successful small group work is to establish a definite objective for student achievement that goes beyond superficial discussion."
>
> *(Cavanaugh and Styles, 1980, p. 24.)*

As Cavanaugh and Styles also point out, small group learning causes some teachers concern:

> "Teachers offer several reasons for keeping to a minimum or avoiding small group work. The learning experiences may deteriorate and lead to idle talk, a mutual pooling of ignorance, disruptive behaviour, confusion concerning the task, bewilderment about how to achieve the objectives, resentment about unequal distribution of workload, the worry that higher noise levels indicate a loss of control, the feeling that group projects are too difficult to organize, and the impression that the time expended will not be justified in terms of student productivity."
>
> *(Cavanaugh and Styles, 1980, p. 24.)*

Perhaps the following reflections of one teacher, who in 1986 attempted to incorporate small group learning into the program, will not only provide insight into the complexity of the process, but also show the potential for positive, constructive learning.

> ## Teacher Log – September 1986
>
> As I walk around the room listening to the group process unfold, I cannot help thinking to myself that I am missing something. Am I really teaching? How do the students feel about this assignment? What dynamic is really at work here? I help them with direction, I clarify, I do not impose my ideas. It takes the first half-hour for them to feel comfortable and to understand what is demanded. There are gaps of silence. Some groups begin to talk about the issues. Some groups do not interact well. What are they thinking? There is an overwhelming desire to impose what I think on them. What are the benefits? They talk more. They collaborate. They **do** discuss ideas. There is more time for them to do this. The process is much more highly interactive. They are limited by background information but they **do** have views/thoughts on these heady topics. They are building confidence. It is my self-confidence/ego that is hurting a bit. … How could the exercise be better designed? Should topic areas be given? Yes and no. The open-ended nature of the assignment is more frustrating for them, but less restrictive for growth/learning. I interacted with a group to clarify a definition and generated further discussion. … One hour and they are variously finished or still discussing issues. The final 15 minutes are for presentation and preparation for individual writing. Whew! Reporting to the group — another important dimension. One group decides that their topic was really a sub-topic and adjusted having heard the others. … What kind of a mark will I assign? The individual writing should be more focused and detailed as a result of their group activity.

(Source unknown.)

Small group learning should be an integral component in all subject areas. Assessment and evaluation of group work needs to be seen as purposeful and just. This is a challenge because many students believe that being assessed on their ability to work in groups is unfair. However, working with other people — on committees, collaborative projects, etc. — is a real world (authentic) situation, and students will likely find that in "real life" they will be assessed for their performance in "group' situations.

Small group learning can be greatly enhanced through the use of co-operative and collaborative learning principles. These lead to greater individual accountability and social skill development.

Traditional Group Learning vs. Collaborative Group Learning

Traditional Group Learning	Collaborative Group Learning	Group Learning Term/Concept
Group members are not required to depend upon one another for materials, ideas, or assistance during the activity.	Activities are structured so that group members depend upon one another for materials, ideas, and assistance.	POSITIVE INTERDEPENDENCE
Individual group members are accountable for their own success or failure; each member is expected to monitor and modify his/her own behaviour and performance. Individual group members are not accountable for the group's success or failure: members sometimes 'hitch-hike' on the work of others.	Individual group members are accountable for their own success or failure: each member is expected to monitor and modify his/her own performance and behaviour. Individual group members are accountable for the group's success or failure; each member is responsible for the performance and behaviour of the other group members. The group 'sinks or swims' together.	INDIVIDUAL ACCOUNTABILITY
Groups are unstructured: group members are randomly selected and there is seldom any pre-planning.	Groups are structured to attend to specific abilities and interests. Care is given to the group's composition.	GROUP STRUCTURE and MEMBERSHIP CONSIDERATIONS
Each group has one leader appointed by either the teacher or the group for the duration of the activity.	The leadership role is shared: no group member is expected or invited to fill this role alone throughout the group activity.	SHARED LEADERSHIP
Task completion is the principal goal of the group and the only criterion used to assess the group's success or failure: the social and interpersonal skills needed for effective group performance are either assumed or ignored.	Task completion is an important part of the evaluation, but the skills and abilities needed to complete the task are also attended to and evaluated both on an individual and a group basis: social and interpersonal skills are developed and reinforced through teacher planning and/or intervention.	ATTENTION TO SOCIAL SKILLS
The teacher's role is predominantly passive once the initial task has been explained. The teacher assumes responsibility for solving problems related to group functioning.	The teacher's role is active and ongoing throughout the activity: the teacher observes interactions and shares his/her observations in order to facilitate the groups' social skills development. The group assumes responsibility for solving problems related to group functioning; the teacher encourages members to develop group problem-solving strategies.	TEACHER'S ROLE
The group is not expected to reflect on the quality of the group's product or on the quality of its social interaction.	The group is expected to reflect on the group's product and process their performance. Reflection allows members to learn from the interactive process and to suggest methods of improvement and modification.	GROUP PROCESSING and REFLECTION

(Growing Collaboratively, 1993, p. 7.)

Evaluation and Co-operative Learning

In Co-operative Learning ...

 **What?** Academic and social objectives demand evaluation of academic and social learning.

 **Why?** Purposes for evaluating include:

Formative

- diagnosis of needs and progress
- modification of objectives
- adjustment of teaching and learning

Summative

- measurement of learning outcomes
- assessment reports

 **Who?** Both teacher and students take active roles in formative and summative evaluation of academic and social learning.

Individual teachers need to decide:

- What the balance will be between teacher and student involvement in evaluation.
- How to facilitate student participation in evaluating self and peers in group work.

(Bennett et al, 1991, p. 130.)

Teachers and students using co-operative group learning and applying group assessment techniques see the advantages:

- students learn by doing — discussing, listening, teaching
- students must co-operate to achieve successful learning
- learning is reinforced
- there are more opportunities for talk to develop critical analysis skills
- the learning environment is seen as authentic
- it is a more receptive forum for ideas that might otherwise be stifled
- it provides greater opportunity for students to be involved in designing and carrying out evaluation tasks
- students evaluate their own learning and become more aware of the way they learn

Rather than list disadvantages, teacher concerns have been expressed as a series of questions. Detailed responses to these questions can be found in Chapter 7 of *Together We Learn*.

1. **What is a good way to introduce evaluation when co-operative small group learning is new for students?**
   - start by evaluating individual learning
   - provide opportunities for informal co-operative learning activities
   - let students first experience how group work enhances individual progress

2. **How do teachers start to involve students in planning and carrying out evaluation of group work?**
   - students must understand the criteria for productive learning
   - gradually students can be involved in selecting the criteria and planning how to use them
   - criteria may be stated in checklist form

3. **How do teachers introduce students to self-evaluation?**
   - once students understand the criteria for evaluation they can begin to apply them in self-evaluation
   - group evaluation is a helpful way for students to begin self-evaluation

4. **When and how should students start evaluating each other?**
   - students need a good deal of experience developing and applying criteria to evaluate their individual learning and the work of their own group **before** they start to evaluate their peers
   - through practice, students will develop competence and understanding of the learning skills which are being evaluated and they will learn to express constructive comments

5. **How do I teach students to evaluate themselves and their peers fairly and realistically?**
   - discussing learning outcomes and criteria for evaluation before and during learning tasks helps students to be realistic and precise in their peer- and self-evaluation

- checklists provide guidelines for progress
- if the teacher uses the same evaluation criteria that students use, the teacher's evaluation helps students learn to evaluate constructively and honestly

6. When should teachers start giving marks for group work?

- when students can apply co-operative skills effectively to complete a piece of work in groups
- as well as giving marks for task completion, the teacher can assign marks for completion of self- and peer-evaluations
- many teachers wait until students reach the senior grades

7. When should students be given a group mark and when should individual marks be given?

- if group work results in a group product, it is important to give one mark to the group for its collaborative work. This reinforces the fact that students are collectively responsible for their work and interaction
- if group work results in an individual product (e.g. a test or essay) it is important to mark individually
- if students make distinct individual contributions to a group product, a combination of both individual and group assessment should be used
- research suggests that motivation is increased by marking both the group product and individual contributions
- it is important that the teacher and students discuss beforehand the way in which marks will be allocated

8. What proportion of evaluation should be based on the learning process and what proportion on the final product?

- when deciding whether to emphasize evaluation of the process or product, teachers must consider the purposes of the evaluation
- if the group task requires learning new skills, the teacher and students will want to monitor the development of skills throughout the learning process. Therefore, emphasis will be on ongoing evaluation of the learning process. Once students have developed skills, the teacher may assign a group task so that students can apply their skills to create a product
- emphasis on process or product is also determined by length of the group work

9. To what extent should group work be reflected in final term grades?

- if the teacher uses group work primarily for the purpose of peer sharing and individual assistance, grades will be based primarily on individual work. Evaluation of group work will be anecdotal and informal
- if group work involves the creation of group products which are marked, then these marks will contribute to the individual student's final grade. The amount of term work done in small groups will influence the weighting in the final grade

10. What combination of weighting should the teacher and student evaluations carry in assigning grades?

- when group work and involvement in evaluation are fairly new to students, the teacher should give more weight to his/her own evaluation
- as student expertise increases, the teacher may move toward averaging student and teacher evaluation
- in general, when using group work, peer assessment should be primarily formative and teacher assessment should be both formative and summative

11. How do teachers assess the group and individuals when a student is absent or not participating?

- whenever possible, plan group activities to occur within one class period
- ongoing self and group anecdotal assessment helps teachers to spot non-participation difficulties early enough to encourage participation
- as students become comfortable working productively in groups, attendance gradually improves and teachers are able to plan more extensive co-operative group tasks

12. What are ways other than marks for assessing group work?

- marks often do not provide information for understanding the development and dimensions of student learning that are important for students, teachers and parents
- anecdotal feedback, group discussion, checklists, and journal writing provide information about the learning that is taking place and help to set directions for future learning

*(Adapted from **Together We Learn**, 1990, pp. 137–148.)*

Following are sample checklists for assessing students in group learning situations.

Sample Collector Form

Fill in one ☞

	Almost Always	Often	Sometimes	Rarely
A. Group Participation				
1. Participated in group discussion without prompting.	○	○	○	○
2. Did his or her fair share of the work.	○	○	○	○
3. Tried to dominate the group — interrupted others, spoke too much.	○	○	○	○
Participated in the Group's Activities	○	○	○	○
B. Staying On Topic				
4. Paid attention, listened to what was being said and done.	○	○	○	○
5. Made comments aimed at getting the group back to the topic.	○	○	○	○
6. Got off the topic or changed the subject	○	○	○	○
Stayed on the Topic	○	○	○	○
C. Offering Useful Ideas				
7. Gave ideas and suggestions that helped the group.	○	○	○	○
8. Offered helpful criticism and comments.	○	○	○	○
9. Influenced the group's decisions and plans.	○	○	○	○
Offered Useful Ideas	○	○	○	○
D. Consideration				
10. Made positive, encouraging remarks about group members and their ideas.	○	○	○	○
11. Gave recognition and credit to others for their ideas.	○	○	○	○
12. Made inconsiderate or hostile comments about a group member.	○	○	○	○
Was Considerate of Others	○	○	○	○
E. Involving Others				
13. Got others involved by asking questions, requesting input or challenging others.	○	○	○	○
14. Tried to get the group working together to reach group agreements.	○	○	○	○
15. Seriously considered the ideas of others.	○	○	○	○
Involved Others	○	○	○	○
F. Communicating				
16. Spoke clearly and was easy to hear and understand.	○	○	○	○
17. Expressed ideas clearly and effectively.	○	○	○	○
Communicated Clearly	○	○	○	○

(Waterloo, *Assessment for Learning*, 1993, Appendix B, p. 5.)

Assess for Success

Individual Self-Evaluation Form

**Fill in the number of squares which best
represents your participation in the group work.**

	Very Little		A Lot

- I encouraged others.

- I shared my materials with others.

- I checked to make sure others understood the work.

- I was willing to give and receive help.

- I accepted responsibility for completing the work properly.

Comments on how you worked in the group.

_____

_____

_____

_____

_____

_____

_____

_____   _____
Signature   Date

*(Waterloo, **Assessment for Learning**, 1993, Appendix B, p. 2.)*

Evaluation Methods
Group Work Assignments

Group Members:

1. Did each member do equal work?   ❏ Yes   ❏ No

   Explain:

   _____

   _____

   _____

2. Was the leadership shared equally?   ❏ Yes   ❏ No

   Explain:

   _____

   _____

   _____

3. Did anyone waste time by not working; talking about other items?   ❏ Yes   ❏ No

   Explain:

   _____

   _____

   _____

Marking		Group	Teacher
Neatness	10		
Completeness	10		
Organized	5		
Total	**25**		

*(Waterloo, **Assessment for Learning**, 1993, Appendix B, p. 3.)*

Application: Mathematics – Geometry

Directions: You will be working in groups of four to determine what specific job or career demands the greatest knowledge, application, or expertise in geometry according to the best thinking of your group members. During this activity, you will be working on the social skill of "asking for clarifying responses of group members when you don't understand something." To begin, appoint someone in your group to serve as Recorder, Time Keeper, Facilitator, and Evaluator so that everyone has an important job to do. Be sure to write down some clarifying phrases or expressions that will help you understand the ideas of one another.

Recording Sheet

Recorder: _____   Date: _____

Group Members: _____

Behaviour indicators of clarifying questions or responses:

1. What are the five most important criteria that your group can agree on when selecting the most geometry-driven career you can think of? Rank order them from most to least important.

2. Who are the nominees from your group as candidates for the most geometry-driven career?

3. Set up the information from numbers one and two above in matrix form, listing the nominees in a vertical column and the criteria (in order of importance) in a horizontal line.

Career Options	*Criteria 1*	*Criteria 2*
1.		
2.		
3.		

4. Who is your group's first choice? _____

5. Give 3–5 reasons why your group made the decision they did.

6. What overall rating would your group give itself on use of clarifying questions or responses during this activity? *Excellent, Good, Fair, or Poor.* _____

    What evidence did you see to document this rating?

(Schurr, 1992, pp. 86–87.)

An Example of Combined Group Assessment

Step 1: If a group of four has been marked for a report, presentation, etc., the teacher may award an initial group mark based on criteria such as the following:

Teacher's Criteria for "Total" Marks	Marks
1. **Content** (e.g., relevance, organization, quality)	10
2. **Clarity** (e.g., facts, presentation, accuracy)	10
3. **Time management** (e.g., preparation, presentation)	10
4. **Use of Organizer/Chart** (e.g., accuracy, clarity, suitability)	10
5. **Answering Questions** (e.g., accuracy, clarity)	10
Total	**50 / 5 x 4**

In this example, the criteria total 50 marks, divided by 5 to obtain a maximum mark of 10 for each member of a group of 4. Thus, a report assessed a 40/50 score would result in a total group mark of 32.

Step 2: If our group of 4 received a total of 32 marks, it is their task to divide that total score into 4 individual marks. This can happen in several ways. One approach follows.

Step 3: Each individual completes a self-evaluation form as outlined below.

Individual Member's Assessment and Marks

Group Number _____   Member Name _____

Topic _____   Total Marks Assigned (from above) **32**

Suggested Criteria	Marks
1. Co-operation	__ / 8
2. Contribution (work)	__ / 8
3. Contribution (ideas and organization)	__ / 8
4. Quality of work	__ / 8
5. Attendance	__ / 8
Total	**= __ / 40 / 4**
	= __ / 10

In our example, the individual group member arrives at a total out of 40, divided by the number of members in the group for a mark out of 10.

Step 4: The four group members compare self-evaluations and fill out the form below. The total number of marks for the individual members must not exceed the total number of marks awarded initially by the teacher — in this case 32. Any discrepancies must be worked out by the group. For example, if all group members feel that they contributed roughly equally to the group product, then each would get 8 marks out of 10. The form below is handed in to the teacher who then records the marks.

Name	Mark	Signature
1.		
2.		
3.		
4.		

Total # of Marks _____   = Teacher's Total _____

Alternative Procedures: Students can help establish the criteria for the teacher's initial evaluation and/or take the major responsibility for setting the criteria for peer- and self-evaluation. It is best to ease into this by getting students comfortable with formative evaluation procedures using at first some, then more, of the above steps.

Disadvantages: It takes some explanation, practice and time. Students must know the criteria for all evaluations.

Advantages: Procedures such as the above combine teacher, self- and peer-evaluation in a way that involves both teachers and students in the evaluation process. Using this procedure can help students develop responsibility for their own learning.

(Myers and Dippong, Toronto Board of Education.)

3. Contracts

Description

Contracts are plans of intended learning that students develop either by themselves or in conjunction with the teacher. In the student evaluation context, attention is directed toward evaluating the contract itself. Techniques for evaluating the product of the contract can be found elsewhere in this chapter — for example in written assignments and portfolios.

Evaluation Context

Students can be encouraged to take charge of their learning by developing a performance contract ahead of time. Usually the contract includes a statement of the goals to be reached, the way in which these will be reached, a timeline, and criteria whereby the performance will be evaluated.

Guidelines for Use

Using the contract as an organizational structure requires an appreciation of the fact that there are two aspects of contract work to consider. First, the contract results in a product, usually a report or artifact of some sort, that is assessed by the means set forth in the initial contract. Second, and less often acknowledged, the student's participation in the act of setting up the contract is itself a performance that can be assessed.

As much attention must be paid to the process of setting up the contract as is paid to the nature of the product that is finally submitted. Students must be made aware that their work in developing their contract is being monitored. Students should be offered some general guidelines. Overly specific guidelines may reduce the opportunities for students to take control of their own learning. A series of teacher-generated questions for students may serve to organize the contract-development process.

- What work do you wish to include in the contract?
- How will you go about it? For example, what books will you use; what other resources will you consult?
- How long will it take you to develop a detailed plan, to gather your resources, and to finish the assignment?
- What criteria are you prepared to meet for an "A", for a "B", or for a pass?

Example

Students reflect on a planning sheet similar to ones on pages 114–121.

The evaluation aspect is covered at the bottom of the sheet under the heading "Evaluation Criteria". Following reflection and initial planning, a contract may be completed between the student and the teacher.

Using the Information for Student Evaluation

If the contract has been well designed, the assessment of the final product is straightforward because the criteria have been established beforehand. Assessing the other aspect, the extent to which the student has been able to take control of his or her learning, is best done by breaking up the exercise into subordinate tasks. Teachers and students need to establish the criteria with which the contract will be assessed. Another set of questions can be generated. Some of these might be:

- How realistic is the contract in terms of the time constraints?
- How appropriate are the contract questions to the objectives of the project?
- How appropriate are the chosen resources to the objectives of the project?
- How realistic was the contract in terms of the student's knowledge of his or her capabilities?
- How comprehensive was the planning?

The assessment questions can be rated by the teacher or by the teacher working with the student. A rating scale would then become the recording instrument for the assessment information. These ratings can then be translated into an overall mark for the student's work in preparing the contract.

Hints

- Be prepared to spend more time than anticipated when setting up the contract system for the first time. One useful strategy is to take a unit of work that has already been completed and, using it as a sample, allow students to develop a contract in a situation where they know the extent of the work involved. "Imagine you had wanted to set up a contract for that last unit on 'Mathematics in the Supermarket'. How would you have found out about the resources you would need?"

- Students vary greatly in their ability to conceptualize what is required for a successful contract. It may be necessary to go through the stages of planning, organizing, and writing a contract with them. The time spent with students teaching them **how** to prepare a contract will ultimately give them greater independence.

Variants

Contracts can also be used to help students take control of their lives in terms of school attendance and behaviour standards. Some students have a learning style that makes independent learning a motivating option for them. Providing them with the learning tools necessary to prepare and fulfill a contract may be an extremely useful instructional method.

*(**Student Evaluation: A Teacher Handbook**, Saskatchewan Education, 1991, pp. 52–53.)*

Setting Up a Contract

Contracted Work: _____

Student: _____ Class: _____ Date: _____

Contract Questions	Answers
1.	
2.	
3.	
4.	
5.	
6.	

Evaluation Criteria	Rating									
A.	1	2	3	4	5	6	7	8	9	10
B.	1	2	3	4	5	6	7	8	9	10
C.	1	2	3	4	5	6	7	8	9	10
D.	1	2	3	4	5	6	7	8	9	10
E.	1	2	3	4	5	6	7	8	9	10

Comments:

Overall Mark: _____

(Student Evaluation: A Teacher Handbook, Saskatchewan Education, 1991, p. 54.)

Example 1 of a Learning Contract

Student Name:

Teacher Name:

Time Period of Contract:

Description of Purpose of Contract:

1. I am planning to do an in-depth study of

2. The reason I have decided to work on this topic is

3. The main focus of my study will be

4. Some questions that I want to answer are

5. I intend to collect information from: (Check (√) at least 5.)

    _____ books

    _____ interviews with experts

    _____ experiments

    _____ magazines

    _____ encyclopedias

    _____ newspapers

    _____ filmstrips, records, pictures, films, videos

    _____ museums

    _____ community agencies, organizations

    _____ my own research (Explain.)

    _____ other sources (List.)

6. The product of my study will be in the form of

7. The learning skills I will be using in order to complete this study are

8. I will make these arrangements to share the information from my study.
   • who I will share it with:

   • when I will share it:

   • how I will share it:

9. My study will be completed by

10. This study will be evaluated by

11. The important things that the evaluator(s) will be looking for are

12. I will evaluate this study and my own learning by

_____   _____
Teacher Signature   Student Signature

_____
Date

(**Student Evaluation: A Teacher Handbook**, *Saskatchewan Education,*
1991, p. 55–56.)

Assess for Success

Example 2 of a Learning Contract

Student Name: _____

Teacher Name: _____

Date: _____

General topic to be studied:

Questions or problems I will try to solve:

Information I already have on this topic:

Information I need to look for:

When I will have this done:

Who will evaluate this project when I am done:

_____   _____
Teacher Signature   Student Signature

Date _____

*(**Student Evaluation: A Teacher Handbook**, Saskatchewan Education, 1991, p. 57.)*

Example 3 of a Learning Contract

Student Name:

What I am going to do:

How I am going to do it:

This is a good thing to do because

I am going to show this to

_____

Student Signature

_____

Teacher Signature

_____

Date

*(**Student Evaluation: A Teacher Handbook**, Saskatchewan Education, 1991, p. 58.)*

CLASSROOM APPLICATION
English: Spelling

Directions: Please complete this contract for learning your 20 assigned spelling words this week. You may choose to do any of the activities in the contract as long as they add up to a total of 60 points. A spelling test will be given in class on Friday and you will receive one point towards your total of 100 points for every word spelled correctly on the test. Good luck and have fun!

A Contract for Learning Assigned Spelling Words

Student Name: _____ Date: _____

I will have completed the following tasks successfully by the end of the week:

_____ 1. I will write my words in alphabetical order. *(10 points)*

_____ 2. I will write each of my words in a complete sentence. *(10 points)*

_____ 3. I will look up each of my words in the dictionary and write out their definitions. *(10 points)*

_____ 4. I will find a synonym and/or an antonym for each of the words. *(10 points)*

_____ 5. I will write an original paragraph using at least ten of my spelling words in the context of the paragraph. *(10 points)*

_____ 6. I will take a practice test on my spelling words with a friend. *(10 points)*

_____ 7. I will create a word finder puzzle or a crossword puzzle using each of my spelling words. *(20 points)*

_____ 8. I will create a collage using pictures from magazines to illustrate each word. *(20 points)*

_____ 9. I will create a secret code and write a message to a friend using at least ten of my words. *(20 points)*

Student's signature _____

(Adapted from Schurr, 1992, p. 133.)

CLASSROOM APPLICATION
Mathematics: Fractions

Directions: Please complete this contract by the end of the week. You are to choose any of the activities to do as long as their total value adds up to 50 points. On Friday, you will be given a short quiz on the multiplication and division of mixed fractions with unlike denominators. Good luck and happy fractioning!

A Contract for Learning Fractions

Student Name: _____ Date: _____

____ 1. Do one of the exercises on page 125 of your math textbook on the multiplication of mixed fractions. Use the answer key to check your results and correct any problems that were wrong. *(10 points)*

____ 2. Do one of the exercises on page 132 of your math textbook on the division of mixed fractions. Use the answer key to check your results and correct any problems that you did wrong. *(10 points)*

____ 3. Make up one story problem that involves multiplication of mixed fractions and one story problem that involves division of mixed fractions. *(10 points)*

____ 4. Browse through the newspaper and find at least five examples of fractions used in the articles, advertisements, or charts/graphs. *(10 points)*

____ 5. Did you ever think about the fact that if there were no fractions, everything would be all or nothing? Make a list of five things that we would not be able to do if there were no such thing as fractions. *(10 points)*

____ 6. Make up three multiplication and three division problems using mixed fractions. Give these to a friend to solve. Check his/her work. *(10 points)*

____ 7. Bring a recipe to school that uses fractions as part of the ingredients called for in preparing the food. Triple the recipe (item by item) using multiplication of fractions. *(10 points)*

____ 8. Develop an argument that you could use with other students to answer the question: "Why do we have to learn fractions?" *(10 points)*

____ 9. Create a comic strip, riddle, or cartoon that uses fractions as a part of its content. *(20 points)*

(Schurr, 1992, p. 134.)

CLASSROOM APPLICATION
Science: Insects

Directions: Please complete this contract by the end of the marking period. You are to choose any of the activities to do as long as their total value adds up to 100 points. You will be asked to set up a display of your work for our "Insect Museum" during Open House. Have fun and don't let this assignment "bug" you too much!

A Contract for Learning About Insects

Student Name: _____ Date: _____

I will have completed the following tasks successfully by the end of the marking period.

_____ 1. Name at least five ways man protects himself from harmful insects. *(15 points)*

_____ 2. Pretend you are a bug found in your backyard. Write your life story, making certain your ideas are as scientific as possible. *(25 points)*
   a. When were you born?
   b. Where do you live?
   c. What is your family history?
   d. What are your hobbies?
   e. What work do you do?
   f. Where do you like to travel?
   g. Who are your friends?
   h. What special skills or talents do you have?
   i. What do you look like?

_____ 3. Find a can of insect repellent in your home or a supermarket. Read the information on the can to learn something about the repellent. Summarize your findings. *(15 points)*

_____ 4. Invent a new kind of bug spray. Be sure to tell what the bug spray is for and what it will do. Think of a clever name for your repellent and draw a picture to show what your repellent does. *(25 points)*

_____ 5. How would you draw each of the bugs listed below if you did not know what each bug was but did know what the words in their names meant? Be creative in your drawings. *(15 points)*
Dragonfly	Silverfish
Yellow Jacket	Walking Stick
Bedbug	

_____ 6. Which insect has the most effect — good, bad, or both — on you and your family? Defend your answer in a detailed paragraph. *(25 points)*

(Schurr, 1992, p. 135.)

Adapting Contracts To Your Classroom

Directions: Choose a skill or concept that is taught in your subject area. Use it to develop a student contract similar to any of the formats modeled here. Try to make the tasks interdisciplinary in nature. For example, if you are a science teacher be sure to include a language arts task or a math task that fits in with the theme of your contract. If you are an English teacher, try to integrate a skill from math, art, music, or social studies as part of your instructional options.

(Schurr, 1992, p. 136.)

4. Self-Assessments

Description

Self-assessment occurs when students evaluate their own work.

Evaluation Context

Self-assessment is a particularly powerful **formative** evaluation method. It is designed to allow students to take more responsibility for their learning by reflecting upon their own activities.

Encouraging the student to become involved in setting criteria for evaluation of his or her work shifts a portion of responsibility to the student. Used selectively, with more emphasis on student growth and self-understanding than on aiming at a final grade, self-evaluation can contribute to a student's ability to structure his or her own learning. It can increase a student's ownership of the learning process.

A further instructional purpose is served when students help in developing criteria. Students learn the expectations concerning their work in greater depth.

Self-evaluation should be reserved for those situations where student self-knowledge about the learning process is important. A major project involving a mix of learning skills such as researching, planning, drafting and bringing to completion is a good example.

Guidelines for Use

In self-assessment, the situation should be structured so that the student feels that he or she is truly in control of the evaluation. A small percentage of the evaluation responsibility totally within the student's control is preferable to a larger percentage ostensibly 'negotiated' between the teacher and the student. Developing the evaluation criteria should be part of the exercise. Students, working alone or in groups, make the initial suggestions and these are modified in consultation with the teacher.

(Saskatchewan Education, 1991, p. 59.)

Using the Information for Student Evaluation

The aim of education is to produce autonomy, not dependency, and it is therefore not only legitimate but important that students become able to evaluate their own work. The more students understand and internalize criteria for assessing their own progress, the less arbitrary will assessment — and education — seem to them. Furthermore, inviting students to evaluate their own work shows respect for them as responsible people. *(Pratt, 1991, p. 86.)*

Hints

If self-evaluation is to be used in the summative mode, the following points should be considered to ensure that the student evaluation result overlaps as much as possible with the teacher evaluation result.

- Offer a sequence of self-evaluation opportunities. Experience in self-evaluation activity increases overlap of student and teacher evaluations.

- Restrict self-evaluation to traditional tasks. For example, assess the relative quality of written products. Overlap is the greatest on such tasks and the least on attitude measures.

- Avoid global ratings. Overlap is greatest on specific tasks rather than on global ratings.

- Take the time and effort to work with the students to develop evaluation criteria together. Overlap increases with student development and ownership of evaluation criteria.

- Avoid evaluating 'effort'. Overlap is minimal for teacher and student estimates of effort.

(Saskatchewan Education, 1991, p. 60.)

Self-Assessment/Metacognition

Student: _____ Date: _____

1. What were you supposed to do?

2. What did you do well? Why?

3. What was your least favourite part? Why?

4. What key things did you learn?

5. With what do you still need help?

6. If you did this task over, what would you do differently?

7. What grade do you think you deserve and why?

8. Can you "connect" this assignment with something you learned in another class? How?

9. Can you connect this assignment with something in your own life? Explain.

10. What are your new goals?

---

*(Burke, K., **Authentic Classroom Assessments**, Workshop presentation, 1993, p. 36.)*

Self-Assessment
ATTITUDES

Name: _____   Date: _____

To the Student

Use the following sentence openers to consider your ideas, feelings, and beliefs about yourself and others.

---

1. The thing I like most about my appearance is

2. I really enjoy

3. If I had only one day to live, I would

4. It really bugs me when

5. When I get angry, I

6. What I value most in a friend is

7. The person I would most like to be is

8. Some day I would like to

9. I hope I never

10. The job I would most like to do is

11. I'm glad that

12. My favourite relative is

13. I like her/him because

14. If I could have one wish, it would be

15. The thought that scares me most is

16. You can tell that someone likes/loves you if

17. My favourite way to use my spare time is

18. My biggest contribution to my family is

19. I wish I didn't have to

20. The thing I do best is

(Basic English OAIP, 1991, pp. 34–36.)

Assess for Success

Rating Scale for Student Self-Assessment
in Cooperative Work Situations

Student Name: _____

Date or Time Period of Assessment: _____

Directions:

Read each question. Circle the phrase that best describes how you feel about each statement.

1. How do you feel about choosing the members of your group on a project?

   I really like it.   It's okay.   I don't like it.

2. How do you feel about having your teacher choose the members of your group on a project?

   I really like it.   It's okay.   I don't like it.

3. How do you feel about deciding in your group how you are going to work together to do a project?

   I really like it.   It's okay.   I don't like it.

4. How do you feel about taking a leadership role in your group when you are deciding how to do a project?

   I really like it.   It's okay.   I don't like it.

5. How do you feel about someone else taking a leadership role in your group when you are deciding how to do a project?

   I really like it.   It's okay.   I don't like it.

6. How do you feel about working together to finish a project in class?

   I really like it.   It's okay.   I don't like it.

7. How do you feel about being part of a group that works together to complete a project for your school work?

   I really like it.   It's okay.   I don't like it.

(Saskatchewan Education, 1991, p. 61.)

Self-Assessment with Essay Question/Assignment

Student Name: _____

Date: _____

Directions: Check (√) appropriate criteria.

Pre-Writing State:

- Have I read the question carefully? _____

- Did I highlight the key words or phrases? _____

- Did I construct an outline that includes the key
  words and the main ideas? _____

The Essay

A. Introduction

- Did I make sure the topic of my essay is included in
  the introductory paragraph? _____

- Did I say what my point of view or theme was in a clear manner? _____

B. Body of Essay

- Does each of my paragraphs link back to my introduction? _____

- Is each of my ideas or details in the introduction followed up
  in the body of my essay? _____

- Do I have enough proof to support my reasoning? _____

C. Conclusion

- Do I have a concluding paragraph that supports what I
  have already stated? _____

- Have I been careful to avoid putting in new data that I
  have not already reported? _____

Post-Writing State:

- Did I read over my final copy to look for possible changes and
  improvements of such things as spelling and sentence structure? _____

(Saskatchewan Education, 1991, p. 64.)

Assess for Success

INDEPENDENT LEARNING
Self-Assessment

Students should do a self-assessment of how they are progressing and what they have achieved. Reflection is a way of consolidating learning and of increasing the likelihood of improved performance next time. Their reflection can include the process, the product, and the learning. The questions below are good "starters" for individual students. They can be adapted for use by groups.

1. To what extent did I achieve what I intended to achieve?

2. What did I achieve that I hadn't even thought about?

3. How valuable was this?

4. What were the best and worst features of this unit of work?

5. Did the products have features beyond the initial expectations?

6. Did the products and skills convey what they were intended to convey?

7. Which aspects or features were most successful, and which would need improvement next time?

8. Are the products and skills likely to continue to be valued and used?

9. How do these products compare in quality with those made last time?

10. Do I understand more about the concepts and ideas upon which the work was based?

11. Can I explain what I know, in talk, in writing, or in some other medium?

12. Can I teach someone else the ideas and concepts that I set out to understand?

13. Can I apply what I learned in new situations?

*(**Senior English OAIP**, Providing Learning Through Assessment (Draft), 1991, pp. 37–38.)*

PHYSICAL EDUCATION
Student Self-Evaluation

Name: _____   Activity: _____

1. PARTICIPATION READINESS

I was on time and present:

> everyday
> absent or late 1 day
> absent or late 2 days
> absent or late more than 2 days
> absent or late more than 5 days (note from parent)

2. EFFORT

In this unit my effort in warmups and drills was:

> outstanding
> good
> did what was asked
> didn't put forth much effort
> didn't participate much at all

3. CO-OPERATION

My co-operation with teachers, students and on assigned tasks was:

> excellent (helped with class management/teaching)
> good
> did most of what was expected
> had to be encouraged to be more co-operative
> demonstrated inappropriate behaviour

4. SKILLS

As a result of taking this unit my skills have:

> really improved
> improved a little
> haven't improved but got good practice
> didn't improve skills

5. THEORY

As a result of this unit I learned:

> a lot more about this activity
> a little more about this activity
> very little I didn't already know

Comments on this unit:

(Adapted from Physical Education Department, Sir Frederick Banting Secondary School, London Board of Education.)

Assess for Success

SELF-EVALUATION SCALE OF WRITING SKILLS

Developmental Stages from Dependence to Independence

STAGE 4 **INDEPENDENT WRITER** (independent, autonomous writer)	• makes highly objective self-assessments • has developed a sophisticated personal style • has developed a writer's voice • takes risks and experiments • is self-motivating and self-aware as a writer • is a craftsperson
STAGE 3 **WILLING WRITER** (peer-involved, willing writer)	• is able to collaborate well with others • requires external feedback to shape progress • is able to profit from criticism • can monitor personal progress • is developing objectivity concerning work • enjoys practising craft • is developing a sensitivity to audience
STAGE 2 **TRANSITIONAL WRITER** (transitional, self-involved, self-delineating writer)	• needs support and coaching in order to develop • learns from modelled behaviours • is developing a degree of comfort with craft • is anxious to stand alone yet is uncomfortable with peer collaboration • is developing an awareness of personal needs, interests, and preoccupations
STAGE 1 **NOVICE WRITER** (unskilled, unaware, teacher-dependent writer)	• has little, if any, individual style • has little awareness of writing process • has undeveloped skills and techniques • seeks approval from teacher • is reluctant to revise any writing • believes good writing comes easily

(Association of Large School Boards in Ontario, 1986, p. I-02.)

Self-Evaluation
FITNESS AND LIFESTYLE

Name: _____

For each of the items below, indicate on the scale where you feel you should be rated for Sept.–Oct.

A. Attitude and Enthusiasm

    Low   1   2   3   4   5   High

B. Fitness Improvement

    Low   1   2   3   4   5   High

C. Physical Involvement – running

    Low   1   2   3   4   5   High

D. Physical Involvement – dancercize warmup

    Low   1   2   3   4   5   High

E. Involvement: Verbal

    Low   1   2   3   4   5   High

F. Involvement: Listening

    Low   1   2   3   4   5   High

G. Co-operation

    Low   1   2   3   4   5   High

H. Consideration of Others

    Low   1   2   3   4   5   High

Days Absent: _____   Note(s) Yes _____ No _____

Days late: _____   Note(s) Yes _____ No _____

Days of non-active participation: _____   Note(s) Yes _____ No _____

I honestly think that I deserve a(n) _____ (letter grade) because

*(Scarborough, **Fitness: A Healthy Lifestyle**, 1992, p. 10.)*

5. Peer-Assessments

Description

Peer-assessment occurs when a student's work is evaluated by some or all of the other students.

Evaluation Context

Peer-evaluation is designed to allow students to take more responsibility for their learning by reflecting upon it and by receiving feedback from their peers. In peer-evaluation, the student is learning about learning through reflecting on the activities of other students.

Peer-evaluation can add a further dimension to a student's growth in self-knowledge. Students who are more concerned with "you scratch my back and I'll scratch yours" considerations than with developing insights into the learning process may experience a shift in attitude. More responsibility for what they do and how they do it will occur when they are in consultation with peers who are providing suggestions for improvement. Great benefits accrue to the students who are doing the evaluation and **are forced to think analytically** about the nature of their peers' performance. In turn, they are able to extend that thinking to their own performance.

Peer-evaluation should be reserved for those situations where student self-knowledge about the learning process is important, and to those situations where a high degree of student interaction is encouraged.

Guidelines for Use

In peer-assessment, the parameters within which the students will evaluate their peers should be narrow and carefully defined. When considering what aspects should be peer-evaluated, **the teacher should emphasize those areas where the act of peer-evaluating will help the student doing the evaluation in addition to helping the student being evaluated.** Not only will this approach maximize the benefits of the exercise, but it will also reduce the influence of any student bias that might exist. Areas to stress are being descriptive rather than judgmental, being consistent, being realistic, being positive, and being reflective.
(Saskatchewan Education, 1991, p. 59.)

Using the Information for Student Evaluation

Assessment is usually viewed as a major responsibility of teachers. However, teaching students to assess one another's work not only shares the heavy load of marking, but also helps students to learn and to take responsibility. It utilizes a potentially rich source of feedback that is always available though usually neglected, right in the classroom. It is necessary that the criteria be discussed with students and be as clear as possible. In awarding marks to the work of peers, students tend to be cautious and use rather a narrow range of marks. Peer-assessment is **particularly valuable for formative assessment**. Sometimes a successful division of labour can be established by peers identifying good and bad points, and teachers awarding marks. If the assessment is summative, the teacher must be certain that the marks awarded can be justified.
(Pratt, 1991, p. 86.)

Hints

Caution should be exercised when using peer-evaluation in a summative mode.

Evaluating Writing as Process

Directions

1. **List three things** you think you could write something about.

2. **Talk with others** about your potential topics.
   (a) Find a partner.
   (b) With your partner, take turns talking about things you could both write about, and explain why you find these things interesting.
   (c) Help your partner find and develop a topic.

3. **Write the first draft.**
   (a) Take time to put on paper some of the ideas you were just talking about with your partner.
   (b) Just write about the topic without stopping to correct your spelling or grammar. The idea is to get all your ideas down on paper.
   (c) Try to write as much as you can, until you are asked to the stop.

4. **Confer with a peer about the first draft.**
   (a) The teacher (or another student) may read the first draft out loud and talk briefly about it.
   (b) Go back to your partner. Read your first drafts aloud to each other.
   (c) As you are reading, you will both notice things you forgot to say and phrases that don't sound right. Just fill in what's missing by explaining it to your partner.

5. **Revise the first draft.**
   (a) Now take a good hard look at the writing you did. What's good about it? What do you like the best? How do you think you could make it better? What changes could you make?
   (b) Revise your first draft.
   (c) There are four basic ways of revising. Experiment with all of them. Which one do you tend to use most often? Least often?
      (i) adding more details or ideas,
      (ii) deleting unnecessary words, phrases, sections,
      (iii) moving things around, and
      (iv) replacing words and expressions

6. **Peer Conference on the revised draft.**
   (a) Find a new partner.
   (b) Using the *Peer Conference Record* form on the next page, your new partner comments on your revised draft and attaches the form to your draft.
   (c) On the bottom of the *Peer Conference Record* record your responses to your partner's comments.
   (d) Hand in both the revised draft and the *Peer Conference Record*.

7. **Revisions and Reflections**

   (a) Make notes in the margins of your revised draft about further changes you think you would like to make.

   (b) Write a learning log entry, explaining how you feel about this piece of writing. What are its strong points and its weak points? What would you do with it next? How did the peer conferences help you? How did they perhaps hinder you?

*(**Senior English OAIP**, "Involving Students in Assessment" (draft), 1991, pp. 17–18.)*

Peer Conference Record

Draft #: _____   Date: _____

Title/Topic:

Purpose:

Audience:

Feedback received from:

Comments made by conference partner:

Writer's Response:

---

*(**Senior English OAIP**, Involving Students in Assessment (draft), 1991, pp. 19.)*

Peer-Evaluation of a Group Presentation

Names of Presenters: _____

Topic Presented: _____

Circle the mark you consider most appropriate for each of the following categories:

1. Evidence of research and preparation

Did the presenters demonstrate mastery of their topic, or did they simply read a prepared text? Did they seem to know about what they were talking? Did they cover all, or most of the suggested topics listed on the Seminar Topics guideline?

1	2	3	4	5	6	7	8	9	10
poor	*adequate*	*average*			*good*	*very good*	*excellent*		

2. Content

Was the material up-to-date? Complete? Was there new information or merely a repetition of common knowledge of which you were already aware? Were case studies included? Were legal aspects of the information emphasized?

1	2	3	4	5	6	7	8	9	10
poor	*adequate*	*average*			*good*	*very good*	*excellent*		

3. Clarity

Was the information presented in language which you could easily understand and follow? Did it make sense to you? Was there an organized and cohesive flow, or was it disjointed? Were terms explained? Was existing law identified, or did the group rush through their topic? Could you pass a test on this topic?

1	2	3	4	5	6	7	8	9	10
poor	*adequate*	*average*			*good*	*very good*	*excellent*		

4. Planning

Was there equal participation by each member? Did each presenter speak slowly enough to permit notemaking? Make eye contact with the class? Were audio-visual materials used and appropriately introduced? Was there a guest speaker, if appropriate, for the topic?

1	2	3	4	5	6	7	8	9	10
poor	*adequate*	*average*			*good*	*very good*	*excellent*		

5. Discussion

Was the discussion on topic? Did presenters ask questions of the class? Were all questions posed by presenters or the class answered to your satisfaction? Did the class interact with the presenters by asking questions or discussing issues?

1	2	3	4	5	6	7	8	9	10
poor	*adequate*	*average*			*good*	*very good*	*excellent*		

6. Overall Impact

What was your general impression of the seminar presentation?

1	2	3	4	5	6	7	8	9	10
poor	*adequate*	*average*			*good*	*very good*	*excellent*		

Total Mark   /60

(Frontenac Secondary School, Business Department.)

Peer Evaluation Rating Scale for Accounting Firm
NAME, LOGO, AND SLOGAN

Observe the company name, logo, and slogan packages of each of the other groups in the class. (Use a separate checklist sheet for each group's package.)

Name of Student Evaluator _____

Name of Firm Being Evaluated _____

Rating Scale: Excellent   2   1   0   Needs improvement

    1. Appropriateness of company name. 2 1 0

    2. Visual impact of the logo. 2 1 0

    3. Recall value of the firm's slogan. 2 1 0

    4. Originality of the entire package. 2 1 0

*(Metropolitan Toronto, **Accounting**, 1989, p. 33.)*

6. Portfolios

Description

A portfolio is a collection of student-produced materials assembled over an extended period of time that allows the teacher to evaluate student growth and overall learning progress during that period of time. It is an organizational structure teachers may use to accumulate and organize student assessment information. Samples of work to be included may be selected by the student, by the teacher, or by the student and teacher in consultation.

Evaluation Context

Since the materials in the portfolio have been collected over a period of time, the student's progress can be judged in a way few other assessment techniques can offer. Portfolios encourage students to collect and reflect on work. Reviewing the materials at the end of the course is like looking at a set of photographs taken during a child's developmental years.

Using Technique to Best Advantage

Portfolios are sufficiently versatile to be used in all subject areas. The particular strengths of this technique lie in allowing a teacher to evaluate students on developmental patterns and on attributes such as creativity and critical thought, responsibility for learning, research skills, perseverance, and communication skills.

Guidelines for Use

The portfolio is more than a collection of student work. Before the portfolio is begun, inclusion rules need to be established. Some decisions are:

- Who will decide what to include? Student? Teacher? Both, working in consultation?
- What will be included? Examples of best work? Examples of worst work? Examples of typical work? Some of each type?
- Will there be an overall limit to the amount of materials that can be included?

The answers to these inclusion rules will provide the framework within which the teacher and the student can operate.

Since the purpose of the portfolio is to record student progress over a long time period, the collection should be started as early in the course as possible. Baseline data is particularly valuable. Subsequent additions should be made according to the prearranged framework, always allowing for unexpected additions. There are really three phases in the development of a portfolio:

1. Before the collection begins, decisions need to be made. Who will decide what to include? What will be included? etc.

2. Collecting the materials.
   Throughout the span of the portfolio, place the selected materials in a folder or large envelope. Each item should be dated and have a note attached to it from the teacher or the student stating why the material was chosen and what special features should be recalled later.

3. Evaluating the materials.
   When the portfolio is complete, teachers will need to examine the contents once again. One method is to prepare a grid — see page 140 for an example of an assessment grid for portfolios — with the list of attributes a teacher decides to assess written down one side and a rating scale across the top. Complete the grid. A complete grid will provide a rich array of assessment information.

Using the Information for Student Evaluation

A grid can serve as an assessment document just as it is. If a teacher wishes to record a mark, he/she can also assign numbers to the 5 points on the scale and convert the assessment into a mark.

Hints

- Limit the number of items as storage can become a problem. For example, teachers or students can leave out things like quizzes or final exams which may not directly fit the portfolio philosophy that emphasizes work created by the student.
- Teachers may wish the student to have the portfolio item available for reference. In that case, file a photocopy in the portfolio. Senior students often produce written work on computers. They will find it easy to produce two copies of products, one for the portfolio and one for themselves.

- Portfolios are powerful ways to report student progress to parents/guardians. Prepare a "typical" portfolio with samples from previously taught students. Be sure to remove names and obtain student permission. Use this sample portfolio to help inform parents/guardians about your expectations of students in your class.

(Adapted from Saskatchewan Education, 1991, p. 65.)

What is in a Portfolio?

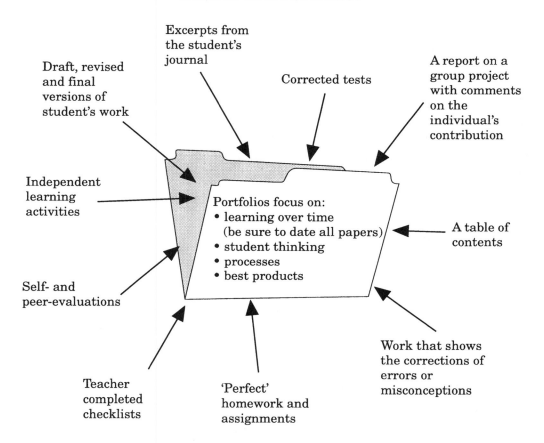

(Waterloo, 1993, Appendix A, p. 10.)

QUESTIONS TO ANSWER BEFORE DESIGNING PORTFOLIOS

What does the portfolio contain evidence about?

- ✧ What is the purpose of the portfolio?
- ✧ Is the purpose the same for all students?
- ✧ Will the portfolio contain evidence of proficiency or progress?
- ✧ To what uses will the portfolio be put?
- ✧ When, how often, and by whom will the portfolio be reviewed?

What will count as evidence in the portfolio?

- ✧ Which pieces are required and which will be selected?
- ✧ Must evidence be produced alone or can it be produced collaboratively?
- ✧ Will the portfolio contain only best work?
- ✧ Where will the portfolio be kept?
- ✧ How much evidence will be kept in the portfolio?

SUGGESTIONS FOR CREATING PORTFOLIOS

- date all samples
- actively involve students in its development and criteria for selection of samples
- devise a management tool to ensure that adequate samples are collected from each student
- include self-evaluations
- include work "in progress" as well as completed work
- provide students with models of portfolios
- place copies of work done by a group into portfolios of each group member
- once or twice per term, have students select their favourite entry and write a paragraph explaining why

ADVANTAGES TO PORTFOLIOS

- focuses on the positive aspects of evaluation
- encourages students to take charge of their own learning
- encourages students to assign value to their own work
- provides evidence of growth and valuable information for reporting and conferencing
- is reflective of different learning styles
- encourages an active role for students in assessment
- having students take portfolios home now and then can open communication and understanding for parents

DISADVANTAGES TO PORTFOLIOS

- can be time consuming in reading and evaluating portfolio
- can be 'messy' to manage
- if students control the portfolios, items can be lost or destroyed
- is challenging to grade a portfolio since it is difficult to reduce the year's work down to one mark

*(Waterloo, **Assessment for Learning**, 1993, p. 28.)*

Classroom Application
ENGLISH: CREATIVE WRITING

Directions: You will be collecting samples of your writing during the school year. Please follow these guidelines for putting together your writing portfolio:

1. Keep your writing samples in the cardboard file box which the teacher has given you for this purpose.

2. Organize each writing sample so that it is in chronological order. Make sure the date is on each item.

3. Select items for your portfolio that will best show your parents what you are doing during writing time in class.

4. Try to include one writing sample for each week of the school year.

5. Once a month, include both your first draft and your final copy for one writing sample.

6. Do not include any writing sample that you do not feel good about or that you do not feel is satisfactory. Of course, the writing samples you do at the beginning of the year will not be as exemplary as those you include at the end of the year.

7. At the end of the school year, select your five best writing samples and write out a rationale for each choice.

WRITING SAMPLES IN POETRY

(Select two writing examples from this group)

___ Haiku	___ Limerick	___ Free Verse
___ Diamante	___ Tanka	___ Other

FOLKLORE

(Choose two writing samples from this group)

___ Legend	___ Tall Tale	___ Myth
___ Fairy Tale		___ Fable

MEDIA

(Include four writing samples from this group)

___ Editorial	___ News Story
___ Book/Movie Review	___ Letter to the Editor
___ Newspaper Advertisement	___ Television Commercial
___ Radio Announcement	___ Advice Column
___ Feature Story	

HUMOROUS WRITING

(Include three examples from this group)

___ Original jokes	___ Original riddles	___ Editorial cartoon
___ Comic strip	___ Puns	___ Tongue twisters

FICTIONAL WRITING

(Include three examples from this group)

___ Short story   ___ Bedtime story   ___ Character sketch
___ Skit or play   ___ Fantasy story   ___ Science fiction story

NON FICTIONAL WRITING

(Include three examples from this group)

___ Autobiography   ___ Biography   ___ Character sketch
___ Encyclopedia entry   ___ Interview   ___ Magazine article

MISCELLANEOUS WRITING

(Include three examples from this group)

___ Pamphlet   ___ Travel brochure   ___ Horoscopes
___ Prayer   ___ Critique   ___ Book jacket
___ Record album cover   ___ Magazine advertisement   ___ Tribute

(Schurr, 1992, pp. 145–155.)

An Example of an Assessment Grid for Portfolios
PORTFOLIO ASSESSMENT

Student Name: _____   Class: _____   Date: _____

Attribute to be Evaluated	Very Good	Good	Scale Average	Poor	Very Poor
originality					

(Saskatchewan Education, 1991, p. 67.)

When designed and used well, portfolios can be very beneficial for student learning, teacher professionalism, communication with parents, and measuring certain types of student learning *(Buell, 1991)*.

There is no one "right" way to design a portfolio system because it depends on context, purpose, and audience. When using portfolios for assessment and instruction, we need to be cautious that such assessments are developed and used properly. We can be misled by work portfolios because the content looks so right. We might not notice that the material was not generated in a way to show what students can do or that it is not representative of student work, etc. There is the danger that if we allow users to rush into use of portfolios for instruction and assessment purposes without thinking through their assessment needs, how a portfolio fits into these needs, and what potential problems they might encounter, they could very likely be confused and disappointed when the portfolio assessment does not fulfill their expectations of "fixing" all assessment problems.

Teachers may want to take the **Self-Test** on pages 142–144 before deciding to use portfolios in their classroom. The Answers to the Self-Test can be found on page 144. Worksheets #1–5 on Portfolio Development Questions can be used by the teacher to gain some focus before using portfolios as a part of their program.

Portfolio Self-Test

1. For your portfolio system, who will be involved in planning? Who will have primary control over the decisions to be made? What leeway will there be for experimentation?

2. Which of the following purposes are of particular importance for the portfolio system you are developing?

   ____ To show growth or change over time

   ____ To show the process by which work is done as well as the final product

   ____ To create collections of favourite or personally important work

   ____ To trace the evolution of one or more projects/products

   ____ To prepare a sample of best work for employment or college admission

   ____ To document achievement for alternative credit for coursework

   ____ To place students in the most appropriate course

   ____ To communicate with students' subsequent teacher

   ____ To review curriculum or instruction

   ____ Large scale assessment

   ____ Program evaluation

   ____ Other:

3. What are two major instructional goals for your program?

   How will portfolios be used for classroom instructional assessment in the system you are designing? What problems (if any) do you anticipate? What issues need to be resolved?

   What questions would you consider asking students in order to prompt them to self-reflect on the work they are choosing for their portfolios?

4. What is the general curricular focus of the portfolio system you are planning?

   ____ Reading

   ____ Math

   ____ Writing

   ____ Integrated Language Arts

   ____ Science

   ____ Social Studies

   ____ Fine Arts

   ____ Cross-disciplinary or interdisciplinary

   ____ Other:

   Keeping in mind the classroom goals for students you listed in #3, consider the kinds of things that might go into the portfolios you are designing in order to promote the attainment of those goals and, at the same time, provide good evidence of the achievement of those goals. First, what might be required to be included in all portfolios, if anything? Second, list four categories of things that should be included in the work students select for their portfolios. How many samples of each of these things should students select?

   Will you allow open-ended choices for the portfolio? How many open-ended items will be allowed?

Who will you get to assist you in finalizing these decisions?

What requirements will you have for when entries are selected for the portfolio, if any?

5. For the portfolio system you are developing, choose one of the types of products that students will be asked to place in their portfolio. What should a good performance look like? What does a poor performance look like? In other words, what are your criteria for judging performance?

For your portfolio system, which of the following considerations do you think are likely to be important in assessing the portfolio as a whole product?

____ Amount of information included

____ Quality of individual pieces

____ Variety in the kinds of things included

____ Quality and depth of self-reflection

____ Growth in performance, as indicated in products or materials included

____ Apparent changes in attitude or behaviour, as indicated on surveys, questionnaires, etc.

____ Other:

What criteria will you use to assess the student metacognition or self-reflection in the portfolio?

____ Thoroughness

____ Accuracy

____ Support of statements by pointing to specific aspects of the work

____ Good synthesis of ideas

____ Self-revelation

____ Other:

Who will help develop, select, adapt the performance criteria?

____ Students

____ Teachers

____ Curriculum experts

____ Evaluation and assessment experts

____ Other:

How will you ensure that your criteria reflect current thinking concerning good performance in the area(s) you chose?

If you intend to aggregate information across students, how will you do this?

6. In your portfolio system, who will select specific work samples for the portfolio?

____ Student only

____ Teacher only

____ Student and teacher

____ Other:

How will storage and transfer occur, if at all?

Who will have ownership of the portfolio?

____ The student alone

____ The teacher(s) alone

_____ The student and teacher(s) together

_____ The school at which the portfolio is created

_____ Parents

_____ The student and parents together

_____ The school at which the portfolio is currently stored and used

_____ Other:

Who will have access to the portfolios?

_____ The student and teacher(s) who created it

_____ Any teacher who needs/wants information provided by that portfolio

_____ Counselors

_____ Anyone in the school where the portfolio is housed

_____ Anyone from the district who shares an interest in the student's educational welfare

_____ Parents

_____ Other(s):

7. Imagine that you are planning to initiate your portfolio system during the coming year. Which of the following types of in-service training would be most helpful to you and others that will be involved?

_____ Overview of the philosophy/rationale for use of portfolios

_____ Practical hands-on workshop on designing/assembling portfolios

_____ Ideas for portfolio management (e.g., ownership, transfer, etc.)

_____ Training in sound assessment practices, including use of portfolios in assessment

_____ Training in development and use of sound criteria

_____ Training in how to teach students good self-reflection skills

_____ Content area training

_____ Other:

Answers to Self-Test

Your self-test is performance based. Evaluate your responses using the following criteria:

1. Completeness. Look for the following:

a. Did you answer all the questions? If not, did you have a good reason for not doing so? If you were unable to answer any of the questions right now, do you have a plan for how you will go about answering the questions?

b. How much would it take to "clean up" your comments if they were going to be used as a discussion piece for a district/teacher committee looking into portfolios?

c. Did you jot down other issues that should be addressed in addition to those listed?

2. Quality. Look for the following:

a. What would be the reaction of each of the following groups to your plan — teachers, district personnel, students, parents, the school board, others? Did you take their points of view into account? If not, did you note why?

b. Does your plan promote good instruction? If teachers carried out your design all year, would their students have received a good education?

c. Does your plan promote good assessment? If your design were carried out, would you have quality information? Would assessment pitfalls be avoided?

d. Is your plan practical?

e. Is your plan flexible?

3. Individuality. Look for the following:

a. Does your plan match the curriculum in your classroom or district?

b. Do your ideas reflect your own personal concept of what a good portfolio can or should be?

(Arter and Spandel, 1992. pp. 36–44.)

Portfolio Development Questions — Worksheet #1
PART 1: PURPOSES FOR A PORTFOLIO
HOW COULD YOU USE A PORTFOLIO?

Which of the following purposes are of particular importance for the portfolio system you are developing?

____ To show growth or change over time

____ To show the process by which work is done as well as the final product

____ To create collections of favorite or personally important work

____ To trace the evolution of one or more projects/products

____ To prepare a sample of best work for employment or admission

____ To document achievement for alternative credit for coursework

____ To place students in the most appropriate course

____ To communicate with student's subsequent teacher

____ To review curriculum or instruction

____ Large-scale assessment

____ Program evaluation

____ Other

(Using Portfolios Workshop, Northwest Regional Educational Laboratory, 1992.)

Portfolio Development Questions — Worksheet #2
PART 2: GUIDELINES FOR SELECTION
WHAT WORK GOES IN THE PORTFOLIO?

What is the general curricular focus of the portfolio system you are planning?

____ Reading   ____ Writing

____ Integrated Language Arts   ____ Social Studies

____ Science   ____ Fine Arts

____ Math   ____ Other

What are two major instructional goals for your program(s)?

1.

2.

What items might be included in the portfolio? Some things may be required; some things may be optional — in which case you might simply list suggestions to give students ideas. Remember, guidelines can range from unstructured (e.g., choose something you feel proud of, something that represents your work as a 6th grader, etc.) to highly structured (e.g., include an essay on a tragic figure in Shakespearean literature).

Must Be Included	Options
1.	1.
2.	2.
3.	3.
4.	4.
5.	5.

SOME IDEAS:

photos of projects	art works	science logs
research project	video tape	drama script
P.E. achievement award	test results	writing samples
affective surveys	rating scales	
personal response to a cultural event		

(Using Portfolios Workshop, Northwest Regional Educational Laboratory, 1992.)

Assess for Success

Portfolio Development Questions — Worksheet #3
PART 3: CRITERIA FOR JUDGING MERIT
WHAT CRITERIA WILL BE USED TO ASSESS
THE PORTFOLIOS AND WHO WILL DEVELOP THEM?

For the portfolio system you are developing, will you have criteria for work in the portfolio? ___ **Yes** ___ **No**. *If so, choose one of the types of products that students will be asked to place in their portfolio. What should a good performance look like? What does a poor performance look like? In other words, what are your criteria for judging performance?*

For your portfolio project, will you have criteria for assessing the portfolio as a whole product? ___ **Yes** ___ **No**. *If so, which of the following considerations do you think are likely to be important?*

___ Amount of information included

___ Quality of individual pieces

___ Variety in the kinds of things included

___ Quality and depth of self-reflection

___ Growth in performance, as indicated in products or materials included

___ Apparent changes in attitude or behaviour, as indicated on surveys, questionnaires, etc.

___ Student self-assessment

___ Other:

For your portfolio system, will you have criteria for analyzing student self-reflection? ___ **Yes** ___ **No**. *If so, what might you include?*

___ Thoroughness

___ Accuracy

___ Support of statements by pointing to specific aspects of the work

___ Good synthesis of ideas

___ Self-reflection

___ Other:

Who will help develop / select / adapt the performance criteria?

___ Students

___ Teachers

___ Curriculum experts

___ Evaluation and assessment experts

___ Other:

How will you ensure that your criteria reflect current thinking concerning good performance in the area(s) you chose?

(Using Portfolios Workshop, Northwest Regional Educational Laboratory, 1992.)

Portfolio Development Questions — Worksheet #4
PART 4: STUDENT PARTICIPATION IN SELECTION
WHO "OWNS" THE PORTFOLIO?

In your portfolio system, who will select specific work samples for the portfolio?

___ Student only

___ Teacher(s) only

___ Student and teacher(s) together

___ Other:

How will storage and transfer occur, if at all?

Who will have ownership of the portfolio?

___ The student alone

___ The teacher(s) alone

___ The student and teacher(s) together

___ The school at which the portfolio is created

___ The student and parents together

___ The school at which the portfolio is currently stored and used

___ Other:

Who will have access to the portfolios?

___ The student and teacher(s) who created it

___ Any teacher who needs/wants information provided by it

___ Counselors

___ Anyone in the school where the portfolio is housed

___ Anyone from the district who shares an interest in the student's educational welfare

___ Parents

___ Other:

(Using Portfolios Workshop, Northwest Regional Educational Laboratory, 1992.)

Portfolio Development Questions — Worksheet #5
PART 5: STUDENT SELF-REFLECTION

What questions would you consider asking students in order to prompt them to self-reflect on the work they are choosing for their portfolios?

1.

2.

3.

Return to the "Guidelines for Selection" worksheet page and decide which items you think would be appropriate for student self-reflection.

Choose one from your list and write a series of self-reflection questions or activities to guide students on their thinking.

1.

2.

3.

(Using Portfolios Workshop, Northwest Regional Educational Laboratory, 1992.)

7. Independent Study

Description

The goal of independent study is to make students responsible for their own learning. Independent study provides students with opportunities to state a definite goal, determine how it is to be achieved, and decide how the process and the goal itself are to be evaluated.

Students ask the following key questions:

1. What do I (we) already know?
2. What do I (we) want to know or find out?
3. How will I (we) go about finding out?
4. How will I (we) know and show that the goal is reached?

Independent study is not carried out in isolation. Small group, pair work and other kinds of interdependent learning may be part of the process and will improve the outcome. Students may do research outside the school and in the community. Students can experiment with final outcomes which may be oral, graphic or dramatic as well as written. The range of possible topics and outcomes is limited only by students' interests, imagination, and time, as well as by the resources available within the school and community.

**Questions to Ask When Developing
the Criteria for an Independent Study**

1. Is the proposed topic or content challenging and engaging?

2. Does it extend and offer points of connection with students' experience and previous knowledge?

3. Is it appropriate in terms of what has gone before?

4. Does it provide opportunities for the student(s) to contribute to the detailed planning of the experience?

5. Has the plan taken account of all the constraints and practical difficulties that may arise?

6. Do the goals seem achievable in the time allotted?

7. Is the plan flexible enough?

8. Is there genuine interest in the topic?

9. Are sufficient resources available?

10. Does the topic seem to generate enthusiasm?

11. Does the topic allow for exploration through a variety of learning media (e.g., art, talk, music, dance, drama, speech, writing, reading, and listening)?

---

*(**Senior English OAIP**, "Promoting Learning Through Assessment", (draft), 1991, p. 36.)*

Suggested Products of Independent Learning

Below you will find a list of various products students may create to demonstrate what they learn.

Essay
Calendar
Pamphlet
Book of fables
Picture book
Frieze
Chart
Promotional materials
Article for a local newspaper or for a magazine
Audio tape, as entertainment or as instruction
Album
Report
Live presentation
Automated slide/tape presentation: informative, evocative, or promotional
Videotape
Design plans
Dance
Folio of art work
Shadow puppetry
Fictional diary or other narrative form
Theatre production
Series of booklets
Animated cartoon
Photographic anthology or portrait gallery
Teaching or directing a group
Tourist guide
Excursion
Speech
Computer program
Poster
Anthology
Scrapbook
Drama
Display window

*(**Senior English OAIP**, "Promoting Learning Through Assessment", (draft), 1991, p. 35.)*

Evaluation Context

Independent study involves student responsibility for planning work and monitoring and assessing the process while the work is ongoing. Such self-evaluation does not occur in isolation. It should be a developing skill learned through dialogue and conversation with the teacher and peers.

It is natural for the teacher and student to observe progress together. To determine a mark for the process is more difficult. Teachers and students need to talk about and identify important steps in the process. One can assess the progress on independent study in several different ways. Have students monitor their own progress in learning journals. In addition, ask that regular reports be submitted. These reports will give the teacher a sense of how the student is progressing.

Students should do a self-assessment of how they are progressing and what they have achieved. Reflection is a way of consolidating learning and of increasing the likelihood of improved performance next time. Student reflection can include the process, the product, and the learning.

PRODUCT AND PROCESS EVALUATION

The following pages give some model forms for summative evaluation of process and product. Teachers can use them as they are or adapt them to fit the specific needs of their subject area.

Evaluation Guideline

Name: _____   Home Form: _____

Subject Class: _____

Subject Teacher: _____

Title or Description of Project: _____

Hours spent on project: _____   Date _____

A. Product Evaluation

1. Originality and Creativity of Idea   _____
2. Clarity and Focus of Presentation   _____
3. Mastery of Content   _____
4. Level and Sophistication of Content   _____
5. Care and Attention to Detail   _____
6. Energy, Enthusiasm, and Vitality   _____
7. Organization   _____
8. Originality and Variety of Presentation   _____
9. Skill, Expertise, and Professionalism of Presentation   _____
10. Value, Interest, and Impact of Product to Immediate or Projected Audience   _____

B. Process Evaluation

1. Definition and Focus of Project   _____
2. Identification of Problems and Problem Solving Strategies   _____
3. Development of Ideas through Logic, Sequence, and Transition   _____
4. Level, Diversity, and Appropriateness of Resources   _____
5. Commitment of Time and Effort   _____

C. Comments

Scale		*Contract*	
4	Outstanding	Completed	_____
3	Above average	Not completed	_____
2	Average		
1	Below Average		

(Independent Learning, 1989, p. 137.)

NARROWING THE TOPIC / ESTABLISHING A THESIS

DISPOSITIONS REQUIRED

SKILLS NEEDED
Use the decision-making strategy.

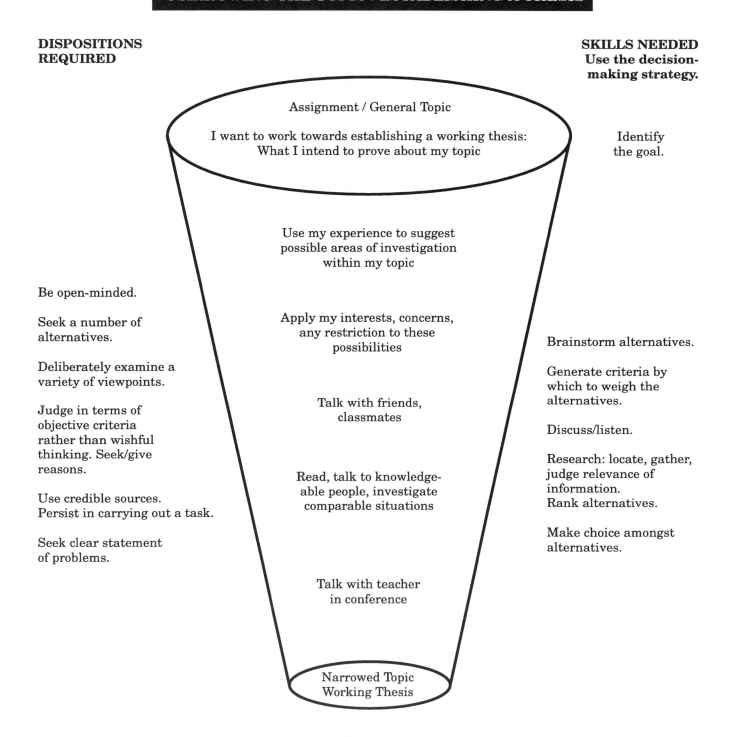

Assignment / General Topic

I want to work towards establishing a working thesis:
What I intend to prove about my topic

Identify the goal.

Use my experience to suggest
possible areas of investigation
within my topic

Be open-minded.

Seek a number of
alternatives.

Apply my interests, concerns,
any restriction to these
possibilities

Deliberately examine a
variety of viewpoints.

Brainstorm alternatives.

Generate criteria by
which to weigh the
alternatives.

Judge in terms of
objective criteria
rather than wishful
thinking. Seek/give
reasons.

Talk with friends,
classmates

Discuss/listen.

Research: locate, gather,
judge relevance of
information.
Rank alternatives.

Use credible sources.
Persist in carrying out a task.

Read, talk to knowledge-
able people, investigate
comparable situations

Make choice amongst
alternatives.

Seek clear statement
of problems.

Talk with teacher
in conference

Narrowed Topic
Working Thesis

Note: This process applies to establishing a specific topic within a general one, a narrower statement of the topic, and generating the specific intention — i.e. theses — in dealing with the topic. Students will probably move back and forth among the stages rather than proceed straightforwardly through them.

(Etobicoke Board of Education, Aitken et al., 1988.)

*(**Independent Learning**, 1989, p. 57.)*

Examples

Sample 1

INDEPENDENT STUDY TIMELINES
DCC OA1 ... Semester 2 ... 1991–92

February 10	• Receive initial handouts and discuss project
February 12	• Meet in resource centre with librarian to be introduced to research procedures
February 19	• Meet in resource centre again to finalize thesis statement
	• Conference with teacher to discuss acceptability of thesis statement
February 26	• Submit thesis statement form and keep photocopy of same *(5 marks)*
	• Receive copy of Independent Study Evaluation form
March 10	• Conference with teacher to show bibliography/reference list *(15 marks)*
April 14	• Conference with teacher to show rough notes produced from previous bibliography/references *(15 marks)*
May 5	• Conference to display Outline of Final Paper *(15 marks)*
May 26	• Submit Final Paper to be marked *(100 marks)*
Total	*150 marks*

(Adapted from Saunders Secondary School, London Board of Education.)

Sample 2

CONTRAT D'ÉTUDE INDÉPENDANTE

Nom _____   Date _____

A rendre à l'enseignant(e)

Voici le sujet de mon étude indépendante: _____

_____

_____

Je vais utiliser les ressources suivantes (livres personnels, bibliothèque de la classe, de l'école, de la ville, etc.). Donnez les titres principaux.

_____

_____

_____

Je serai aidé(e) dans mon travail par les étudiants suivants.

Nom _____

Il/Elle a accepté de m'aider à: _____

Nom _____

Il/Elle a accepté de m'aider à: _____

J'aurai deux entrevues avec mon enseignant(e) de français pour lui faire part de l'évolution de mon travail et pour discuter le plan de ma présentation orale.

La première sera le _____

Pour cette date, j'aurai terminé _____

_____

que je montrerai à l'enseignant(e).

La deuxième sera le _____

Pour cette date, j'aurai terminé _____

_____

que je montrerai à l'enseignant(e)

Je remettrai la partie écrite de mon projet le _____

Je ferai ma présentation orale le _____

Signature de l'étudiant(e):

Signature des étudiants-réviseurs:

Signature de l'enseignant(e):

(CENTRE ÉDUCATIF ET CULTUREL INC.)

Sample 3

INDEPENDENT STUDY WORK PLAN / LOG

Student: _____

Presentation Date:_____

Independent Study Period	Date	Planned Activities	Accomplishments
1			
2			
3			
4			
5			
6			
7			
8			
9			
10			
11			
12			
13			
14			
15			
16			

Date

Teacher
Check

1 _____   _____
signature

2 _____   _____
signature

3 _____   _____
signature

(*World Issues – OAC*, Scarborough, 1988, p. 26.)

Sample 4

INDEPENDENT STUDY PROGRESS CHART

Name: _____		
Thesis Statement	5	
Bibliography/References	15	
Rough Notes	15	
Outline of Paper	15	
Final Paper Evaluation	100	
Optional Presentation		
Total	150	

Sample 5

WORDPERFECT PRESENTATIONS

1. Using the HELP files and texts provided, experiment with all items in your assigned topic until you feel comfortable with it.

2. Prepare a clear, concise user manual (to be handed out to your classmates) on the topic selected. Include step-by-step instructions, examples and pitfalls to avoid.

3. Make up review sheets that others can use to try out these new features immediately.

4. The handouts will be evaluated according to the following criteria:
   - Aesthetic appeal
   - Notes condensed into authors' own words
   - Ease of interpretation
   - Comprehensive coverage of all topics
   - Effectiveness of review sheet(s)
   - Spelling and grammar

5. The presentation will be evaluated according to these criteria:
   - Equal contribution by all members in explanation and/or demonstration
   - Attentiveness of classmates during presentation
   - Voice dynamics
   - Pace of presentation
   - Thoroughness of explanation
   - Overall impression

6. The handouts must be handed in to the teacher to be run off no later than 8:00 a.m. on the day of presentation in order to be run off before the presentation (a day or two before is even better).

(Adapted from Saunders Secondary School, London Board of Education.)

WORDPERFECT HANDOUTS

Presenters _____   Mark ____ / 35

_____

	Poor				Excellent
Handouts are esthetically pleasing.	1	2	3	4	5
Written work is free from spelling errors.	1	2	3	4	5
Proper grammar and sentence structure has been used.	1	2	3	4	5
Notes have been condensed into the author's own words.	1	2	3	4	5
Text is easily understood.	1	2	3	4	5
All assigned sub-topics were covered completely.	1	2	3	4	5
The review sheets were quite helpful.	1	2	3	4	5

Comments:

Evaluator: _____

(Saunders Secondary School, London Board of Education.)

WORDPERFECT ORAL PRESENTATION

Presenters _____   Mark ____ / 35

_____

	Poor			Excellent	
Members contributed equally to the explanation and/or demonstration.	1	2	3	4	5
Classmates were attentive during the presentation.	1	2	3	4	5
Suitable voice dynamics were used.	1	2	3	4	5
Awareness of audience understanding was evident in pace of presentation.	1	2	3	4	5
Material was explained quite thoroughly.	1	2	3	4	5
Questions were answered well.	1	2	3	4	5
Overall impression.	1	2	3	4	5

Comments:

(Saunders Secondary School, London Board of Education.)

Sample 6: MARKING SCHEME FOR CREATIVE PERFORMANCE

Topic Format

Presented by   Marked by

Time started   Time completed

First Impression	Qualities	Assessment	Total
Performance Values /5	• Did the performance have audience appeal? • Were properties and costumes sufficient and appropriate? • Could you hear and understand the presentation well? • Did the presenters know their parts? • Was attention paid to all parts of the performance?	1 2 3 4 5 6 7 8 9 10 1 2 3 4 5 6 7 8 9 10 1 2 3 4 5 6 7 8 9 10 1 2 3 4 5 6 7 8 9 10 1 2 3 4 5 6 7 8 9 10	
Adherence To Form /5	• Was the performance within acceptable guidelines for its mode? (Teachers will have to make agreement with performers and markers on criteria.)	1 2 3 4 5 6 7 8 9 10	
Content /5	• Did the performance enrich the guidelines for its mode? • Was the performance on topic? • Was the content a suitable product for this level?	1 2 3 4 5 6 7 8 9 10 1 2 3 4 5 6 7 8 9 10 1 2 3 4 5 6 7 8 9 10	
Organization /5	• Did the performance start on time? • Were the presenters prepared and ready to take control?	1 2 3 4 5 6 7 8 9 10 1 2 3 4 5 6 7 8 9 10	
Creativity /5	• Did the presentation give you a fresh look at the topic? • Did you feel that the performance was creative?	1 2 3 4 5 6 7 8 9 10 1 2 3 4 5 6 7 8 9 10	

What were the strengths of this performance? Give two suggestions for expansion or improvement on the back of this sheet. *(Wellington County Board of Education.)* **(Independent Learning, 1989, p. 135.)**

Sample 7

INDEPENDENT STUDY SELF-EVALUATION				

Name: _____   Topic: _____

Scale:

To a great extent		Somewhat		Not at all
5	**4**	**3**	**2**	**1**

1. I consulted a variety of resources.	5	4	3	2	1
2. I made a special effort to acquire some unique resources.	5	4	3	2	1
3. I have a thorough understanding of the resources in my annotated bibliography.	5	4	3	2	1
4. I used the inquiry model to organize my independent study.	5	4	3	2	1
5. My presentation strategy is organized.	5	4	3	2	1
6. I maintained a good liaison with the teacher.	5	4	3	2	1
7. I used rough drafts to prepare my presentation.	5	4	3	2	1
8. I gave my best effort to this assignment.	5	4	3	2	1
9. I organized my time wisely during this assignment.	5	4	3	2	1
10. Because of my research I have an in-depth understanding of this topic.	5	4	3	2	1

TOTAL _____ x 2

= _____ %

*(Scarborough, **World Issues – OAC**, 1988, p. 17.)*

Sample 8

ADA OA1 INDEPENDENT STUDY PEER EVALUATION

Title _____ Playwright _____

In each of the following areas consider what the playwright has accomplished. Make extensive and detailed comments and rate each area with a letter grade A to E.

Characterization:

Grade _____

Plot:

Grade _____

Setting:

Grade _____

Stage Directions:

Grade _____

Theme or observation of some aspect of human truth:
(what does the play SAY to its audience?)

Grade _____

Comments on the overall success of the play and any suggestions that you feel might improve the script or help the writer.

Overall Evaluation   *Grade* _____

Name of evaluator _____

(Sylvia Valevicius, Sir Frederick Banting Secondary School, London Board of Education.)

Sample 9

GROUP MEMBER EVALUATION

Name: _____

This is a strictly private evaluation.

Rate each person on a scale of 0 to 6 (decimal fractions accepted).

Take your time … make this an honest evaluation. Your tally here is what percent of the final case study mark you think you and your partners deserve.

0	did nothing
1	poor
2	did just enough to get by
3	put forth a solid effort
4	did more than was required
5	could not reasonably expect more
6	did it all while others "watched"

Group Member Name	Leadership	Initiative	Co-operation	Time & Effort	Responsibility	Quality of Work	Total
Myself							

Explanation

1. **Leadership**   took an active role in organizing efforts and leading activities.

2. **Initiative**   took an active role in suggesting ideas and wasted no time in getting down to work on the task at hand.

3. **Co-operation**   worked well as a group member, helped others, shared ideas, listened, encouraged group performance.

4. **Time and Effort**   the degree to which the person put forth the necessary time and effort on a consistent basis to ensure that a quality case study was produced.

4. **Responsibility**   accepted jobs given by the group, had tasks completed on time.

6. **Quality of Work**   a thorough understanding of ideas, a desire to polish the final product, intelligent and articulate presentation.

Assess for Success

Sample 10

INDEPENDENT STUDY: TEACHER EVALUATION

Name: _____

	Excellent				Poor
Selection of Topic	5	4	3	2	1
Narrowing Skills					
Webbing Skills					
Information Gathering	5	4	3	2	1
Use of Resources					
Variety of Resources					
Time Management	5	4	3	2	1
In-Class					
Meeting Deadlines					
Interpersonal Skills	5	4	3	2	1
With Peers					
With Instructors					
Organizational Skills	5	4	3	2	1
Creative Approach					
Imaginative Approach					
Self-Discipline	5	4	3	2	1
Independent Work					
Seeks Assistance as Needed					
Presentation Skills	5	4	3	2	1
Well Organized Presentation					
Imaginative Format					

Strengths   ***Suggestions***

Summary Comments

Final Grade: _____

*(Waterloo, **Assessment for Learning**, 1993, p. 6.)*

Sample 11: Independent Study

PART A — ENG 4A1

CREATING A PERSONAL ANTHOLOGY

Reading widely with eagerness and enthusiasm can give life new meaning and broaden limited horizons. This independent study allows you to test this statement.

I Aim:

— to encourage a search for those works that best connect with your own personality, interests, and literary tastes.

II Objectives:

— to become more familiar with the literature of your own country and of our neighbours
— to read widely in various literary genres
— to formulate a personal philosophy
— to follow directions in completing a project
— to become familiar with the conventions of editing an anthology.

III The task:

A. Find and read from literature that is unfamiliar to you (i.e., not previously studied):

   1. *Works by Canadian authors:*
      1 poem   1 essay/article
      1 work from a genre of your choice   1 work of short fiction

   2. *Works by American writers:*
      1 poem   3 works from 2 genres of your choice

   3. *Works by your fellow students:*
      3 works from genre of your choice

   4. *Longer works, one of the following:*
      1 play (full length)   1 nonfiction work
      1 biography or diary   1 novel

   5. *A report/review of two of the following (seen between Feb. 1, '89 and May 1, '89):*
      The final review should be based on the format sheet given
         1 live performance (play, concert, talk, etc.)
         1 movie
         1 television show

B. Reading process:

   As you read, you should keep the following journals as a basis for the finished anthology:

   — a personal journal in which you comment on the suggested topics or record your day-to-day ideas
   — a reading journal based on the suggestion sheet. Each shorter work should have one entry, the longer works should have at least ten entries
   — a working log to keep track of times, places, work accomplished, and problems

C. Present the Anthology; it must have the following components:

Title page/Cover
Table of contents
Preface and dedication
Works
Your biography
Bibliography

IV Process (100 marks)

		Marks	*Due Dates*
A.	Exploratory search and reading (work group discussions and personal journal)	25	May 1
B.	Reading/Working log and notes	50	May 1
C.	At least one interview with teacher	10	
D.	Outline and rough copy of Preface	15	May 23

V Finished product (100 marks)   **June 5**

It must be typed, organized, bound, and presented according to the guidelines in the *Centennial Communications Guide*.

PART B: PERSONAL ANTHOLOGY MARK SHEETS

INDEPENDENT STUDY: PROCESS MARK SHEET		
Personal Anthology	**Your Mark**	**Total**
I Journals/logs		
A. Personal	15	
B. Reading	20	
C. Working	10	

II Collected works
  — correct number and categories
  — appropriate
 	
25		

III Reviews (rough copies) 20		
IV Work habits/use of time and resources 10		
Total 100		

```
┌─────────────────────────────────────────────────────────────────┐
│              INDEPENDENT STUDY: FINAL MARK SHEET                 │
│          ─────────────────────────────────────────              │
│  I    Process mark (previously evaluated)          100           │
│                                                                   │
│  II   Final copy                                                  │
│       A.  Title page                                              │
│       B.  Table of contents                                       │
│       C.  Preface and dedication                                  │
│       D.  Presentation of works                                   │
│           1.  Collection                                          │
│           2.  Reviews                                             │
│       E.  Biography                                               │
│       F.  Bibliography                                            │
│                                                                   │
│  III  Overall impression                            15            │
│                                                                   │
│  Total                                             200            │
│                                                                   │
│  Mark                                              100            │
└─────────────────────────────────────────────────────────────────┘
```

*(Adapted from **Independent Learning**, 1989, pp. 151–152.)*

Sample 11: Independent Study

MATHEMATICS — GRADES 7 TO 10 PROJECT ASSIGNMENT SHEET

Topic	Golden Section or Golden Ratio
Objectives	1. To understand and explain the meaning, the mathematical development and the application of the Golden Section or Golden Ratio.
	2. To be able to identify and locate the Golden Section or Golden Ratio in art and architecture.
	3. To express in written form the understanding of this mathematical concept.
	4. To be able to research a mathematical concept as it applies to art and architecture.
The Task	From sources such as the *Life Science Library: (Mathematics)*, encyclopedias and other resource books on drawing and painting, locate and record all facts, diagrams and calculations needed to complete your assignment. Your final report should include a title, an explanation or definition of the Golden Section, diagrams and calculations showing how the ratio is developed, a brief history of its application in works of art, two or three examples, and a written summary in which you briefly explain why you think this ratio is so often selected by artists and architects. Some class time will be provided to do the project. However, you should expect to do most of the work out of class. Your final report, including the title page, should be no more than four pages.
Due Dates	Project assigned *Nov. 1*
	(A) Rough copy to show to, and discuss with, your teacher *Nov. 12*
	(B) Final submission date *Nov. 20*

Criteria for Marking

25%   *Originality:*

Are the diagrams, comments and written work, and the structure presentation your own work?

30%   *Mathematical Thought and Application to Art and Architecture:*

Is there a clear indication of your understanding of the mathematics of the topic and its application to art and architecture?

Is there evidence that you have researched the topic?

20%   *Appearance and Workmanship:*

Is your presentation attractive and neat?

25%   *Clarity:*

Would the concepts, as you have explained them, be understood by readers?

Are the diagrams, pictures and explanatory notes orderly and relatively simple?

Note: This project will be worth ____ per cent of your term mark.

Note: This specific example is one of a group of topics that would be prepared for a class. Every student in the class need not receive the same assignment sheet.

(***Making the Grade***, 1987, pp. 105–106.)

References

Please see page 282.

Chapter 5
Types of Student Assessments

Types of Student Assessments

"Effective assessment uses a broad range of information and involves a variety of techniques to collect the data." ...

"Assessment consumes a large portion of classroom time and has a powerful effect on what and how material is learned and taught. The choice of assessment directly effects the outcome. Familiarity with the strengths and limitations of a number of assessment tools allows for informed choices that are reflective of what we want to assess."

(Waterloo, 1993, p. 9.)

TYPES OF STUDENT ASSESSMENT HAVE BEEN ORGANIZED UNDER THREE HEADINGS:

Paper and Pencil (Tests):

true/false

matching

completion

short answer

multiple choice

essay questions

Personal Communication (Direct Discussion):

instructional questions

conferences and interviews

journals and logs

Performance Assessment (Products and Observation):

A. written assignments, demonstrations, presentations/seminars, projects, oral tests and exams

B. anecdotal records, checklists, rating scales

Paper and Pencil Assessment

The focus for this section is the paper and pencil test that has been the traditional staple of classroom assessment from upper elementary to senior secondary grades. This section will begin with an overview of the principles involved in the development and use of tests/quizzes/examinations; this will be followed by a detailed review of each of the types of questions that are commonly used on teacher designed tests. The section will conclude with some summary comments and recommendations for effective paper and pencil assessment.

Planning the Year or Semester Tests

Teachers planning a course of study should give as much emphasis to planning assessment as they do to planning other course components. This planning should ensure that there is a balance between assessment and learning activities and that a variety of assessment methodologies are used. Using a sheet such as "Matching Student Assessment to Learning Outcomes" may help ensure this balance. (See page 177.)

Having decided on a balanced assessment program which includes testing, teachers must decide the frequency of testing and the type of testing which will occur. The basic decision that will have to be made is when to use objective tests and when to use essay questions. Each have advantages and limitations which teachers should be aware of; a detailed comparison can be found on page 179.

Planning should also allow for modification for exceptional students and for reteaching and retesting so that students have the greatest possible opportunities to successfully demonstrate that they have achieved the learning outcomes.

Above all these considerations, the basic guiding principle for testing should be **no surprises**; students should know the what, when, where and how they will be tested as soon as possible in the semester or year. In order for this to happen, teachers must carefully and comprehensively plan all the assessment procedures for each course they teach.

One example of this sort of planning is provided in the curriculum resource guide for senior Physical Geography developed by the Scarborough Board of Education. The writers of this guide decided that the critical outcome of this course was that students would demonstrate their ability to analyze the visual characteristics of landscape. In order to make this completely clear to the students taking this course, they are provided with the final examination below on the first or second day of the course. Throughout the course teachers emphasize the visual aspect of all the components of physical geography and students are given numerous opportunities to practice interpretation and description of the visual aspects of physical geography. Near the end of the course, students are randomly assigned a photograph of a physically distinct landscape and they are required to complete the final evaluation over a two or three day period. This example is from Physical Geography, but the same principles could be applied to other subjects.

Final Evaluation

The Questions

Carefully observe the assigned photo. Based on the materials discussed throughout the course:

1. Describe the landscape in detail. This description should include bedrock, landforms, natural vegetation types, soils, weather/climate characteristics as well as an indication of the impact human activity has had/ is having on all aspects of the environment.

2. Account for the patterns you observe. In this section you must explain the following:

   (a) how you know your identifications in the part 1 are correct;

   (b) what the present features tell us about the original formation processes that created this landscape and how and why it has changed over time; (Where appropriate explanations can be accompanied by labelled diagrams.)

   (c) how the various aspects of landscape development have had an impact on one another.

Evaluation

Part 1: Description

(a) completeness	10
(b) accuracy of descriptions	25
(c) organization	5

Part 2: Analysis

(a) accuracy of explanations	25
(b) depth of understanding	10
(c) ability to observe and explain relationships	25
Total	100

The completed evaluation must be handed in no later than _____.

*(Scarborough, **Physical Geography**, 1993, p. 18.)*

1. Paper and Pencil Tests

Description

These are assessment techniques structured to allow students to put on paper what they know and are able to do.

Evaluation Context

Paper and pencil tests may be quizzes, tests or examinations; variations in name usually relate to length, location, formality and scheduling. They used to be the focus of assessment, but they are now seen as one of a variety of assessment techniques. Paper and pencil tests are particularly valuable for assessing student knowledge of content but well designed tests can also assess processes and skills.

Using Technique to Best Advantage

Testing must be planned as an integral part of the teaching/learning process. Students should see testing as a vital and valuable part of their learning process.

Guidelines for Use

(For an expanded list see "88 Key Questions about Tests and Examinations", **Making the Grade***, pp. 112–118.)*

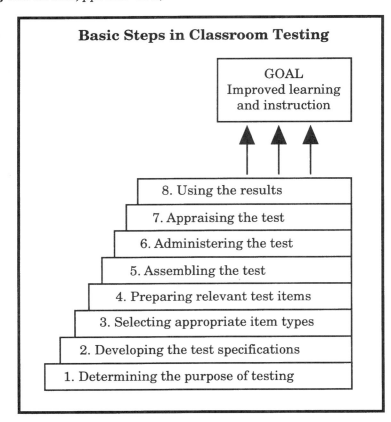

(Gronlund and Linn, p. 110.)

1. ***Determine the purpose of testing:***
   - diagnostic or formative or summative

2. ***Develop test specifications:***
   - to ensure that the test will appropriately sample the intended learning outcomes some type of chart should be used. (Samples are included on pages 180–182.)
   - involve students in the development of the table of test specifications, so as to provide them with a clear vision of the learning outcomes (target).

3. ***Select appropriate item types:***
   - choice is basically between objective items and essay questions. "Each type should be used where most appropriate, with **appropriateness determined by the learning outcomes to be measured** and by the advantages and limitations of each item type." *(Gronlund and Linn, p. 121)* For a detailed review of the advantages and limitations of each item type, see page 179.

4. ***Prepare relevant test items:***
   - each item should measure an important learning outcome with "the most direct measure of the performance task described in the intended learning outcome*s*".
   - each item should be stated in clear, simple language
   - write test items well before the test and write more items than needed
   - avoid providing clues within and between items
   - provide clear directions for each type of item
   - a suggested approach is provided on page 182. A sample using 'reducing air pollution' as the topic is provided with examples of five types of questions. This is followed by a blank sample sheet which could be photocopied and used.

5. ***Assemble the test:***
   - follow the test specification table and indicate the mark value of each question
   - ensure that the test length and difficulty is appropriate for the students being assessed

	• be consistent in the presentation of each item-type and group questions by item-type
	• check that the test is free from gender, class and race bias
6. *Administer the test:*	• proofread the test carefully (ask a colleague to help for a fresh view)
	• distribute clear, readable copies
7. *Appraise the test:*	• draw up a grid to find patterns of success and errors; where there are consistent errors determine whether the problem was with the test or with the instruction
8. *Using the results:*	• provide individual feedback to students which focuses on improving learning (and instruction)
	• review or **reteach** any necessary topics **using a different method of presentation** as required
	• **provide a re-testing opportunity for students**
	• revise instruction as indicated by the review of the test

Using the Information for Student Evaluation

Information from paper and pencil tests should be used to provide students with information on how they are progressing (i) relative to their own previous performance, (ii) relative to the standard of performance expected or required and (iii) relative to other students. (This last standard should be used infrequently and it should be de-emphasized by teachers.)

Information from paper and pencil tests should be incorporated into grades and should be included in reports to parents.

Oral exams and collaborative exams may be seen as variants of paper and pencil tests; for further information see pages 246–254.

Variants

Instead of using paper and pencil assessments, devise "authentic" or "performance" assessments that require students to demonstrate that they have acquired knowledge or skill.

*(See Wiggins, Grant, "Creating Tests Worth Taking", **Educational Leadership**, May 1992, pp. 26–33.)*

Oral tests and exams may be used instead of paper and pencil tests (see page 246).

Limitations

> In school we ask students to tell us what we told them; we test them on our lectures. They figure out the system, party and procrastinate, then cram and feed it back to us to get the grades. They often think all of life operates on the same short-cut system.
>
> *(Covey, Stephen, **Principle Centred Leadership**, Simon and Schuster, New York, 1992, p. 16.)*

Test anxiety, personal factors and environmental factors may prevent students from performing at their best. Paper and pencil tests give clear advantage to certain learning styles and suggest that the only things we value are what we test.

Testing often causes the "cram and forget" syndrome described in the above quote from Covey.

It is external to the learning process and overemphasizes reading ability. It must also be recognized that paper and pencil tests cannot measure all the important learning outcomes.

STUDENT INSTRUCTIONAL OR ASSESSMENT GROUPING

Matching Student Assessment to Learning Outcomes

Learning Outcomes	Assessment Techniques Used Now	Additional Assessment Techniques To be Included	Uses? Diagnostic? Formative? Summative?
Outcome #1.			
Outcome #2.			
Outcome #3.			
Outcome #4.			

(Adapted from Saskatchewan Education, 1991, p. 31.)

Types of Complex Learning Outcomes Measured by Essay Questions and Objective Interpretive Exercises

Type of Test Item	Examples of Complex Learning Outcomes That Can Be Measured
Objective Interpretive Exercises	Ability to — identify cause-effect relationships identify the application of principles identify the relevance of arguments identify tenable hypotheses identify valid conclusions identify unstated assumptions identify the limitations of data identify the adequacy of procedures (and similar outcomes based on the pupil's ability to select the answer)
Restricted Response Essay Questions (i.e. short answer completion)	Ability to — explain cause-effect relationships describe applications of principles present relevant arguments formulate tenable hypotheses formulate valid conclusions state necessary assumptions describe the limitations of data explain methods and procedures (and similar outcomes based on the pupil's ability to supply the answer)
Extended Response Essay Questions	Ability to — produce, organize, and express ideas integrate learnings in different areas create original forms (e.g., designing an experiment) evaluate the worth of ideas

(Gronlund and Linn, 1990, p. 215.)

A Comparison of Essay and Objective Test Items

	ESSAY	OBJECTIVE
MODE OF RESPONSE	• Student answers in own words. • Most time spent thinking and writing. • Good writers have advantage over poorer writers.	• Student selects answer from options, or indicates true-false, or writes brief answer. • Most time spent reading and thinking. • Good readers have advantage over poorer readers.
LEARNING OUTCOMES TAPPED	• Can tap high levels of thinking at an EXPRESSIVE level. • Can tap ability to express oneself in written form. • Not appropriate to measure rote memory of facts/definitions.	• Can tap high levels of thinking at a RECOGNITION level. • Cannot tap writing ability directly. • Measures knowledge of facts and definitions efficiently.
SCOPE OF COVERAGE	• Essay test contains fewer items; does not permit extensive course coverage. • Depth is emphasized.	• Objective test contains many items; permits extensive coverage of course content. • Breadth is emphasized.
PREPARATION AND QUALITY	• Relatively easy to design. • Quality of item is determined largely by skill of reader/scorer. • Majority of teacher time is spent reading responses.	• Some skill required to design items that do not give "clues" to correct answers. • Quality of item is determined largely by skill of item-writer. • Majority of teacher time is spent designing items.
DIRECTIONS	• Fairly extensive instructions may be needed for understanding.	• Student understands what is expected with a minimum of instructions.
GUESSING / BLUFFING	• Susceptible to bluffing: fluent student can write a lot even when unsure of content.	• Susceptible to guessing: especially a problem with True-False items and poorly written Multiple Choice items.
MARKING	• Time consuming, tedious, difficult to mark. • Prone to "halo effect"/bias (e.g., teacher may be influenced by what is already known about student's ability or performance).	• Rapid and accurate marking. • No "halo effect"/bias, since marking is completely objective. • Almost anyone can mark these items/ tests, when provided with a "key". • Distribution of final scores is determined by the number correct.
RELIABILITY	• Tends to be low because marking is subjective: two different readers often assign widely different marks.	• Tends to be high because marking is quantifiable and thus objective: marking is consistent time after time, or when done by different markers.

(Peel, Book 2, 1990, p. 2. See also page 42 in the same booklet. A similar chart can be found in Gronlund and Linn, p. 124.)

Sample 1

Test/Examination Preparation Matrix

Cognitive Skills

	Knowledge/ Comprehension 0–15%*	Application 10–30%*	Analysis 30–40%*	Syntheses 15–25%*	Evaluation 15–25%*	Totals:
Conceptual Frameworks and Theories						
Between Families: The Young Single						
The Newly Married Couple						
The Family with Young Children						
The Family with Adolescents						
Launching						
The Family in Later Life						
Totals:						

Course Outline

* suggested range of marks

(OAC Evaluation Handbook, Family Studies, 1993, p. 33.)

Sample 2: Science Test Specification Chart

	Performance Levels							
	Knowledge	Comprehension	Application	Analysis	Synthesis	Evaluation	Total	Percent
Vocabulary	Number of Items							
1. Students will define velocity, speed ...	4	4					8	16%
2. ...	1	1					2	4%
Facts/Principles								
1. Working from a list of animals and environments, students will match animals and habitats.	3						3	6%
2. Students will calculate force for objects of different mass and acceleration.			1				1	2%
3. Students will decide whether statements are consistent with Darwinian views.			6				6	12%
4. When given unfamiliar diagrams, students will answer questions about the genetic processes involved.		2					2	4%
5. ...	2						2	4%
6. ...	1	9	3	2	1		16	32%
Applications								
1. In response to an unfamiliar passage, students will infer author's assumptions about the role of science in everyday life.				5			5	10%
2. Students will critique an unfamiliar experiment.						5	5	10%
Total	**11**	**16**	**10**	**7**	**1**	**5**	**50**	

(Sparzo, p. 17.)

Sample 3: Table of Specification for a Weather Unit

Objectives / Content	Knows			Understands	Interprets	Total Number of Items	Percent of Items
	Basic Terms	Weather Symbols	Specific Facts	Influence of Each Factor on Weather Formation	Weather Maps		
Air Pressure	2	2	2	3	3	12	20
Wind	1	4	2	8	2	17	28
Temperature	2	2	2	2	2	10	17
Humidity and precipitation	3	2	1	2	5	13	22
Clouds	4	2	2			8	13
Total number of items	12	12	9	15	12	60	
Percent of items	20	20	15	25	20		100

(Gronlund and Linn, 1990, p. 116.)

Sample 4: Test Specification Chart

Subject: Biology   Date: _____

Grade: 10   **Unit/Topic: Cells**

Content	Educational Outcomes			Total
	Recall	Analysis	Comparison	
1. Cell Structure	5 questions	2 questions	1 question	8
2. Cellular Reproduction	3 questions	2 questions	1 question	6
3. DNA	2 questions	2 questions	4 questions	8
Total	10	6	6	22

(Classroom Assessment Training, Northwest Regional Educational Laboratory, Portland, Oregon.)

Sample 5: Writing Test Items: Air Pollution

To develop questions for a table of specification linking "reducing air pollution" with "inferential thinking"

Proposition: If you wanted to reduce air pollution from auto vehicles you could search for alternative energy sources for cars, reduce the number of cars on the road, and/or develop technologies to reduce auto emissions. (Assume this had not been explicitly taught in class.)

TRUE T/F ITEM:

One viable way to reduce air pollution by autos is to search for alternative sources of power for cars.

FALSE T/F ITEM:

One viable way to reduce air pollution due to autos is to increase the number of cars on the road.

SHORT ANSWER OR FILL-IN ITEM:

What is one way to reduce air pollution by autos?

MULTIPLE CHOICE ITEM:

What is one way to reduce air pollution by autos?

    A. Outlaw catalytic converters

    B. Find alternative energy sources for cars

    C. Increase the number of cars on the road

    D. Tax the use of methanol

ESSAY ITEM:

Discuss three specific ways to reduce air pollution from autos. Explain how each would contribute to the reduction.

(Stiggins, Richard, Workshop on Paper and Pencil Test Development, NWREL, Portland, Oregon, p. 7–2.)

Writing Test Items

Objective: (You choose)

_____

_____

Proposition: (You choose)

_____

_____

TRUE T/F ITEM:

FALSE T/F ITEM:

SHORT ANSWER OR FILL-IN ITEM:

MULTIPLE CHOICE ITEM:

ESSAY ITEM:

(Stiggins, Richard, Workshop on Paper and Pencil Test Development, NWREL, Portland, Oregon, p. 7–3.)

The Meaning of Quality

The objective of this section is to promote the development and use of effective, high quality tests in our schools. In this as in all aspects of assessment, the meaning of quality can be summarized in four words — target, sample, interference and purpose.

1. There must be a clear vision of the assessment **target** and the proper assessment method must be matched with the target. Paper and pencil tests are best suited to assessing knowledge and, to a lesser extent, thinking and may be used in the form of questionnaires to assess the affective domain.

2. Student performance must be **sampled** sufficiently to represent all the key aspects of the target without wasting time with too much assessment (marking).

3. Extraneous **interference** must be controlled as much as possible. Teachers should seek to ensure that the test, its marking and the environment where the test is held provide no barriers to optimum student performance. Teachers must also be sensitive to factors affecting students which legitimately interfere with their performance on a test.

4. Classroom tests must arise from a clear sense of **purpose** which is known to the teacher and the student. For example, it must be clear whether a test is for diagnostic, formative or summative purposes and whether the resultant "mark" will be included in the student's report card grade.

(a) True/False (sometimes called Alternative Response)

Description

True/false questions require a student to indicate whether an item is true or false, right or wrong, fact or opinion, yes or no, and the like.

Evaluation Context

True/false questions are used mainly to assess content knowledge, such as the correctness of statements or facts, definition of terms, and the ability to distinguish fact from opinion. They provide a way to ask many questions in a short time/space.

Using Technique to Best Advantage

True/false questions are used mainly to assess content knowledge; with careful construction can measure a broader range of thinking skills. They are more effective when used in conjunction with other types of items.

Guidelines for Use

The following guidelines should be followed:

- ensure that statements are **entirely** true or false **as stated;**
- identify key ideas and express them in own words; do not copy statements directly from textbooks;
- have an approximately equal number of true statements and false statements;
- use language that is simple and clear; avoid words like "often", "never", "none", "always", "all", "more", "few", "large", "good";
- ensure that only **one** idea is contained in each item;
- use negatives sparingly if at all; double negatives test logic not knowledge;
- avoid over-generalization and trick questions; and
- provide clear directions and letters for students to circle or boxes for students to mark; use a template for quick marking.

Using the Information for Student Evaluation

Calculate the total number of correct answers and use as a mark. To discourage guessing, the number wrong can be subtracted from the number right, but this is **not** a recommended practice; never give a negative mark.

Variants

Have students go beyond the simple choice of true/false and give reasons for their choice (this now becomes a short answer type of question).

Questions may use maps, diagrams or charts which require interpretation to determine the correctness of a statement.

Limitations

True/false questions assess identification rather than production of an answer and are usually limited to factual recall. They may be more of a reading test than a test of knowledge. It is difficult to write statements that are absolutely true or false and/or unambiguous.

Results may be unreliable because of 50/50 chance of guessing the correct answer. This type of question has little diagnostic value. Another problem is that cheating is relatively easy.

> Based on the above limitations and the views of experts like Gronlund and Linn, *Measurement and Evaluation in Teaching*, 6th Edition, New York, Macmillan, 1990, pp. 153–154, **true/false questions are of dubious value and should have limited use.**

Examples

Directions: Read each of the following statements. If the statement is true, circle the T. If the statement is false, circle the F.

(T) F 　1. The green colouring material in a plant leaf is called chlorophyll.

T (F) 　2. The corolla of a flower includes petals and sepals.

(T) F 　3. Photosynthesis is the process by which leaves make a plant's food.

(Gronlund and Linn, page 150.)

Directions: Read each of the following questions. If the answer is yes, circle the Y. If the answer is no, circle the N.

(Y) N 　1. Is 51% of 38 more than 19?

Y (N) 　2. Is 50% of 4/10 equal to 2/3?

Y (N) 　3. If 60% of a number is 9, is the number smaller than 9?

(Y) N 　4. Is 25% of 44 less than 12?

(Gronlund and Linn, page 150.)

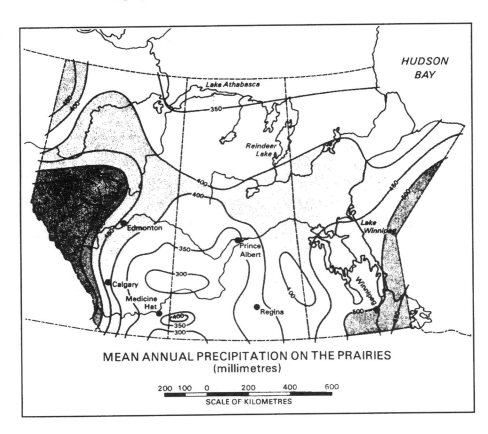

MEAN ANNUAL PRECIPITATION ON THE PRAIRIES
(millimetres)

For each of the following statements, indicate whether the information given

A. is TRUE, based on evidence given on the map;

B. is FALSE, based on evidence given on the map;

C. CANNOT BE DETERMINED from evidence given on the map.

In each case, circle the letter indicating your choice in the space to the left of the statement.

A B C Medicine Hat receives more precipitation on the average than does Calgary.

A B C Areas to the north and west generally receive more precipitation than does the south central area.

A B C Regina receives on the average more precipitation in winter than in summer.

A B C Winnipeg receives more precipitation on the average than does Edmonton.

A B C Throughout the area, precipitation in winter falls mainly as snow.

(Making the Grade, 1987, page 172, adapted from O.A.I.P. Geography.)

(b) Matching Items

Description

Matching items consists of a set of problems or questions ('premises') in one column (usually the left hand column) and a set of possible responses ('options') (usually the right hand column).

Evaluation Context

Matching items are most commonly used to test recall of factual information and association of information. They provide broad coverage of facts in an efficient manner. This type of question is easy to mark and less prone to guessing than true/false items

Using Technique to Best Advantage

Matching items are particularly appropriate whenever learning outcomes emphasize the relationship between two things. They are most effective when used in conjunction with other types of items.

Guidelines for Use

The following guidelines should be used:

- make sure directions are clear and provide all the necessary information

    e.g. indicate if a response can be used more than once or if an item has more than one match;

- limit the number of premises and responses; maximum is 10, less is better;

- list a few more responses than premises as this reduces success by guessing;

- list premises and responses randomly

    e.g. verbal alternatives in alphabetical order and numerical alternatives in numerical order;

- make sure that the material in each matching exercise is homogeneous; do not mix events, dates, names; do not mix point form and sentence form;

- ensure that the entire matching question is included on one page;

- identify premises with a number and responses with a letter; provide a clear and obvious space for students to record the response letter; never ask students to draw lines from premise to response; and
- do not use irrelevant options.

Using the Information for Student Evaluation

Marking will normally be based on one mark per correct response. These questions can be used for formative, diagnostic or summative evaluation.

Limitations

Matching items assess identification rather than production of an answer. They are usually limited to factual recall or association. Care must be taken not to overuse this type of question.

They often present a difficult reading problem so become a test of reading rather than knowledge.

Example

Directions: The column on the left lists some important inventions; the column on the right contains the name of some inventors.

On the line to the left of each invention, write the letter of the person's name who invented it.

Each letter may be used once or not at all.

_____ 1.	Atlantic cable	A.	Colt
_____ 2.	cotton gin	B.	Edison
_____ 3.	electric starter	C.	Field
_____ 4.	sewing machine	D.	Franklin
_____ 5.	steam engine	E.	Howe
_____ 6.	wireless telegraphy	F.	Kettering
		G.	Marconi
		H.	Watt
		I.	Whitney

(Adapted from Peel, Book 1, 1990, p. 9.)

(c) Completion Items

Description

Completion questions require students to fill in a blank or supply a missing phrase, number or symbol.

Evaluation Context

Completion questions are mainly used to test factual recall. They can cover a wide range of material efficiently as they are relatively easy to develop and mark.

Using Technique to Best Advantage

Completion questions require more thought by students as they have to supply rather than select an answer.

Guidelines for Use

The following guidelines should be followed:

- ensure that there is only one correct answer by asking direct, clearly worded questions;
- place equal-length fill-in blanks at or near the end of the question/ statement;
- do not use multiple fill-in blanks in the same item;
- avoid giving clues to the correct answer;
- give clear directions

  e.g. whether each blank represents one or more words, whether synonymous terms are acceptable, whether spelling "counts", etc.; and
- where an answer is to be expressed in numerical units, the unit should be stated.

Using the Information for Student Evaluation

Marking will normally be based on one mark per correct response.

Variants

This type may be seen as a variant of the short answer type where the answer is very short!

Limitations

Great care must be taken to carefully word items as students may consider that there is more than one correct answer. This type of question may test reading ability rather than knowledge. They take longer to mark than other objective formats.

Examples

Directions: Fill in the blank with the appropriate word or number.
Marks will/will not be deducted for incorrect spelling.

1. Lines on a weather map which join places with the same temperatures are called _____.

2. Vessels which carry used blood back to the heart are called

   _____.

3. A member of the United States Senate is elected to a term of office of _____ years.

(d) Short Answer (or Structured Response) Items

Description

Short answer questions require students to provide an answer to a specific question.

Evaluation Context

When used to test the ability to recall knowledge, short answer questions usually require a one word or one phrase answer.

When used to test higher levels of thinking, a sentence or two, or maybe a paragraph is usually required.

Using Technique to Best Advantage

Short answer questions are useful to assess how well students have learned content. This type of question requires more thought by students as they have to supply rather than just select an answer.

They are useful in mathematics, science and other subjects where solutions to problems can be indicated by numbers or symbols. These questions have better diagnostic value than other objective formats.

Guidelines for Use

The guidelines listed here should be followed:

- make sure that a clearly worded, unambiguous question is asked;
- students must be told how much they are expected to write; in general, the shorter the better; and
- if the answer is to be expressed in numerical units the unit should be stated.
- give clear directions as to length required, the format expected (point form or sentences) and requirements with regard to spelling and grammar

Using the Information for Student Evaluation

The number of marks for each question should be clearly identified. The mark obtained by a student is the total or some predetermined percentage of it.

Diagnostic information can be obtained by analyzing student responses.

Variants

This type of question may be seen as a variant of the completion type where the statement is phrased as a question.

Multiple-choice and true/false items can be expanded into short answer questions by requiring students to select the correct response and write an answer justifying their choice.

Limitations

- see Completion Items (page 189)
- may encourage rote learning, especially if statements are taken straight out of textbooks
- marking is more subjective than other types of objective tests
- limited value for assessing complex thought or expanded body of knowledge

Example 1

Directions: Answer the question with a one word or number answer. There is one mark for each question. Marks will/will not be deducted for incorrect spelling and grammar.

1. Fluorine was first isolated in what year? _____

2. In which gland is insulin produced? _____

3. What is the value of x in the equation $2x + 5 = 9$? _____

4. How many syllables are there in the word "Argentina"? _____

5. Milk sells for $0.96 a litre carton and $3.68 for a 4 litre jug. How many cents would you save on **each litre** if you bought it in a 4 litre jug? _____

Example 2

The following statement has been made concerning the Maritime Provinces of Canada.

> "From a geographic and economic point of view, it would make better sense for the Maritime Provinces to join the United States than to remain as part of Canada."

Do you agree with this statement? Indicate your view by circling the appropriate letter from the choices below.

- A. strongly agree
- B. agree
- C. disagree
- D. strongly disagree

In the space provided below, outline three reasons why you hold the position you have indicated above. Write your answer in full sentences.

1.

2.

3,

(Making the Grade, 1987, p. 181.)

Example 3

Below is a list of some suggestions that have been made to help deal with an energy crisis. Choose two suggestions, and for each choice state one argument supporting the suggestion and one argument opposing it. State each argument in one sentence.

Suggestions:

1. Raise the price of gasoline.
2. Limit the amount of gasoline each car may use per week.
3. Place a tax of $300 to $500 on big, gas-guzzling cars.
4. Encourage large businesses and factories to switch from oil to coal.
5. Encourage the development of nuclear energy sources.
6. Close schools during January and February and extend classes through July.

First Suggestion:

Argument For:

Argument Against:

Second Suggestion:

Argument For:

Argument Against:

(Making the Grade, 1987, p. 182.)

(c) Multiple Choice

Description

Multiple choice questions consist of a problem ("stem") and a list of suggested solutions ("options"); the correct option is called simply the "answer" and remaining options are called "distracters". Students select the correct **or** best option.

Evaluation Context

Multiple choice questions should be used when there is only one right or best answer but there are several plausible alternatives to the correct answer.

They can measure a variety of learning outcomes from recall to higher level thinking and can cover lots of material efficiently.

Using Technique to Best Advantage

This type of question needs a great deal of time to plan and devise but is easy to mark. They are most effective when used in conjunction with other types of items; so, a wide range of student learning can be assessed.

Guidelines for Use

The guidelines listed below should be followed:

- ensure there is only one correct or best answer;
- avoid wordiness and complex or ambiguous language; e.g. "sometimes", "could be", "may be";
- state the whole question in the stem; i.e. stem should be meaningful by itself;
- the stem should be worded in positive terms; if a negative is used it should be **bold**;
- options should be brief and parallel in length, grammatical construction and generality;
- avoid complex formats and repetition in response items;
- limit use of "all of the above" or "none of the above" as options;
- the number of options in each question on the same test **may be varied**;
- options should be listed in alphabetical or numerical order and should be indicated by letters;
- all distracters should be plausible (see page 193);
- be prepared to accept that there may be two or more correct answers and adjust all marking accordingly; and
- before using multiple choice questions try them out on colleagues to ensure that they are accurate, understandable and fair.

Using the Information for Student Evaluation

Award the same number of marks for each correct answer and no marks for incorrect answers.

Use of a correction formula for guessing is not appropriate on classroom tests.

Results have diagnostic value.

Variants

To encourage higher level thinking and to ensure that guessing is not rewarded, students may be asked to give reasons (in sentence or point form) to defend or support their choices.

Limitations

Multiple choice questions assess the selection not the production of an answer.

They are difficult to design, especially the selection of plausible distracters.

This type of question may test reading ability more than any other factor.

Care must be taken to ensure that there are logical and clear reasons to support the answer when students are asked to select the "best" answer.

Ways to Make Distracters Plausible

1. Use the students' most common errors.

2. Use important-sounding words (e.g., "significant," accurate") that are relevant to the stem.

3. Use words that have verbal associations with the item stem (e.g., politician — political).

4. Use textbook language or other phraseology that has the "appearance of truth."

5. Use incorrect answers that are likely to result from pupil misunderstanding or carelessness (e.g., forgets to convert feet to yards).

6. Use distracters that are homogeneous and similar in content to the correct answer (e.g., all are inventors).

7. Use distracters that are parallel in form and grammatically consistent with the item's stem.

8. Make the distracters similar to the correct answer in length, vocabulary, sentence structure, and complexity of thought.

Note of Caution

Distracters should distract the uninformed, but they should *not* sresult in "trick questions" that mislead the knowledgeable pupils (e.g., don't insert *not* in a correct answer to make it a distracter).

(Gronlund and Linn, 1990, p. 184.)

Example 1

Directions: Circle the letter beside the **correct** answer.

1. The device on a car that mixes fuel and air in the correct proportions is called:
    A. an alternator
    B. a carburetor
    C. a distributor
    D. a manifold

2. The value of 0.3 x 0.02 is

   A. 6.0

   B. 0.6

   C. 0.06

   D. 0.0006

*(Waterloo, **Assessment for Learning**, 1993, p. 15.)*

Example 2

Directions: Circle the letter beside the **best** answer.

1. Which one of the following factors contributed most to the selection of Toronto as the capital of Ontario?

   A. central location

   B. distance from U.S.A.

   C. good highways

   D. large population

2. What is the most important purpose of city zoning bylaws?

   A. attract industry

   B. encourage apartment building

   C. protect property values

   D. provide land for schools

* For other examples and detailed "Guideposts for the Construction of Multiple-Choice Questions" see Making the Grade, *pages 160–166.*

(f) Essay-Style Questions

Description

Essay style questions require students to respond comprehensively in written form to an assigned topic.

Evaluation Context

Essay style questions should be used to measure complex learning outcomes such as a student's ability to communicate through writing and to synthesize, organize, interpret and/or evaluate a broad base of information.

Using Technique to Best Advantage

It is important to ensure that the essay question approach is aligned with learning outcomes. Students should be adequately prepared for this type of question; i.e. they should have practiced with the same format — criteria, marking scheme, time limits, length of answers expected, etc. Teachers should determine appropriate modification for exceptional students.

Sampling validity suggests that several short essay questions are better than one long question.

Guidelines for Use

Constructing the Essay Question(s)

- make sure the question identifies exactly what the student has to do;
- ensure that students understand the directing word(s) by providing an explanation with the question or a sheet (see examples on pages 197, 201) with a comprehensive list of directing words;
- indicate clearly the criteria and marking scheme that will be used in assessing the essay; also indicate the length of response expected and how much time each student should devote to the question;
- restrict choice to ensure equal difficulty for all students;
- ensure that the question is an extension of or logical follow up to classroom instruction/activities; and
- word questions so that they require application of knowledge to new situations, i.e. require selection and organization of knowledge not just recall.

Marking the Essay Question (see page 199)

- write a model answer in advance to help develop criteria and marking scheme, to identify difficulties and to enhance empathy;
- mark all responses to one question at the same time;
- mark answers anonymously if possible and shuffle papers before and during marking;
- redraft the initial marking scheme if it becomes evident that there are problems; students must be informed and all papers must be marked on the basis of the new scheme;
- eliminate factors that are irrelevant to the learning outcomes being measured, e.g., legibility, and separate mechanics of writing from content;
- try to (plan, design and) mark questions collaboratively with other teachers; this is particularly desirable if important decisions are to be based on the results; and
- while marking look for diagnostic information, e.g., topics that need reteaching, students who need help.

After the Test

- maintain student's self-esteem by giving results as anonymously as possible;
- use class time so that the essay question and student responses are a basis for further learning and instruction; and
- provide feedback, remediation and second chance testing for each student.

Using the Information for Student Evaluation

Use either holistic or analytic scoring (students **must** have this information).

Holistic scoring comes from an overall impression based on a list of attributes. In *analytic scoring*, a stated proportion of the available mark is assigned to each attribute. (See page 279.)

Hints

Developing the criteria for assessment with students will help to ensure that they have a better understanding of what is expected.

Variants

Emphasis on organization and selection rather than writing skill can be obtained by requiring the response in point form rather than sentence and paragraph.

Limitations

Developing criteria for marking is difficult and marking is often unreliable and time consuming. Most approaches to improving marking require even more time.

Essay questions provide a limited sampling of content areas.

The ability to write can interfere with the ability to show understanding.

This type of question is inefficient for testing knowledge; it should be used for higher order thinking.

In the light of these limitations and the frequency of use of essay questions, the following comments by David Pratt of Queens University should be considered carefully:

In any assessment, it is necessary to ask what real-world capability is being assessed? The normal essay test requires learners to produce, from their internal resources, quality prose under timed conditions. While this may be a valuable skill for journalists and diplomats, it is one that will rarely be used by most adult citizens. The argument that essays test higher-order thinking is plausible. But analysis of university examinations shows that the great majority of essay questions require simple recognition and memory of facts, with some ability to apply factual information in fairly routine ways *(Beard and Pole, 1971)*. Furthermore, essays are relatively inefficient; they can assess only a few areas of learning per hour of assessment time, and therefore may not validly sample a student's learning *(Lorber & Pierce, 1990)*.

The question of authentic assessment is particularly germane to the use of essay tests. If nurses are being taught "how to give an intramuscular injection" it is more appropriate to have them demonstrate this skill on one another, using injections of distilled water, than to have them write an essay on intramuscular injections. In preparing an assessment of students' abilities in such a subject as History or English, we need to ask, in what ways will our students use these knowledges and skills in the real-world (or the after-school world) context? **When this question is asked, the ritualized formal essay examination in the school gymnasium often begins to appear bizarrely inappropriate. Sometimes its only defense is that it is preparation for the same kind of questionable ritual at the university level.** People do use essay-type skills in their private and occupational lives: when writing letters, memoranda, and reports. But typically they have the opportunity to draft and revise several times, with considerable time flexibility, and with access to human and reference resources. In such circumstances, the take-home essay will be a more appropriate measure than an essay examination under timed and artificial conditions.

(Pratt, 1991, pp. 94–96.)

In order to increase the value of essays as assessment instruments Pratt notes a number of suggestions (most of which have been included above in the "Guidelines for Use"). One interesting idea that could be implemented and should be considered is that "essays (should be used) primarily for formative assessment, where the purpose is to obtain insight, and to comment on the learner's progress, rather than for summative assessment in which marks are awarded and recorded."

(Pratt, 1991, p. 95.)

Example

In divorce settlements today, judges more frequently tend to award joint custody of the child(ren). In such cases, the children will spend a portion of their time living with each of their parents and the parents share equally in decision-making about the welfare of the children.

As this family structure becomes more wide spread, evaluate the impact that this might have regarding:

- the process of socialization
- styles of parenting and childcare
- parent-child relationships

Total marks 15

Content: 12 marks

- answer should show depth of thought
- inclusion of factual information — not opinion
- use of relevant theories and conceptual frameworks

Organization: 3 marks

- correct essay format used

(Adapted from **OAC Evaluation Handbook: Family Studies**, *p. 43.)*

Sample Student Sheet of "Directing Words" with Examples

Students must clearly understand the meanings of frequently used directing words. It is important that students understand what their teachers mean by these directing words. Some directing words and the usual meaning for each are listed below.

CONTRAST

- Bring out the points of difference.
  Example: Contrast Jane Austen's *Pride and Prejudice* with William Thackeray's *Vanity Fair*.

COMPARE

- Bring out the points of similarity and points of difference.
  Example: Compare the games of basketball and lacrosse.

CRITICIZE

- State your opinion of the correctness or merits of an item or issue. ("Criticize" may involve approval, disapproval, or both.)

  Example: Criticize the use of nuclear power as a means of generating electricity.

DEFINE

- Give the meaning of a word or concept by placing it in the class to which it belongs and setting if off from other items in the same class.

  Example: Define the term "archetype."

DESCRIBE

- Give an account of; tell about; give a word picture of.

  Example: Describe the Pyramids of Giza.

ENUMERATE

- Name or list in some order and in concise form.

  Example: Enumerate the Dutch painters of the seventeenth century studied this term.

EVALUATE

- Give the good points and the bad ones; appraise; give an opinion regarding the value of; explore the advantages and disadvantages of.

  Example: Evaluate the use of teaching machines in classroom learning.

EXPLAIN

- Make clear; interpret; make plain; tell "how" to do; tell the meaning of.

  Example: Explain how scientists can, at times, trigger a rainstorm.

ILLUSTRATE

- Use a picture, diagram, chart or concrete example to clarify a point; using words, make clear by using examples. (The wording of a question using the directing word "illustrate" must make clear to the student whether or not a sketch or diagram should be used to answer the question.)

  Example: Illustrate, through sketches, the use of catapults in medieval warfare.

  Illustrate, by giving three examples from *To Kill a Mockingbird*, how Atticus Finch was a good father.

INTERPRET

- Make plain; give the meaning of; give your thinking about the meaning of.

  Example: Interpret the line "He jests at scars who never felt a wound," and relate it to …

JUSTIFY/SHOW HOW

- Show good reasons for, or give evidence and present facts to support your position.

  Example: Justify the American entry into World War II.

OUTLINE

- Give, in order, the main points of; sketch in general terms.

  Example: Outline Nevill Chamberlain's argument for trying to appease Hitler in the late 1930s.

PROVE

- Establish the truth of something by giving factual evidence or logical reasons.

  Example: Prove the reflector property of the parabola and relate it to the use of dish antennae.

SUMMARIZE

- Briefly give or review the main points.

  Example: Summarize the ways in which food can be preserved.

TRACE

- Follow the course of; give a description of the development of.

  Example: Trace the development of counting machines from the abacus to the microcomputer.

*(Cornfield, et al., **Making the Grade**, 1987, pp. 138–139.)*

HINTS ON MARKING ESSAY QUESTIONS

Prepare a "Model" or "Ideal" Answer in Advance.

Check this model answer against a few papers selected at random before beginning to mark. Grading criteria may have to be adjusted if your expectations were too high. **Remember** this must be done before actual marking begins; after that, standards should not be changed, nor should they vary from paper to paper or from reader to reader.

Randomly Shuffle Papers Before and During Grading.

The assigned mark can be influenced by the position of the paper in the package, especially if the preceding answers were very good or very poor. There might be some pattern in how papers were handed in which would determine "clusters" of very good or poor papers within the package — e.g., better students may finish first and hand their papers in early; or students may be grouped (formally or informally) within the class by ability/skill.

Periodically Re-Establish a Marking "Baseline".

Since "mind set" can be a problem in marking essay questions, the teacher should refer from time to time to the first few papers graded. This will help maintain a baseline for the consistent application of marking criteria.

Mark Only One Question at a Time, Across All the Papers.

Marking one question at a time, rather than each entire paper separately, helps reduce the "halo effect." It also increases the reliability of grading by making the marker thoroughly familiar with the grading criteria for each individual question.

Mark the Answers Anonymously.

It is natural that teachers will have different impressions of different students, and these might bias subjective grading of essay questions. To reduce the influence of this potential bias, teachers should not know whose paper is being graded. Students can write their names on the backs of their papers or else be assigned an identifying number.

Mechanics of Writing Should Be Judged Separately from the Content of the Answer.

If legibility, spelling, punctuation, grammar, etc., are to be considered in grading, this should be decided ahead of time and a proportion of the question's value assigned to this aspect of the answer. Teachers must try to see past these distractions in evaluating an answer. Research shows that when told to disregard these things, teachers still give lower grades to papers containing such errors — even if all the relevant information is included in the answer.

Try to Mark All Answers to a Particular Question Without Long Interruptions.

If a lengthy break is unavoidable while marking, re-read some of the first few papers when marking is resumed. This is especially important with holistic scoring. Variations in mood, energy level, etc., from one marking session to another can affect decisions. Take short coffee breaks, but if possible don't interrupt marking for long periods of time.

Provide Comments and Correct Errors.

This step is time-consuming, but important. It provides students with valuable information on their performance and progress; it gives the teacher some justification for assigning the overall score; it helps the teacher be more aware of the type of errors made by individual students and by the class as a whole. The process also helps the teacher analyze the questions themselves: were the types of errors made by students attributable in part to the question being unclear? to the use of an inappropriate directing word? was a particular area/skill not covered thoroughly enough in class?

Have Two Independent Readings of Essay Answers if Marks Are To Be Used as the Basis for Important Decisions.

If the marks are to be used as the basis for making decisions about awards, admittance to special programs, scholarships, etc., two readers should grade the essay. The marks of the two readers can be averaged. "Group marking" is an excellent way to make marks more reliable. If two independent readers are to mark the essays, the first reader's grade should not be placed on the test paper (where it could influence the grade given by the second reader). Another approach — although not quite as objective — is to have the same teacher grade the essay twice, with several days intervening.

*(Peel, **Book 2**, 1989, pp. 25–26.)*

Examples of the Use of Directing Words Appropriate to the Different Levels of Thinking

This ladder lists some directing words and the levels of thinking they generally call for. Steps may easily overlap; "application" must include factual recall and may also require some analysis, synthesis and evaluation. Moreover, some directing words may lead to thinking at varying levels, depending on the rest of the question.

Example:

Identify five parts of a flower.

Identify the similarities and differences between flowers which self-pollinate and those which cross-pollinate.

EVALUATION
- draw conclusions...
- what errors...
- what inconsistencies...
- defend...
- judge...
- evaluate...
- compare...

SYNTHESIS
- propose an alternative...
- devise...
- how else would you...
- construct...
- compare...
- show relationship...

ANALYSIS
- what motive(s)...
- what relationship exists...
- identify the main idea or theme...
- analyze...
- distinguish...
- examine...

APPLICATION
- apply...
- what would happen if...
- what elements or statements best illustrate...
- explain how would react to...
- illustrate...
- prove...
- demonstrate...

COMPREHENSION
- why...
- how...
- state in your own words...
- condense...
- show or demonstrate...
- paraphrase...
- re-tell...
- interpret...
- summarize...

KNOWLEDGE
- what...
- where...
- when...
- who...
- define...
- outline...
- state...
- list...
- describe...

*(**Making the Grade**, 1987, p. 142.)*

2. Personal Communication

> ### Direct Discussion
>
> Instructional Questions
> Conferences and Interviews
> Response Journals and Learning Logs

Introduction

In order to give students opportunities to develop their personal communication skills, teachers should provide programs which offer a range of types of "direct discussion" activities. Ongoing assessment and evaluation of these activities should provide students with a sense of their growth and achievement in personal communication. For assessment and evaluation, a distinction should be made between process and product. The **product** should be the final outcome and will usually take the form of an oral performance (speech, debate, seminar presentation). The **process** should be the **speaking**, **listening**, and **personal writing** that students engage in as they work towards the final outcome. Assessment methodologies for "direct discussion" would, for the most part, serve diagnostic and formative functions.

Personal communication includes the receptive skill of listening which can only be assessed through direct discussion. Diagnostic and formative assessment, which helps to foster a concern for good listening skills, may make students more conscious of their attention and response to speakers. Such assessment should help students to improve listening habits which contribute directly to more successful learning.

The assessment methodologies presented in this section support the development of direct discussion skills. The strengths and limitations listed here apply in general to all methodologies detailed in this section.

Strengths

- can assess quickly
- can sample group achievement
- permits follow-up questions
- encourages valuable personal contact

Limitations

- can be difficult to sample achievement of all individuals
- can be difficult to sample broad domains
- demands time for one-to-one contact
- record keeping can be difficult

ORAL LANGUAGE IN ACTION

> Thinking Capabilities Develop Through the Immediate Testing of Ideas in Oral Language Activities

Thinking Capabilities

discriminating differentiating distinguishing modifying reasoning
generalizing particularizing evaluating synthesizing organizing
reflecting questioning comparing categorizing classifying
assimilating analyzing speculating outlining deliberating
summarizing imagining associating relating

lead to a variety of:

Oral Language Processes ⟶ Oral Language Activities

Narrating
- storytelling, reader's theatre, oral reading, monologues, conversation, dictation

Describing
- conversation, discussion, monologues, oral reports

Explaining or Expounding
- public speaking, monologues, debates, oral reports

Persuading
- public speaking, monologues, debates, reports

Arguing and Defending
- debates

Reporting
- oral reports

Informing
- oral reports, brainstorming, interviews, conversation

Discussing
- panels, roundtables, seminars, oral reports

Instructing or Directing
- oral directions and instruction

Presenting
- roundtable discussions, seminars, role play, symposia, panels, announcements, oral reports, introductions, thank you's, dramatic monologues

Questioning
- panels, seminars, roundtable discussions, interviews, (formulating, asking, and answering) questions, conversations, debates

Problem-Solving
- discussion panels, brainstorming, monologues

Conversing
- roundtable discussions, greetings, conversations

Entertaining
- oral reading, choral reading and speaking, storytelling, recitation, dramatic presentations, monologues, public speaking, debates

(Pro-File: Language Aloud ... Allowed, 1987, p. 13.)

(a) Instructional Questions

Description

Oral assessment occurs when the student responds to an assessment item by speaking rather than by writing.

Evaluation Context

It is known that questions before, during, and after instruction, assist students' learning. Classroom questions, insofar as they provide feedback to the teacher, are an important form of assessment.

Using Technique to Best Advantage

Research indicates that most classroom questions tap only low levels of knowledge. Students learn more if classroom questions are thought-provoking. This technique permits follow-up questions and encourages valuable personal contact. The teacher can assess quickly, and can sample group achievement.

Guidelines for Use

Because there is a natural tendency to ask more questions of more able students, teachers should take care that their questions are evenly distributed among the learners in a class.

Example 1

A question such as "When did Canada change its flag from the Union Jack to the Maple Leaf?" requires only recall. The question "What does the change of the Canadian flag from the Union Jack to the Maple Leaf tell us about the differences in Canadian society between 1967 and today?" requires deeper thought on the part of students.

Example 2

A question such as "What is the area of a rectangle 3m x 4m?" requires simple multiplication. "What is the maximum perimeter of a rectangle of area 12 m^2?" requires more sophisticated thought.

Limitations

This technique demands time for one-to-one contact. It can be difficult to sample achievement of all individuals. Record keeping can be difficult.

Using the Information for Student Evaluation

Objective questions asked during instruction and answered right or wrong can indicate mastery of knowledge. Thinking-skills questions, followed up by additional probes, can provide insights into thought processes. We can find out how students feel about things by talking to them.

Hints

It has been shown that pausing between the question and naming a student — e.g., "How would our mathematical system be different if humans had twelve fingers? … … … Thomas?" — increases the quality of student thought and response.

Variants

Oral English Outside the Classroom

The most natural, valid and reliable assessment of oral language occurs as students use language over a period of time, for authentic reasons. Assessment and evaluation do not have to be limited to the context of the classroom. Increasingly in the senior years, students will take some of their work out of the classroom into the larger context of the community, for example, in work experience and co-op programmes. Some of the assessment of students' work may well be undertaken in these contexts. In addition, some of the assessment may be done not only by the student, fellow students, or the teacher, but also by other members of the community. Many of the instruments which are identified for use by students or teachers can be used effectively by other members of the community. These people, as partners in the assessment process, may also provide anecdotal assessments, either in writing or on tape.

*(**Senior English OAIP**, "Promoting Learning Through Assessment", 1991, p. 19.)*

	Oral Question
Purpose	• Assess knowledge during instruction
Typical Exercise	• Open-ended question
Student's Response	• Oral answer
Scoring	• Determine correctness of answer
Major Advantage	• Joins assessment and instruction
Potential Sources of Inaccurate Assessment	• Poor questions, students' lack of willingness to respond, too few questions
Influence on Learning	• Stimulates participation in instruction, provides teacher immediate feedback on effectiveness of teaching
Keys to Success	• Clear questions, representative sample of questions to each student, adequate time provided for student response.

(Adapted from Northwest Regional Educational Laboratory.)

The Oral Language Folder

The richness and range of oral language can be synthesized into a record of the student's growth and achievements. This record, the Oral Language Folder, parallels the Writing Folder. It is a place to set contractual goals, to store ideas, to record work initiated, and to evaluate work brought to completion. The Folder records not only the variety of work attempted, but also the criteria by which it should be assessed and evaluated.

By encouraging students to have, and keep, and update an Oral Language Folder, you are teaching them to be more aware of the whole picture of their language development. You are moving them towards seeing that learning to use oral language for a variety of purposes is as important as the writing process.

The Oral Language Folder documents growth and achievement in oral language. It may consist of a three-ring binder for written records, and some kind of box or container for audio and video tapes.

It may include the following:

    (a) a record of oral language work to be done;

    (b) a record of all work begun;

    (c) a record of all work brought to completion;

    (d) a list of possible topics for the future;

    (e) a section to store records of work in progress;

    (f) copies of assessment instruments on work completed and in progress;

    (g) a folio section, for work which has been completed which may be selected for summative evaluation.

*(**Senior English OAIP**, "Promoting Learning Through Assessment", 1991, p. 20.)*

(b) Conferences and Interviews

Description

Conferences and interviews are one-to-one meetings between a teacher and a student for a specific purpose. Formal conferences should be planned and directed and students should know the purpose and expectations. A written record of the interview is necessary if the results are to be used for evaluation purposes.

Evaluation Context

Conferences can be effective for diagnostic assessment and formative evaluation. They allow teachers to individualize feedback, clarify misconceptions, and report on progress.

Using Technique to Best Advantage

Conferences are extremely useful for students involved in major projects or independent study.

Example: Student Conference on Planned Project

Date: _____   Topic Chosen: _____

Student: _____

Strengths of Topic	Weaknesses of Topic
❏ focuses	❏ too difficult
❏ clearly expresses	❏ resources not accessible
❏ worthy of research	❏ not related to aims
Other Comments	Other Comments

Next Conference Dates: _____

*(Waterloo, **Assessment for Learning**, 1993, p. 33.)*

Guidelines for Effective Conferencing

1. Approach the interview as if you (the teacher) were the learner, and the "student" were the author who has something he or she wants to share with you .

2. Assume the role of a good listener and initiate discussion by asking the student-author some sequence of the following questions:
   a) What is there about this topic that excites you?
   b) What particular angle or focus do you want to take in presenting your topic?
   c) What feelings do you want to express? What feelings do you want to arouse in your reader?
   d) What do you hope your reader will do as a result of reading your essay?

3. React to the student's replies in a way that suggests empathy with the writer's feelings, or with appropriate emotions in light of the writer's feelings.

4. Guide the discussion in the direction of helping the student clarify the reasons for his or her feelings.

5. Ask the student to tell you what he or she likes best about the essay in its present form.

6. Ask the student to tell you what areas of the essay could still be improved.

7. Ask how these improvements might be made. If the student runs thin on ideas, ask the student what techniques other authors use to get across their ideas or create certain effects.

8. Help the student pinpoint a target for the next step in the writing.

9. Attempt to fan the flames of the student's enthusiasm for revising and writing the best final copy possible.

10. Encourage the student to keep a running log of what he or she has learned in conferences with the teacher.

11. When the conference is completed, jot down any pertinent notes for future reference in your record book.

(Cavanaugh and Styles, 1985, p. 2.)

CONFERENCE RECORD

The conference record is a written account of a planned interaction between the teacher and a student. It is usually a formal individual conference regarding a subject area (writing, reading, math, independent study, etc.).

The conference record can be simply a blank loose-leaf page, or a more structured format where the teacher records what (s)he sees and hears in a conference.

<table>
<tr><td colspan="5">SAMPLE CONFERENCE RECORD
(Writing)</td></tr>
<tr><td colspan="5">Name: _____   Skill/Subject Area: Writing a report</td></tr>
<tr>
<td>Date</td>
<td>Focus of Conference</td>
<td>Question(s)</td>
<td>Answer(s)</td>
<td>Comments/Observations/ Program Notes</td>
</tr>
<tr>
<td>Oct. 14</td>
<td>• Report (transactional)

• "Frogs"</td>
<td>• Where did you get your information?</td>
<td>• From books and filmstrips (list of titles attached).</td>
<td></td>
</tr>
<tr>
<td></td>
<td></td>
<td>• Why did you organize your report this way?</td>
<td>• I watched the frog in the terrarium.

• I don't know; it made sense.</td>
<td>• A. explains how she recorded information gathered at the terrarium.

• Helped A. clarify how she saw the organization of her report. (At a later date, show her different ways to organize a report.)

• A. is able to pick out sections of the report. She shows the beginnings of outline construction.

• Directed A. to expand section on frogs' habitat by finding out what needs frogs have and how these needs connect with the habitat.</td>
</tr>
</table>

(Peel, Book 5, 1990, p. 28.)

CONFERENCE RECORD

Name: _____   Skill/Subject Area: _____

Date	Focus of Conference	Question(s)	Answer(s)	Comments/Observations/ Program Notes

*(Peel, **Book 5**, 1990, p. 55.)*

Assessment, Evaluation and Reporting for Successful Learning

The personal interview is an excellent method of obtaining self-assessment information from students except that it is time consuming, and the information gained is not standard from one individual to another. Therefore, the self-assessment inventory or questionnaire is commonly used in place of the personal interview. It consists of a set of questions pertaining to a particular area of behaviour, and enables the efficient collection and summarizing of a relatively large amount of information (see *Student and Teacher Evaluation Checklist*). If correlation between teacher and student assessment is high, a brief interview is all that is required. Discrepancies serve as a basis for focused and, if necessary, more detailed discussion.

Student and Teacher Evaluation Checklist

[S] Check boxes [√] in the student column which apply to you.
[T] This column is for the teacher to check.

S   T

EFFORT

❐ ❐ Does more than expected.
❐ ❐ Completes work without supervision.
❐ ❐ Requires a little supervision.
❐ ❐ Does required work when forced to do it.
❐ ❐ Works as little as possible.

USE OF TIME

❐ ❐ Uses time to best advantage.
❐ ❐ Well organized most of time.
❐ ❐ Requires guidance.
❐ ❐ Easily distracted.
❐ ❐ Unable to organize him/herself.

CONFIDENCE

❐ ❐ Self-assured.
❐ ❐ Needs little support.
❐ ❐ Needs occasional support.
❐ ❐ Needs encouragement and approval.
❐ ❐ Requires constant reassurance.

EMOTIONAL CONTROL

❐ ❐ Happy, even-tempered.
❐ ❐ Shows adequate control.
❐ ❐ Becomes angry sometimes.
❐ ❐ Often moody.
❐ ❐ Easily upset.

S	*T*	

INITIATIVE AND CREATIVITY

❐	❐	Works out new ideas.
❐	❐	Able to adapt and work out ideas from plans.
❐	❐	Able to choose plans well.
❐	❐	Follower, tries things which others try.
❐	❐	Never tries **anything** new.

DEGREE OF INSTRUCTION NEEDED

❐	❐	Goes ahead on his/her own.
❐	❐	Needs only initial instruction,
❐	❐	Needs some additional instruction.
❐	❐	Tries to follow instructions.
❐	❐	Needs repeated instruction.

CO-ORDINATION

❐	❐	Handles tools expertly.
❐	❐	Above average skill.
❐	❐	Average co-ordination.
❐	❐	Awkward but tries.
❐	❐	Often has trouble.

GROUP RESPONSIBILITY

❐	❐	Does more than his/her share.
❐	❐	Co-operative, conscientious.
❐	❐	Usually dependable.
❐	❐	Unreliable.
❐	❐	Unco-operative.

How does your self-evaluation compare with the teacher evaluation?

(Source unknown.)

(c) Journals and Logs

Description

Response journals and learning logs are used as a method for recording both content information and reflective thoughts. They can be used in **all subject areas** to provide students with a forum to summarize their learning, express opinions and feelings, or explain concepts in their own words.

Using Technique to Best Advantage

Learning logs and response journals provide unlimited opportunities for students to read and write on a consistent and personalized basis.

Guidelines for Use

The emphasis in response journals should be on the process of "reflective thinking":

- to record personal responses to independent reading, viewing, listening, and discussion situations;
- to record ideas, thoughts, opinions, and first drafts which can be used later in other contexts;
- to record observations and questions;
- to monitor individual development and progress; and
- to "dialogue" in written form with teacher or peers.

Learning logs (course diaries) should be used:

1. to record classroom notes (from lectures and textbooks);
2. to record concise summaries of important information (key diagrams, formulas, rules, anything students tend to forget); and
3. to record personal reactions, interpretations and opinions.

Using the Information for Student Evaluation

Evaluation is most often anecdotal but if a mark is to be assigned, it is normally based on 'doing' the journal or log, not for the quality or quantity of what was written.

Variants

Interdisciplinary: expand to include other subjects.

Examples

Adapting Learning Logs/Response Journals In Your Classroom

Develop a set of guidelines for students to use in maintaining both a Learning Log and a Response Journal in the classroom. The guidelines for the Learning Log should include a list of important subject matter concepts (to be covered from teacher lectures/demonstrations/discussions), a list of key diagrams/rules/assignments (to be learned from readings), and a list of provocative questions or points to ponder for student input. The guidelines for the Response Journal should include a list of questions for students to reflect on during a given assignment or task. The questions should require the student to think and to express his/her feelings, opinions, and reactions. The guidelines for the Learning Logs should focus on the Knowledge, Comprehension, and Application levels of Bloom's Taxonomy while the Response Journals should focus on the Analysis, Synthesis, and Evaluation levels of Bloom's Taxonomy.

(Schurr, 1992, p. 125.)

ASSESSING WRITING FOR ONESELF

There are some basic principles underlying the assessment of private writing or writing for oneself.

1. Eliciting writing for oneself regularly should be part of all work in any curriculum.
2. Such writing may take any or all of the following forms: journals, learning logs, notes, work diaries, exploratory drafts. Much of this kind of writing should be taking place naturally, as part of typical classroom activity in all subjects.

3. For at least some entries, there should be a response to the substance of what has been written, either by the teacher or a peer.

4. Students should be encouraged to select the entries which they wish to share; in responding the reader or listener is expected to respond solely and honestly to the content of what has been written.

5. The best response to the content of such writing is to respond to the ideas, either by agreeing, extending, modifying, or by questioning, disagreeing, or qualifying.

6. If the work is to be evaluated, the simplest and most effective strategy is to reward quantity on a contract basis. At the beginning of each semester or unit, negotiate with students the quantity and range of writing necessary to achieve specific grades.

This kind of assessment and evaluation ensures that students will try out the various forms of writing for oneself in a non-threatening environment, where risks are possible without any cost to grades, and where the power of writing as an instrument of discovery and learning may be experienced.

*(**Senior English OAIP**, "Promoting Learning Through Assessment", 1991, (draft), p. 23.)*

JOURNAL

1. **WHO** should write in your Journal?
   You should.

2. **WHAT** should you write in your Journal?
   New words or new ideas or new formulas or new concepts you've learned.
   Profound thoughts you've had.
   Wonderings, musings, problems to solve.
   Reflections on the class.
   Questions — both answerable and unanswerable.
   Writing ideas.

3. **WHEN** should you write in your Journal?
   After class each day.
   As you are preparing, reading, or studying for class.
   Anytime an insight or question hits you.

4. **WHERE** should you write in your Journal?
   Anywhere — so keep it with you when possible.

5. **WHY** should you write in your journal?
   It will record ideas that you might otherwise forget.
   It will be worthwhile for you to read later on so that you can note your growth.
   It will facilitate your learning, problem-solving, writing, reading, and discussion in this class.

6. **HOW** should you write in your journal?
   In wonderful, long, flowing sentences with perfect punctuation and perfect spelling and in perfect handwriting
   Or in single words that express your ideas, in short phrases, in sketches, in numbers, in maps, in diagrams, in sentences.

(McIntosh, 1991, p. 431.)

Learning Journals in Mathematics

Learning journals are a means of providing a record of the student's own involvement with the learning experience.

Implementation Activities

1. A starting point might be to have students write entries during the last five minutes of each period, responding to activities of the day, specific questions, etc. If students are summarizing what they learned and questions they still have, the journal serves as both a closure activity and a means of checking for understanding. In early stages and/or earlier grades you may want to consider a class journal where different students/teams take responsibility for the entry and then move to individual journals. Entries may/may not be made every day. Make it work for you.

2. Additional types of entries might include having students

   a) respond to specific questions;

   b) write on any aspect they choose;

   c) make predictions/list expectations about new topics;

   d) list what they think they know about a topic;

   e) write down new definitions/concepts in their own words;

   f) explain something to a third party;

   g) write about how they felt about learning;

   h) identify connections to their experience (e.g., where might it be useful);

   i) react to math related news articles, reports, etc.; and

   j) assess their own performance.

3. Anticipate that early attempts will be less than desired. Improvement will come with time and sustained effort as well as by providing specific feedback and encouragement. Be prepared to respond to students in ways which maintain open communication and help them improve their communication skills. In short, they need to be taught how to use a journal. Students will need to see models of entries. The teacher should model the expectation that everyone will write, by writing in his/her journal also.

4. Once lines of communication are open and students feel comfortable with writing, they may want to share and discuss excerpts from their journals.

Writing Questions/Topics

What did I learn today?

What puzzled/concerned me?

What did I enjoy, hate, accomplish in class today?

How did I learn from today's math lesson?

How was my performance? How could I improve? Next time I will …

Talk to your stuffed bear and tell it how you felt about math today.

Do an evaluation T. This activity helps increase specificity. Students make a big T on their page. On one side they list three specific things they liked and on the other three specific things they did not like, were concerned about, etc. Then they use these ideas to write their entry.

What did you say about the test that wasn't true?

What misconceptions did you have about today's topic?

What was most difficult for you today? Why?

How/where/when would you use the information learned today?

What kinds of errors did you make? Why?

What would make math class better?

(Ann Beyer, Workshop materials, 1991.)

YOU AND YOUR WRITING LOG

1. Like a professional author, you may want to capture your personal thoughts and feelings on paper before they evaporate.

2. If you do not write down accurate observations when you experience them, they can elude your memory.

3. You may wish to keep part of your log like a diary with dated, ongoing entries.

4. You can negotiate the use of your log for a purpose unique to your interests.

5. Your log will often take the form of written-down talk; at other times, you may choose a structured approach to recording your ideas.

6. Sketchy jottings and point-form lists are also perfectly acceptable as a means of capturing ideas before they are fully developed or forgotten.

7. You may want to record subjective responses to course activities, to literature studies, to shows you have seen, to books you have read, and to conversations you have enjoyed.

8. You should feel free to try different forms of expression in different parts of your writing log — impressions, reflections, drawings, doodlings, images, arresting words and phrases, poetic forms, anecdotes, personal experiences, humorous incidents, or virtually anything you feel motivated to write.

9. Most of the time you will decide what to write in your log; at certain times, you will be asked to write in your log in a particular way about a specific topic.

10. The writing you do in your log is experimental and will not normally be graded.

11. The writing in your log is private and the pieces you select to share with others will be your decision.

12. At times you will find material in your writing log a useful source for developing and completing assignments to be included in your writing folio.

(Cavanaugh and Styles, 1985.)

Problem-Solving Log

Name: _____   Date: _____

Class: _____

My problem is ...

1. I'm stuck on ...

2. The best way to think about this ...

3. Something that is similar to this problem is ...

4. A question I still have is ...

5. One solution I think could work is ...

6. I need help with ...

*(Burke, Kay, **Authentic Classroom Assessments**, Workshop presentation, 1993. p. 32.)*

Learning Log

Name: _____   Date: _____

Course: _____   Topic: _____

Circle one: Lecture   Discussion   Video   Written Material   Other

1. Key ideas:

2. Questions I have:

3. Connections I can make with other subjects:

4. How I can apply these ideas to my own life:

5. My insights or reflections from these learnings:

*(Burke, Kay, **Authentic Classroom Assessments**, Workshop presentation, 1993. p. 33.)*

Assess for Success

DOUBLE-ENTRY JOURNAL

Name: _____ Date: _____

Topic: _____

Initial Observation:	Upon Reflection:

*(Burke, Kay, **Authentic Classroom Assessments**, Workshop presentation, 1993. p. 34.)*

JOURNAL STEMS

Student: _____ Date: _____

Topic: _____

Select one of the following stem statements to use in your journal entry:

Stem Statements

A. The best part about …   E. How …

B. An interesting part is …   F. Why …

C. I predict …   G. A connecting idea is …

D. I wonder …   H. I believe …

Stem statement:

*(Burke, Kay, **Authentic Classroom Assessments**, Workshop presentation, 1993. p. 35.)*

3. Performance Assessments

Introduction

> "[Performance] assessments will focus on the integration of knowledge, skills, and attitudes and will employ principles of active and collaborative learning. They may be of short or extended duration and include the development of portfolios, simulations, extended projects, and exhibitions."
>
> *(Joan Baron, Connecticut Board of Education.)*

Performance assessments are active displays of learning, and are characterized by teacher observation and professional judgment. Performance assessments require that the teacher watch as a student or group of students do a particular task to demonstrate their learning and assign a level of proficiency based on the performance. Performance may be individual- or group-based, may be organized into contracts, be self- and/or peer-assessed, and be included in portfolios. Checklists, rating scales, and anecdotal records may be used to record assessment information. Performance assessment is used here as a broad category of assessment strategies. Performance assessments should be planned carefully using forms similar to the *Performance Assessment Blueprint* found on page 220.

Characteristics of Performance Assessments

- Students are asked to perform, create, produce, or do something.
- Tasks are meaningful instructional activities.
- Tasks are 'real-world' applications.
- People, not machines, do the scoring.

(Waterloo, 1993. p. 19.)

Section A — Products

1. Written Assignments

A teacher may wish to collect student progress information by having students plan, organize and produce a written product. This may be done on an individual or a group basis and may occur in the form of a contract or as an ongoing task. The written report may accompany a presentation or it may be the sole focus. Teachers may assess the content, skill development, attitudes of the student toward the task, and learning processes found within the task of producing a written product by using checklists or rating scales. They may be included in a portfolio. Self-assessment or peer-assessment may be used in conjunction with teacher-assessment of the written report.

2. Demonstrations/Performance

Demonstration within the context of ongoing student activities refers to assessing student learning progress in tasks that require students to be actively engaged in some activity such as manipulating materials, demonstrating a skill, solving a multi-stage problem, or participating in a debate.

3. Presentations/Seminars

Presentations may accompany written assignments and student demonstration assessment. They may be done on an individual or group basis, be organized in a variety of ways, e.g. contracts, portfolios, self- and/or peer-assessment. Checklists, rating scales, and anecdotal records may be used to record assessment information. A seminar is a common type of oral presentation.

4. Projects

A project is a formal assignment given to an individual student or small group of students on a topic related to the curriculum and which may involve some out-of-class research and development. A project may include constructing models and/or preparing written reports with or without diagrams, pictures, tables and graphs. It may also include producing sound or video tapes, films, collages, collections of photographs, plays and mime.

5. Oral Tests and Examinations

This form of testing assesses student learning through oral responses. It can be seen as a variant of paper and pencil tests.

Section B — Observation

Observation is the evaluation of a student's mental, physical or social activity while he/she is performing some educational activity. Observation is not only the evaluation of a finished product or a skill. The most important aspect of observation is the assessment of the student's performance during the creating of the product or the performance of the skill. The emphasis should be on both the degree of successful completion of the activity, and on the identification of physical, psychological, and social factors which help or hinder the acquisition of skill or appreciation. Teachers may find it advantageous to involve students in the development of checklists and rating scales.

1. Anecdotal Records

Anecdotal records are ongoing written notes of progress that are kept and later analyzed to inform an evaluation of process or an analysis of growth that has taken place.

2. Checklists

The observation checklist is a listing of specific concepts, skills, processes, or attitudes, the presence or absence of which you wish to record. If the observation checklist is used relatively frequently and over time, a longitudinal profile of a student can be assembled and ultimately evaluated.

3. Rating Scales

Rating scales are measuring instruments that allow representation of the extent to which specific concepts, skills, processes, or attitudes exist in students and their work.

Performance Assessment Blueprint

CONTEXT

1. What performance will you evaluate?

    Content: _____

    Skill(s): _____

2. How will proficiency manifest itself?

    ❑ Behaviour(s) to be observed [What behaviours(s)?]

    ❑ Product(s) to be observed [What product(s)?]

3. Why will you conduct this assessment?

    ❑ To inform decisions (What decisions?)

    ❑ Diagnosis   ❑ Grading   ❑ Grouping

    ❑ Evaluating your teaching   ❑ Other

    ❑ To convey information to students (What information?) _____

4. What kind of assessment result will you need?

    ❑ Rank order

    ❑ Attainment of specific target(s) (mastery)

CRITERIA

5. By what standards will you judge proficiency?

Criterion	Continuum		
	Poor	*Good*	*Excellent*
1.			
2.			
3.			

METHOD

6. How will you elicit this performance so you can observe it?

    ❑ Structured exercise (Example:) _____

    ❑ Naturally occurring events (What events?) _____

7. How will you rate performance and create a record of your assessment?

    ❑ Checklist

    ❑ Rating scale

    ❑ Portfolio

    ❑ Audio or video tape

    ❑ Anecdotal record

8. Who shall evaluate performance?

    ❑ Teacher

    ❑ Student

    ❑ Peer

    ❑ Other (Who?) _____

(Northwest Regional Educational Laboratory, Classroom Assessment Based on Observation, Portland, Oregon.)

Assess for Success

Section A: Products

1. Written Assignments

Description

Written assignments are designed to allow the student to plan, compose, and report upon a unit of learning. Students may be given the opportunity to choose their topic and to design their research plan, or they may be provided with a structured framework. Written assignments are ongoing student activities that provide information for teachers on student progress.

Evaluation Context

Written assignments are powerful instructional methods. Evaluating plans prepared in advance and communicated to students, can provide structure to the whole exercise, as well as indicate to the student the teacher's criteria for assessing the quality of the work.

There is a wide range of student activities that fall under the category of written assignments:

essays	laboratory reports
short response questions	journal entries
letters	articles
poetry	written dialogue
written solution to a math puzzle	research

Major projects often have a written component. Learning logs and journals can also be considered under the heading of written assignments.

- Describe overall expectations for the written assignment in as much detail as possible. A student's first assignment should be more tightly structured; whereas, later ones can be left more in the student's control. The more structure provided, the more comparable the assignments will be.

- If the assignment has a number of development stages, construct assessment criteria for each segment of the written assignment. For example, if students are doing a project on how local government operates, they may:
  - interview council members;
  - research the stories from the local newspaper;
  - trace the path of a local issue through the stages from initial submission to council to the final decision;
  - prepare a display or presentation for their classmates;
  - hand in a final report to you.

Each of these segments can have its own assessment scheme developed by the teacher or by the student. (Refer to self- and peer-assessment.) By designing the assessment pattern in this way, teachers can help the student direct his or her efforts appropriately.

Guidelines for Use

- Schedule regular consultations with students. During these times, reinforce the assessment criteria and adjust them if necessary (for example, if certain segments of the project become unworkable).

- If students work in groups, another variable has been introduced into the assessment. Three students working in a group may not produce a project or report that is three times as good as a single student's. Maintaining the group integrity can take an appreciable amount of effort. This will need to be factored into the assessment scheme.

- If an outsider is used as a judge, remember that only part of the report, usually the final display, will be involved. The other segments must not be neglected in the overall evaluation.

- Use a variety of techniques, matching each technique to the objective of that segment of the assignment that is under consideration. Observation checklists and rating scales offer potential.

(Adapted from Saskatchewan Education, 1991, p. 94.)

A Framework for Marking a Project or a Written Assignment

Student Name: _____

Date or Time Period of Assessment: _____

Topic or Project Description: _____

A. Organizational Features	Yes	No	Comments
1. Student understood the objectives of the assignment.			
2. Student understood the specific terms/requirements of the assignment.			
3. Student understood the timeline and due date for the assignment.			
4. Student understood the method/procedure/criteria by which the assignment would be marked.			
5. Student had an opportunity to discuss the assignment topic and have input into the assignment direction.			
6. The assignment is within the capabilities of the student.			
7. Consultation has occurred with the student throughout the stages of development of the assignment.			

B. Student Learning	Yes	No	Comments
1. Student formulated her/his own questions and found answers to them.			
2. Student showed evidence of individual initiative.			
3. Student exchanged ideas with other students in developing the assignments.			
4. Student brought in references to learning prior to this experience or from other areas that relate to this experience.			
5. Student worked in a methodical manner to produce the assignment.			
6. Evidence exists in the assignment of the following. • planning • organization • interpretation • inference • analysis • application • synthesis • hypothesis • prediction • evaluation			
7. Technical aspects of the assignment reflect accuracy and suitability of the following. • sentence structure • vocabulary • grammar and punctuation • spelling • handwriting • information included in assignment			

(Saskatchewan Education, 1991, pp. 95–96.)

2. Demonstration (Performance)

> Performance assessments are levers to make assessment maximally useful. They direct a different conception of the place of assessment in the educational process.
>
> *(Waterloo County Board of Education, **Assessment for Learning**, 1993.)*

> Unlike standardized multiple choice tests, performance assessments require individuals to engage in tasks that mirror as closely as possible the conditions under which a particular competence is performed in 'authentic' settings.
>
> *(Waterloo Board, 1993.)*

Description

Performance assessments help teachers assess how well a student performs a practiced behaviour, the attainment of which is the primary goal of the teaching. This is a limited definition of performance. If a teacher's use extends to include process skills such as working cooperatively, then there are other assessment techniques that would apply.

Evaluation Context

Demonstrations are used in those situations where the student is required to demonstrate competence directly such as playing a musical instrument, driving a car, solving a mathematical puzzle, demonstrating skill with technology, giving a speech, or identifying and repairing a fault in a piece of machinery. They are also used in simulation situations. Two examples are using a driving simulator or practicing a tennis serve in slow motion without the ball. In simulation situations, the emphasis is upon mastery of the fundamentals of a performance skill.

Guidelines for Use

Demonstrations, as with other test formats, have to be thoroughly prepared. Some points to remember are:

- The manner in which the performance test is constructed and administered should be equivalent for all students. Otherwise, it is impossible to claim that the same assessment has been conducted for all the students. For example, have all candidates in a music examination play the same piece on the same piano. There are other variables such as the order of playing that may affect both the performer and the evaluator. Careful preparation can help teachers control many external variables.
- Give the students clear information on what will be required of them. As with any assessment technique, students should be informed well ahead of the time of the assessment.

- The information given to students should include a list of the performance attributes that a teacher will be assessing and the criteria he/she will be using. For example, "the student will hem a skirt of cotton material so that the hem is straight, the material is not gathered, and the ends of the stitching are neat." These detailed criteria can be incorporated into a rating scale, an anecdotal record, or an observation checklist that will guide the assessment of the performance. The criteria should, where appropriate, include elements from both the process and the product. In the example above, the finished hem represents the product and the correct preparation and use of the sewing machine represents the process.

Using the Information for Student Evaluation

The information from the various data-gathering and recording techniques can be converted into a mark, grade, or qualitative evaluation statement.

Variants

Demonstrations are frequently organized in assessment stations. More than one station can be set up in a series to test a variety of skills.

In designing a performance task, here is a framework for design that a teacher may find useful in thinking through the process. For each of the headings, attempt to be as specific as possible.

- the objective of the task
- the design of the task
- previous knowledge students need in order to complete the task
- knowledge directly related to current in-class work with which students need to have a reasonable level of familiarity or skill in order to complete the task
- processes involved in completing the task
- attitudes that may be observed during the students' interaction with the task
- technical skills students need to complete the task
- materials that the student would use to complete the task
- the location of the performance of the task
- number of students working at the task at the same time
- assessment instruments used to record information
- method of communicating evaluation information to the students

By completing this framework, a basic plan for the assessment task will be in place.

(Saskatchewan Education, 1991, p. 104.)

Sample Rubric for a Performance Test

CRITERIA FOR THE DELIVERY OF A SPEECH PERFORMANCE TEST

1. **The delivery is *inadequate* in meeting the requirements of the task.**
   - volume is too low to be understood
   - rate is too fast to be understood
   - pronunciation and enunciation are so unclear that the message is not understandable

2. **The delivery is *minimal* in meeting the requirements of the task.**
   - volume is too low or too loud
   - rate is too fast or too slow — pauses are too long
   - pronunciation and enunciation are unclear (**many** "ahs", "uhms", "you knows")
   - listeners distracted by delivery or have difficulty understanding words (listener has to work)

3. **The delivery is *adequate* in meeting the requirements of the task.**
   - volume is audible
   - rate is measured — pauses are appropriate
   - pronunciation and enunciation are clear (**few** "ahs", "uhms", "you knows")
   - listeners are not distracted by delivery
   - listeners have no difficulty understanding words

4. **The delivery is *superior* in meeting the requirements of the task.**
   - delivery is lively, enthusiastic and enhances meaning of message
   - volume varies to add emphasis or interest
   - rate varies and pauses are used to add emphasis or interest
   - pronunciation and enunciation are clear (**very few** "ahs", "uhms", "you knows")

---

*(Adapted from Waterloo, **Assessment for Learning**, 1993, p. 20.)*

Evaluation of Oral Reading

Name: _____

Instructor's Comments:

	Superior 1	2	Average 3	4	Poor 5
Selection					
1. Significance and quality of material					
2. Appropriate for speaker, audience, occasion					
Introduction					
1. Appropriate information					
2. Conversational directness					
Meaning					
1. Communicated author's intended meaning					
2. Accurate phrasing to convey meaning					
3. Appropriate emphasis					
Emotion					
1. Communicated emotion the author intended					
2. Communicated the climax					
Voice					
1. Pleasant, clear quality					
2. Appropriate pitch level					
3. Appropriate inflection					
4. Adequate volume					
5. Appropriate rate					
6. Clear articulation					
7. Correct pronunciation					
Delivery					
1. Reader physically poised and at ease					
2. Unobtrusively handled script					
3. Body action co-ordinated with thought and emotion					
4. Adequate eye contact with audience					

Additional suggestions:

(Sylvia Valevicius, Sir Frederick Banting Secondary School, London Board of Education.)

Dance/Drama Evaluations

Group Members: _____

_____

Theme: _____

Unity of movement:	0	1	2	3	4	5
Originality and effort:	0	1	2	3	4	5
Costumes:	0	1	2	3	4	5
Musical selection:	0	1	2	3	4	5
Extras (lights, etc.):	0	1	2	3	4	5

Comments:

Total: /25

(Sylvia Valevicius, Sir Frederick Banting Secondary School, London Board of Education.)

Scene Study/Monologue Evaluation Sheet

Name: _____

Date: _____

Title of Scene: _____

	Mark
Characterization	/5

     — is it honest?
     — is it realistic?
     — is it believable?
     — is careful preparation evident?

Voice   /5

     — is it controlled?
     — is it varied?
     — does it reveal character?

Movement   /5

     — is it controlled?
     — is it purposeful?
     — does it reveal character?

Preparation   /5

     — has a character analysis been done?
     — has a blocking sheet been prepared?
     — are lines learned?
     — are costumes and props used?

Total   /20

(Sylvia Valevicius, Sir Frederick Banting Secondary School, London Board of Education.)

Assess for Success

3. Presentations/Seminars

Definition

Presentations involve students in a variety of activities that are both process- and product-oriented. Students collect information and organize it. They analyze what is needed for a specific purpose and bring together various elements into a whole. They record the material in a manner they have chosen that will best display their learning process. They communicate to an audience what they have learned through visual, audio, and/or kinesthetic means. In becoming involved with a presentation, students interact with the material they are learning.

Evaluation Context

Presentations are extraordinarily rich in possibilities for assessing student progress. Knowledge, skills, attitudes, and processes all become evident throughout the stages of development. A presentation may be used as a summative assessment activity at the end of a unit or course. It may also be used formatively to assess student progress while the unit or course is proceeding. A presentation may accompany a written report as part of a major project. If a teacher wants to improve students' actual presentation styles, having them become involved in a presentation can serve a diagnostic function as well. Suggestions for improvement can be made based on their performance.

There are many possibilities for using presentations within a student evaluation program. Students may present to the class individually, or to each other in small groups. Such a situation is conducive to peer-assessment. A teacher may assess more globally on the presentations as he/she circulates among the groups, gathering more general student information such as attentiveness, listening behaviours, and active involvement with the topic through questioning.

If presentations are on a broad topic, the topic may be divided into sections with groups within a class presenting each section. A teacher could then use group evaluations with the added benefit that the students would be teaching each other at the same time.

A third possibility is to have students individually present on a topic to the teacher and to the class on an ongoing basis. If the content of the presentations is secondary to the processes and skills a teacher wishes to assess, students could take turns over the course of the year presenting on a topic of interest to them. Students may choose their topics or they may be related to ongoing units of work. The structure would then remain the same for each student, allowing for comparisons, but the topics would change from student to student.

Guidelines for Use

- Students come with varying experiential backgrounds in conceptualizing, organizing, and delivering a presentation. To use presentations as a diagnostic assessment technique, have the students use what they currently know. To use presentations in formative or summative assessment may require teaching presentation skills.

- As with all other assessment activities, students must know how they will be assessed — what you are looking for and what standard of performance is expected.

- Not all students have the self-confidence necessary to stand up in front of their peers and teachers to give a presentation. Consider some of the following questions prior to assigning a presentation to students.
  - Has an atmosphere of acceptance been established in the classroom so that students will feel confident that what they present will be well received?
  - Are there students who have disabilities that would hamper their ability to give a presentation? If so, what modifications can be made so that they can present to their best ability?
  - Have expectations been established about how and why these presentations will be assessed?
  - Has thought been given to assistance or modifications for students who might find this activity extremely stressful?

(Adapted from Saskatchewan Education, 1991, p. 97.)

SEMINAR PRESENTATIONS

Student Instruction Sheet

- You must choose one topic from the list provided for detailed study.
- Your topic must be chosen no later than _____.
- You should work in groups of two (2). (Any variation from this must be approved by your teacher.)
- Presentations will take the form of a seminar.
- Seminar dates will be allocated by _____.
- To do a proper seminar presentation, you must develop a hypothesis about your topic and you must substantiate this hypothesis in your presentation. Your hypothesis will also be the "organizer" for your presentation because you must focus on all aspects of your hypothesis.
- The following timetable must be followed when preparing for your presentation:

4 weeks before the presentation	an annotated bibliography with at least 5 items. (An annotated bibliography consists of a full bibliographic reference, a brief summary and a brief statement on the usefulness of the material for your presentation.)
3 weeks before the presentation	hypothesis to be discussed with your teacher.
2 weeks before the presentation	hypothesis and content outline in writing given to and discussed with your teacher. The outline must include any AV material you plan to use during your presentation.
1 week before the presentation	presentation strategy to be discussed with your teacher.
2 classes before the presentation	your teacher **must** receive a minimum 1 page, maximum 2 page summary of the presentation. This material will be distributed to the class before the presentation to prepare the class to be able to participate in discussion of your topic.

- Presentations should be planned to last all or most of one period including any AV material used.
- You should plan to use about half your Independent Study periods to work on your presentation.

Evaluation

- Concepts and information from the presentations will be included in tests/exams.
- Using the Presentation Preparation and Evaluation Sheet, presenters will be marked out of 10 on each of the preparation requirements. (total – 50)
- The presentation itself will be marked out of 50. The mark for each member of the presenting group will be a blending of teacher and student assessment.
- The total of the above three will count for 20% of your final mark.

*(Scarborough, **World Issues — OAC**, 1988, p. 24.)*

Presentation Preparation Sheet			
Topic: _____			
Group Members: _____			
Session	**Date**	**Comments**	**Mark**
1. Annotated Bibliography			/10
2. Hypothesis (Oral)			/10
3. Hypotheses and Outline (Written)			/10
4. Presentation Strategy			/10
5. Summary			/10
6. Presentation			/50
Total			/100

*(Scarborough, **World Issues — OAC**, 1988, p. 25.)*

NOTES TAKEN ON PRESENTATIONS

Name: _____

Topic: _____

Presenter(s): _____

Questions raised:

Main ideas presented: **Details:**

Conclusions reached:

*(Scarborough, **World Issues — OAC**, 1988, p. 29.)*

         Assess for Success

Class Presentations — Peer/Teacher Evaluation Sheet

	E Poor	D Fair	C Average	B Good	A Excellent	Mark out of ___
Organization and Preparation	not prepared and unorganized	poorly prepared	acceptable	good preparation and most effective	extremely well organized and prepared	
Use of Aids charts, models, samples, board	none used or ineffective	used but obscure	moderately well used, sometimes obscure	acceptable, mostly effective and well used	very vivid and effective	
Knowledge of Topic	lost and misleading	not sure	sometimes uncertain	knowledgeable	extremely knowledgeable	
Presentation	boring	dull	adequate	interesting	outstanding	
Class Response and Participation	none	some	interested	well involved & very interested	extremely interested & totally involved	
Remarks						

(Bruce Southern, Sir Frederick Banting Secondary School, London.)

Seminar Evaluation

Topic:

Name: _____   Date: _____

RESEARCH			MARKS
0 • insufficient breadth or depth	**5** • adequate coverage • recognized authorities	**10** • valid and relevant research, pertinent reading selections	
INFORMATION			
0 • factors left out, misunderstood or misinterpreted	**7** • important ideas conveyed • adequately and understandably	**15** • socio-cultural data and all key concepts presented comprehensively and precisely	
ANALYSIS			
0 • describes or • defines only	**4** • finds relationships among ideas	**8** • explains, justifies interprets and predicts	
DISCUSSION			
0 • limited, off topic • little leadership • no class participation	**2** • adequate, relevant • meaningful class participation	**5** • stimulating • relevant, productive class participation	
PRESENTATION			
0 • too long or short • vague, off topic • disorganized • barely interesting	**6** • adequate length • on topic • satisfactory coverage • interesting	**12** • challenging • comprehensive • relevant, clear • precise, provocative	
TOTAL MARKS:			**/50**

*(Waterloo, **Assessment for Learning**, 1993, Appendix B, p. 1.)*

Assess for Success

Seminar Evaluation Sheet

Name: _____

Seminar Topic: _____   Date: _____

Group Members: _____

Criteria for Evaluation:

1. **Research:**
   - is there any evidence that a variety of sources have been used?
   - is there any evidence of thorough research?
   - is the seminar prepared in so far as content is concerned?

2. **Organization:**
   - does the speaker know what he/she is trying to do?
   - is there a clear purpose in the seminar?
   - does the speaker emphasize the main ideas or concepts?

3. **Presentation:**
   - is the speaker understandable?
   - does the speaker use notes and avoid reading his/her presentation?
   - does the speaker utilize time effectively?
   - is the material presented in an interesting manner?

4. **Group Involvement:**
   - does the seminar leader(s) encourage discussion?
   - does he/she create opportunities for discussion?
   - does he/she handle questions well?
   - does he/she try to bring about some resolution of the discussion?

5. **Summary:**
   - have related ideas and suggestions been pulled together?
   - has a clear picture of the main ideas, problems been given?

Evaluation (Circle mark for each criteria):

1.	Minimal research and thought indicated	1	2	3	4	5	6	7	8	9	10	Well researched and thought out
2.	No clear issue or problem presented	1	2	3	4	5	6	7	8	9	10	Clearly analyzed the issues and problems
3.	Material presented poorly	1	2	3	4	5	6	7	8	9	10	Material well presented
4.	No attempt made to involve the group and questions handled poorly	1	2	3	4	5	6	7	8	9	10	Interesting, relevant questions involve everybody in discussion
5.	Discussion rambles and is not summarized	1	2	3	4	5	6	7	8	9	10	Well directed and summarized discussion

Total:

*(Scarborough, **World Issues — OAC**, 1988, p. 28.)*

AEROBIC WARM-UP ROUTINE

Names: _____

_____

	DUE DATE	REC'D	MARK
1. Music Selection	_____	_____	___/5
2. Music Analysis	_____	_____	___/10
3. Exercise Checklist Cards Submitted	_____	_____	___/5
		Total	___/20

4. Presentation Date _____

Routine Evaluation

1. Music
   • proper tempo
   • appropriate to exercise category _____ _____ ___/5

2. Composition
   • exercises appropriate to category
   • flow from one to other
   • checklist for complete workout covered
   • keeps interest without being complicated _____ _____ ___/10

3. Knowledge of Routine _____ _____ ___/5

4. Presentation of Routine
   • good voice
   • proper verbal cues given in advance _____ _____ ___/10

| | | Total | ___/50 |

*(Scarborough, **Fitness: A Healthy Lifestyle**, 1992.)*

4. Projects

Description

A project is a formal assignment given to an individual student (or occasionally to a small group of students) on a topic related to the curriculum. It may involve some out-of-class research and development. A project may include constructing models and/or preparing written reports with or without diagrams, pictures, tables and graphs. It may also include producing sound or video tapes, films, collages, collections of photographs, plays and mime.

Suggestion

> Whenever possible, have a sizable portion of the work on a project during class time in order that process can be assessed and the grading differentiated between contributing members of the team.

Evaluation Context

Projects can be an extremely valuable and rewarding learning activity, but a frustrating evaluation activity. The reason is that when marks are assigned, the activity becomes comparative. The comparison can be very difficult to make and justify when the normal constraints of time on task, resources used, and contribution by the student are no longer controllable or directly observable by the teacher.

Advantages of Projects

- provides a student or group an opportunity to direct their learning, demonstrate initiative, and pursue interests
- allows students to acquire the skills of an independent learner
- allows for integration of learning in several disciplines
- can be designed at differing levels of difficulty to encourage success for all students
- is a valuable alternative to tests

Disadvantages of Projects

- is difficult to evaluate since the teacher is unsure how much is the student's own work
- is influenced by access to resources
- is time consuming to organize
- is demanding on the library/resource centre

*(Waterloo, **Assessment for Learning**, 1993, p. 31.)*

Suggestions for Projects

Evaluation can be confrontational and controversial when it is only summative and product oriented. Use project proposals, preliminary reports, 'rough drafts', project outlines, learning logs and journals, tracking sheets, interviews, observation, and peer and self-evaluation to 'spread' the evaluation over time.

❏ **Assess both process and product.**

Process includes willingness, effort, engagement, self-direction, ability to use library resources, classroom work, time management, etc. Product includes completeness, accuracy, logical organization, visual impact, originality, concise and precise, method of presentation, etc.

❏ **Projects should never be "choose a topic and do it".**

It is essential that students clearly understand what is expected of them. Description of the project should include topic choices, scope, criteria for evaluation and mark allocation, length, time commitment, due date, objectives, and possible sources and resources.

❏ **Teach the necessary skills.**

These skills include:
- information skills of retrieving and accessing information, recording, organizing and presenting
- personal management skills of task management and time management

❏ **Involve students in discussing the evaluation criteria**

A collaboratively agreed upon list of criteria will reduce the judgmental nature of teacher evaluation.

*(Waterloo, **Assessment for Learning**, 1993, p. 32.)*

Guideposts for Assigning and Marking Projects

A. Ensure that students understand what a project is and how they are to go about doing it. Students must be directly taught how to do a project before it is assigned.

B. Ensure that students have ample opportunity to discuss various aspects of a general topic and to select a manageable smaller aspect of that topic for their own project. For example, the topic "The Inuit" would be too broad, but "Inuit Methods of Hunting" would be manageable for most students.

C. Ensure that the project is within students' capabilities so that they can derive personal satisfaction from completing it.

D. Provide students with opportunities to practice the skills of project preparation in the classroom, especially in Grades 4 to 10.

E. Ensure that students know precisely and in advance the teacher's expectations regarding the project.

F. Provide students with a written outline of the assignment, including the following information:
- the objectives of the project;
- the specific terms of the assignment;
- the due date or, where appropriate, a deadline for each phase of the project;
- the criteria on which the project will be evaluated, including the marking scheme.

Suggestions could also be included in the outline regarding sources and/or location of sources. In order to avoid confusion and delay at home, students in Grades 4 to 10 should be encouraged to show the written outline of the assignment to their family as soon as possible after it has been distributed.

G. Prepare the project assignment in close consultation with the resource center teacher. Ensure that sufficient resources, including non-print materials, are available for each project and in sufficient quantity for all students. If other teachers will be involved or affected, also consult with them.

H. Maintain continuous consultation with individual students on their plans and progress. This will ensure that projects will not be inappropriate, unmanageable or unrealistic in either time or scope.

I. Ensure that exactly the same project topics are not assigned in one or more succeeding grades.

J. Provide, where applicable, each student with a written evaluation based on the criteria announced when the project was assigned. Be prepared to spend time discussing the written evaluation with individual students.

K. **Provide the marks or comments regarding the student's completed project on a sheet of paper separate from the project.** This practice will allow projects to be displayed in the classroom, school or community, if deemed appropriate and agreed to by the student. A child's work should never be exhibited against his or her will or for purposes of comparison or competition. The manner in which a child's work is displayed reflects the teacher's respect for individuality and effort.

L. Use the completed projects, where feasible, as part of the teaching and learning program.

M. Provide opportunities for students to generate their own topics for project assignments and to suggest how they could be developed and evaluated.

N. Provide opportunities for some students, at some times, to choose a project, rather than another type of assignment, such as a major essay.

O. Consider providing an opportunity for a small group of students to volunteer to work together to complete a project, with the understanding that each member of the group will receive the same mark, grade or comment.

*(**Making the Grade**, 1987, pp. 98–99.)*

Sample Outline of a Project Assignment Sheet

The following sample outline of a project assignment sheet provides a framework of headings for five essential components of a good project. Each heading is followed by suggestions regarding the information to include under each heading.

The outline containing the detailed information for a specific project should be given to each student when a project is assigned. There should be an appropriate amount of time devoted to discussing with the students the **five essential components** of the project assignment sheet.

PROJECT ASSIGNMENT SHEET

Topic Choice(s):

Assign a specific topic, provide a group of topics from which students can select, or allow students to propose their own topics within the general subject area.

Objectives:

Provide a short list of specific objectives, for both the project and student learning related to the project. These objectives should be stated in student terms.

The Task:

Include in the task description what the students may do, how they might do it, where the work will be done and what form the completed project might take.

Due Dates:

Preliminary Dates:
Indicate several dates for each teacher/student consultation, peer discussion and consultation, and progress report.

Final Submission Date:

Criteria for Evaluation:

Include the specific criteria directly related to the stated objectives upon which the projects will be evaluated.

*(**Making the Grade,** 1987, p. 100.)*

Evaluation for Individual Project

Person: _____   s = self   p = peer   t = teacher

Rating: *5 = excellent   4 = above average   3 = average   2 = below average   1 = poor*

		1	2	3	4	5
1. Time Total hours spent	s p t					
Organized time	s p t					
2. Research Scope and nature of study	s p t					
Number of resources used	s p t					
3. Content Relevant to topic	s p t					
Information given is complete	s p t					
4. Creativity New or original lay-out	s p t					
Personal skills used	s p t					
5. Organization Logically and orderly presented	s p t					
Maps, charts, bibliography presented	s p t					
6. Style Carefully proofread	s p t					
Interesting and mature writing	s p t					
7. Appearance Neat cover and title	s p t					
Use of colour, lines, printing, etc.	s p t					
Mark	s p t					

Name: _____

(London, Regional Geography — Travel and Tourism, 1992, p. 14–17.)

GEOGRAPHY PROJECT EVALUATION

(A) Resource Materials   **(5)**
- variety
- suitability
- dates
- bibliography

(B) Technical Skills   **(5)**
- maps (situation, site, thematic)
- graphs (quality, suitability)
- diagrams, profiles
- choice of construction methods
- photographs

(C) Overall Quality of Project   **(5)**
- suitability of materials used
- appearance (writing, labels, neatness, packaging)
- table of contents
- titles and headings
- title page
- durability of displays or models

(D) Amount of Work Put Into Project   **(5)**
- size of project
- originality
- type of work done
- time spent in planning

(E) Academic Quality   **(10)**
- stated theme or introduction
- suitability of topic to this Geography course
- level of work done
- organization
- conclusion or summary
- spelling, grammar

Total Mark out of 30 =

*(London, **Regional Geography — Travel and Tourism**, 1992, p. 14–17.)*

Assess for Success

PHYSICAL AND HEALTH EDUCATION
PERSONAL FITNESS

Topic: *The development of a personal fitness plan using the range of available programs in the school.*

Objectives:

1. To determine the range of programs available in the school related to physical activity.

2. To develop a personal fitness plan based on the programs available in the school and the components of physical fitness which you have learned about in your various classes.

The Task: *What you should consider including in your project:*

1. Activities and programs that you think are appropriate for learning about and developing your physical fitness. Give reasons for your choices.

2. A realistic long-term plan or program for you to follow in order to develop your own physical fitness.

3. A personal weekly schedule of physical activities that you might follow.

4. Direct reference to the fitness kit. When making these references, include:
   – the *name* of each instrument;
   – what physical fitness *component* each instrument measures:
   – *how* each instrument measures the fitness component.

5. A pre-test schedule and form.

6. A post-test schedule and form.

7. A list of references (people, books, magazines, visuals) that you used.

Your personal feelings about this project. (Written on a separate page attached to the project.)

Your project assignment, including any schedules, forms, charts, graphs or diagrams, should be submitted according to the dates stated.

Due Dates: *Preliminary Dates:*

   A. Classroom work and group discussion   _____

   B. 1st Student/Teacher Consultation   _____

   C. 2nd Student/Teacher Consultation   _____

   D. Draft Submission   _____

   Final Submission Date: _____

It is suggested that you allot the following amounts of time to completing this project:

in class _____ periods

out of class _____ hours

How Your Project Will Be Marked

Marks will be awarded for:

30%	— developing a personal fitness plan which is balanced, reflects the appropriate activities and programs available in the school and includes references to the fitness kit, and an example of a pre-test and a post-test;
20%	— information that is complete, on topic, and accurate for each aspect of your project;
10%	— ideas that are developed in an organized manner;
15%	— including materials such as charts, graphs, pictures, schedules, models, photographs, and drawings to support or illustrate the information in your project;
10%	— indications that you have done research and that you have presented the information from this research in a manner that is easy to read, brief, and to the point;
10%	— originality of content and method of presentation;
5%	— attractiveness, neatness and visual impact.

*(**Making the Grade**, 1987, pp. 103–104.)*

EVALUATION OF NEWSPAPER ON SOCIAL PROBLEMS

Name: _____

Part A	Front Page Story	10 marks	Poor	Fair	Good	Excellent
1.	Creativity		2	3	4	5
2.	Accuracy (including quantity and quality)		2	3	4	5
3.	Clearly identifies and explains social problem		2	3	4	5

Part B   Feature Articles   10 Marks

Causes

1.	Factually accurate and complete		2	3	4	5
2.	Organized sequence		2	3	4	5
3.	Applies skills on BACKGROUND and IMMEDIATE causes		2	3	4	5

Solutions

1.	Describe **three** different solutions clearly		2	3	4	5
2.	Provides positive and negative criticisms for at least two		2	3	4	5

Part C   Editorials   5 marks

1.	Focuses on issue of problem		2	3	4	5
2.	Takes a stand and defends it		2	3	4	5

Part D   Letters to the Editor   5 marks

1.	Creativity		2	3	4	5
2.	Reflects different viewpoints		2	3	4	5
3.	Provides additional information and ideas		2	3	4	5

Part E   Interview   5 marks

1.	Asks related and significant questions		2	3	4	5
2.	Able to obtain additional info on problem		2	3	4	5

Part F   Overall Impression   5 marks

1.	Includes spelling, grammar, and layout of newspaper		2	3	4	5

*(Scarborough, **A Resource Guide for Senior History/Contemporary Studies, Grade 11 and 12**, p. 554.)*

5. Oral Tests and Examinations

Description

Oral tests and examinations assess student work through oral responses.

Evaluation Context

Oral tests and examinations are often the main method of assessing fluency in a foreign language and performance tests in drama. Procedures similar to those used for paper and pencil tests should be followed.

Using Technique to Best Advantage

Oral tests can be used for both formative and summative assessment. The more positive, supportive and non-comparative the test or examination, the greater the likelihood of a quality result.

Guidelines for Use

Oral examinations can be stressful for a student when this approach is first used. This stress can be reduced significantly if the testing is done privately or if the testing is conducted within an atmosphere of acceptance.

Oral examinations may cover less content. Attention must be focused on selecting the most important areas to be examined. Make the questions as clear as possible so that time is not spent on clarifying the questions.

Oral examinations are a more intimate form of communication than written ones. Consequently, teachers may be tempted to 'fill in the blanks' in what the student says with the result that they feel that the student has said or explained more than she or he actually has. Body language can also provide the student with clues that are not available in the written situation. It is important that the teacher concentrate on what is actually being said and the student's reactions.

Oral examinations, being interactive in nature, accentuate any cultural or gender differences. Be alert to such influences, and take them into account. In extreme cases, consider enlisting the help of a colleague whom the student would find more compatible.

When examining some of your students orally due to a physical handicap such as blindness or motor paralysis while the other students are being assessed by written tests, teachers should verify that the test content and procedures are reasonably equivalent.

To keep the time requirements for oral assessment to a minimum, make sure that the task students are asked to perform is one that is truly inaccessible in other ways. By knowing exactly what is to be assessed, teachers can ensure that their techniques are appropriate.

Using the Information for Student Evaluation

Oral tests and examinations are often used as an alternative to paper and pencil tests for special needs students. They are the only realistic way to test proficiency in a foreign language, job interview skills, and debates.

Hints

If students have input into the criteria for assessment and the weightings to be used in the evaluation, the oral test or examination, is much less likely to be threatening or stressful and the performance is likely to be better.

Ensure that the examination period is long enough to provide adequate information for assessment.

Be consistent about what is recorded. Use checklists and rating scales.

Limitations

Oral tests and examinations take a great deal of time to administer.

Bias can interfere with validity.

Variants

The Co-operative Examination (see Brock High School example on page 253.)

Sample: Essay Question – Responding Orally

1. Was the student able to paraphrase the question?

2. Did the student answer the question asked?

3. Was the answer organized for presentation so that it developed logically with a beginning, a middle, and an end?

4. Did the student choose significant details to support a position taken?

5. Was the student able to express the response precisely and succinctly?

6. Was the student able to diagram simply on paper the basic structure of the answer?

7. Did the student speak easily and confidently in expressing the answer?

(Pro-File: Language Aloud ... Allowed, 1987, pp. 56–57.)

Descriptive Oral Proficiency Scoring Scheme
(Individual or Group)

Date: _____

Names:	1 Low	2 Fair	3 Good	4 Exc't	Comments

1 = Low
Not at all fluent; hesitates frequently
Very limited vocabulary
Uses occasional short phrase
Hard to understand
Errors

2 = Fair
Not very fluent; hesitates often
Limited vocabulary
Can answer simple questions; uses simple sentences; begins occasional short
 conversations
Sometimes hard to understand
Some errors

3 = Good
Reasonably fluent; hesitates occasionally
Good grasp of vocabulary
Able to ask and answer simple questions; able to start and maintain a simple
 conversation
Fairly easy to understand
Occasional errors

4 = Excellent
Fluent; hesitates rarely
Broad range of vocabulary
Asks and answers a wide range of questions easily; able to start and maintain
 a conversation very easily
Very easy to understand
Errors rare

(Ullman, 1990, p. 45.)

How to Develop Communicative Tests

Thinking the Test Through: French Program

The following steps are important inasmuch as if you attend to them all, you will be confident that the testing task you design will in fact carry out your intention. The order in which the steps are to be carried out is flexible; sometimes your particular focus in testing makes one of the steps of special importance, so that you would consider it first. For example, you might want to exploit the students' interest in a specific social situation or a community event, or to emphasize certain vocabulary, therefore working around that focus. Whatever decisions you make, however, you will want to keep a record of them, so that you will have a descriptive summary to accompany the test when you add it to your files.

1. **Identify where the test fits into the French program.** You will want to record the grade and where in the year's program the test belongs: for example, at the end of the semester, or at the end of a unit, or following instruction and practice on a specific point of usage.

2. **Decide whether your objective for this test is summative or formative.** If your objective is to measure performance for grading, the test must be designed so that uniform conditions of administration are possible and scoring criteria are clearly defined beforehand for the students. If your objective is to obtain diagnostic feedback, administration could be relatively informal.

3. **Decide on the communicative purpose or function of the task.** Communicative purpose includes both the mode of language use and the tone. Modes include narrating, discussing, describing, negotiating, asking questions, apologizing, inferring, ordering, informing, giving directions, expressing emotions, explaining, hypothesizing, etc. Tone can be formal, informal, or colloquial, persuasive or hesitant, approving or complaining, courteous or curt, etc. For example, the communicative purpose could be describing a movie; the tone would depend on whether the student was to describe the movie to a friend or make a formal presentation to the class.

   As both mode and tone are connected to choice of grammatical form, it may be that your choice of a specific linguistic focus for the task (see next step) suggests an appropriate communicative purpose. For example, to verify that students can use the conditional tense, you might set a speculative task (*Si j'étais riche, je ...*).

4. **Decide on the linguistic focus of the task.** You may want to emphasize one or more of the following:
   - affirmative, negative, imperative, or interrogative structures
   - topical vocabulary
   - specific verb tenses, reflexive verbs, or irregular verbs
   - adverbs or adjectives
   - connectors (conjunctions, prepositions)
   - language registers (formal, informal, colloquial)
   - conventional openers and closers of oral or written communication.

5. **Decide on the skill focus of the task.** A communicative task could emphasize listening or reading comprehension, or oral or written production, or any combination of listening/speaking, reading/ speaking, listening/writing, or reading/writing. Particularly with more advanced students, tasks would involve balanced comprehension and production skills.

6. **Specify the topic.** Like the topics you introduce in your lessons, the topic for a testing task should be within the students' world knowledge and be seen by them as relevant and interesting. Topics related to their immediate environment (school, community, etc.) are appropriate for all levels; topics involving current events or other subject areas are appropriate depending on the maturity of your students. Do not overlook topics related to francophone culture.

7. **Decide on the communicative context.** When you have chosen a topic, consider the numerous ways in which communication takes place and choose one appropriate to the topic: for example,
   - an article, letter to the editor, want ad, or product ad in a newspaper or magazine
   - an announcement on a billboard or bulletin board
   - a telephone message
   - a telephone consumer survey
   - an announcement, report, commentary, critique, commercial, etc. on radio or TV
   - a letter (invitation, request for information, solicitation, postcard, etc.)
   - a dialogue (student/student, student/family member, student/storekeeper, student/reporter, etc.)
   - an announcement on a PA system
   - non-verbal "information" such as a series of pictures or a sequence of sounds.

8. **Specify what the students must do to complete the task.** In the chosen communicative context, decide what type of activity the student is required to do. For example, the task may consist of one or more of the following:
   - choosing the correct answer from alternatives
   - completing a dialogue
   - initiating and sustaining a dialogue
   - writing a letter, ad, paragraph to convey specific information
   - writing an open-ended response to a question or instruction
   - reading to find specific information
   - guessing and hypothesizing from clues (auditory, written, or non-verbal)
   - responding orally to a question or instruction.

In communicative tests, the instructions must be prepared with great care to ensure that the context and the communicative purpose are clearly presented. And if the test is to produce meaningful results, the students must understand clearly, before they begin, what the task is and what they are expected to do.

Another major consideration is that the instructions must be worded in such a way that they do not contain virtually all the French the students need to perform the task. Otherwise the test fails to be a true measure of their ability. As you will see in the examples worked through later in this chapter, the wording of the instructions can be a step requiring repeated revision. If the problem cannot be resolved in any other way, the answer may be to use English in the instructions, much as we prefer to avoid it.

9. **Decide on the format for the test**. If the test involves listening comprehension, will the students be listening to you in person or to yourself or someone else on tape or video? Will oral responses be direct or taped? Will instructions be on the board or overhead or on a handout? This step involves working out in practical terms what you and the students will be working with.

10. **Decide on a scoring technique.** Your decision whether to use an objective or a subjective method of scoring will influence the design of the test item. Items that have only one correct answer can be scored objectively (e.g., *Oui / Non, Vrai / Faux*, multiple choice, "exact word"), requiring no judgment or opinion on the part of the scorer. Items that allow a range of possible answers must be scored in a more subjective way; however, specifying the criteria and the levels of achievement for each criterion helps you to arrive at a reasonably good rating of performance.

11. **Note any practical considerations in administering the test.** Depending on the nature of the test, the physical characteristics of your classroom, the equipment you have access to, the maturity of your students, and the availability of resource people, you can make various decisions about how to administer the test.
    - Specify whether the test is given to individuals, partners, small groups, or the whole class at once.
    - Consider whether administering the test to one or a few students can be done in the classroom or whether a quiet space must be arranged elsewhere. If the latter, you will have to arrange for help to supervise either the class or the test-takers.
    - List materials and equipment needed, such as handouts, tape recorder and microphone, VCR, overhead projector, visuals.

Summarizing Your Decisions

When you eventually put the completed test in your files, you could enclose with it a "cover sheet" like that shown on page 252 to record its essential features.

(Ullman, 1990, pp. 51–54.)

Sample Cover Sheet: The Test at a Glance

Student Name: _____

Grade: _____   Date of test: _____

Stage in year's work: _____

Objective:

    Summative _____   Formative _____

    Is the test suitable for either objective? _____

Communicative function:

    Mode of language use: _____

    Tone: _____

Linguistic focus: _____

Skill focus(es): _____

Topic: _____

Context: _____

Type of task: _____

Format: _____

Scoring method: _____

_____

Materials/equipment/special arrangements: _____

_____

Comments: _____

_____

_____

(Ullman, 1990, p. 55.) (D.C. Heath Canada Ltd., 1990.)

Brock High School
English Law Co-operative Examination

Heterogeneous groups of four will be determined by lot at the start of the examination. The only stipulation on groups will be that both sexes are represented in each group. The method of determining groups will be through selection from one of four boxes. Each box will have a label: writer, artist, speaker, physical manager. A student will select a number from the box that most closely represents the part of the team that most suits his/her strengths. Each team will be represented from all of the areas.

The year is 1599 A.D. The Lord Chamberlain's Company has just arrived in your town to perform its new play *A Midsummer Night's Dream*. Your advertising agency has been asked to prepare an advertising campaign to sell the play to the public. Mr. Shakespeare has purchased one column, (250 words), in the local newspaper, and space for one poster on the community bulletin board. You are to spend the next 60 minutes preparing a poster that combines a picture that, in Shakespeare's words, "Says it all," with a caption that ,"Catches the imagination while accurately representing the play," and a press release of exactly 250 words that has a catchy heading, outlines what is most important in the play, encourages people to come, and tells the public when, where, and how much the show will be.

At the end of the 60 minutes, you will be required to present your advertising campaign to Mr. Shakespeare. Be prepared at that time to answer any questions that he may ask about the strategy you have chosen.

Marks will be assessed as follows:

Process

> Each student will be checked at intervals during the examination a total of 5 times. The group skills being assessed are positive interaction, participation, and task commitment. If the student, when observed, is acting appropriately, (s)he will receive 2 marks. If the student is not clearly displaying appropriate actions,(s)he will receive 1 mark. If the student is displaying contrary actions, (s)he will receive 0 marks. The maximum process mark is 10.

Product

> Each group will present a poster, a newspaper article, and an oral presentation to William Shakespeare. Those people involved in the presentation must be prepared to answer any questions that Mr. Shakespeare might ask. Each of these is worth 10 marks, but each student receives marks in his/her own area.

Integration

> A mark will be assessed for the success of the group at tying all of the different parts together. The article, the poster, and the presentation should all belong together. This provides a product mark for the group cooperative skills. This mark is 10.

> The student who chose a number from the writer box will have the responsibility of writing the newspaper article.

> The student who chose a number from the artist box will have the responsibility of preparing the poster.

The student who chose a number from the speaker box will have the responsibility of preparing and delivering the oral presentation. This student should also chair the opening group meeting that will determine the overall concept for the advertising programme. (i.e., colour, style, format, materials...)

The student who chose a number from the physical manager box will have the responsibility of making or securing everything that the other members need, keeping track of the time, and assisting with the oral presentation.

At the end of the presentations the teacher will review the process part of the examination to highlight the activities for which marks were given.

Time frame

Group process, written article, poster, preparation for presentation	*60 minutes*
Presentations and questions	*15 minutes per group*
Process review	*20 minutes or remainder of period*

Each student may earn up to 30 marks for the examination, 20 of which will be an individual mark, and 10 of which will be a shared group mark.

Group Skills Check List

Every student will be evaluated 5 times during the examination. The students will be evaluated on the following skills: positive interaction, task commitment, and equal participation. Each time a student is observed he/she will earn 2 marks if (s)he is displaying a positive behavior in one of the areas, 1 mark if (s)he is displaying a neutral behavior, and 0 marks if (s)he is displaying a negative behavior. The student may earn up to 10 marks or down to 0 marks on this portion of the examination. At the end of the examination the process will be reviewed in detail.

Skills\Names							
Positive Interaction support help mediate probe other							
Task Commitment on task role other							
Equal Participation verbal non verbal							

Assess for Success

Section B — Observation

Observation should be an integral part of an evaluation program for all students in all grades. It involves watching, listening and collecting information about what a student says and/or does. It is an excellent way to monitor student progress and make judgments about what has been learned. It can provide qualitative information about a broad range of student behaviours and consequently a more comprehensive understanding of a student's strengths and weaknesses. Observation is not only the evolution of a finished product or a skill. Its most important aspect is the evaluation of the student's performance during the creation of the product or the performance of the skill. The emphasis should be on both the degree to which the activity is successfully completed and the identification of physical, psychological and social factors which help or hinder the acquisition of skill or appreciation. Observation should provide the teacher with clues for individual assistance and encouragement. No single piece of information or evaluation technique is sufficient in itself as a basis for making decisions about students. Observational data takes into account evaluation of certain aspects of student performance or behaviour which cannot be measured using many other evaluation techniques. Incorporated into a developmental learner profile, it can help the teacher get to know the student as an individual person and make appropriate program decisions.

Observation complements paper-and-pencil tests by providing information in areas that are critical for assessing student learning, in particular non-cognitive outcomes.

> *Teachers of all subject areas use observation for a variety of reasons, including to assess:*
> - a student's ability to follow the correct procedure in using a welding torch;
> - a student's participation in a group;
> - a student's development in the use of oral language;
> - student perseverance and confidence in analyzing and solving problems;
> - a student's skill in dribbling a basketball;
> - a student's vocal and physical performance in Dramatic Arts;
> - a student's attitudes and awareness in the process of creation in Visual Arts;
> - the safety procedures during a laboratory experiment or physical activity in the gymnasium; and
> - a students' fluency in a foreign language as they talk in pairs.

(Waterloo, 1993, p. 22.)

When teachers know what they are looking for, observation can work and be of value. When evaluating students through observation, a record must be made, either while the observation is being conducted (preferable), or as soon as possible thereafter.

Observations can be best recorded using:

- *checklists:*   which record whether a specific action has been completed or a particular quality is present
- *rating scales:*   where a judgment is made on the degree or quality of an action or product
- *anecdotal records:* where a very brief comment is recorded to describe an observed action or characteristic

When constructing observational instruments, the following points should be remembered:

- They should be based on the outcomes for the course, unit or lesson.
- They should be comprised of a limited number of items so that the observation can be focused.
  - Each item should be clear and precise.
  - Each item should focus on specifics and avoid generalities.
- They should be designed so that they can be used as a basis for a discussion by the teacher with a student or parent. Therefore, they should be written in such a way that they can be readily understood by a student or parent.
- They should be developed in such a way that students can understand them; hence, they may be used for self- and peer-evaluation.
- They can be designed either for a single evaluation or a cumulative record.

Observational instruments can be used as the basis for diagnostic, formative and/or summative evaluation. One of the most important uses is as a basis for anecdotal comments.

In summary:

- Planned, systematic observation is an essential tool for comprehensive student assessment.
- Observation provides information on types of outcomes not measured by paper-and-pencil tests.
- Observation is helpful in programming for individual needs and in discussions with students, staff, and parents.

*(Peel, **Book 5**, 1990, p. 42.)*

Sample Checklist and Rating Scale

> The checklist helps the teacher keep track of **whether or not** a student showed each of the listed behaviours.

CHECKLIST OF ORAL PRESENTATION (BOOK REVIEW)

Student: _____ Date: _____

Check if student shows these behaviours:

- Positions self so others can easily see him/her _____
- Introduces the topic of the book _____
- Describes the plot and character _____
- Reads illustrative passage to show why s/he liked the book _____
- Talks about the illustrations and/or author _____
- Provides additional information relating to the book _____
- Answers questions from the group _____

> The rating scale assumes that all students will show the listed behaviours but in **varying amounts or at different rates**.

RATING SCALE OF ORAL PRESENTATION (BOOK REVIEW)

Student: _____ Date: _____

Rate the student on each of these behaviours by choosing a number from the scale:

Excellent   Satisfactory   Unacceptable

  1   2   3   4   5

- Positions self so others can easily see him/her _____
- Introduces the topic of the book _____
- Describes the plot and character _____
- Reads illustrative passage to show why s/he liked the book _____
- Talks about the illustrations and/or author _____
- Provides additional information relating to the book _____
- Answers questions from the group _____

> - Behaviours to be observed are defined precisely and stated in objective terms.
> - Behaviours are organized in some logical sequence.

(Peel, Book 5, 1990, p. 32.)

Threats to Objectivity

Below are some examples of how the "halo effect" (drawing premature conclusions) and the teacher's own past experience, can be "threats" to objectivity.

- A student is known to be quite intelligent and functions at a high level in academic work. A teacher observing this student in social situations may find it difficult to conclude that s/he is immature in social interactions with peers.

- A student is rude, inattentive, and restless in class. When the teacher hears any disruptive talking, it is always attributed to this student. The teacher may tend to mark this student's work more severely than the work of other students, regardless of its actual quality.

- A student has performed exceptionally well on the first test of the term. A teacher tends to expect that subsequent work will live up to this early promise and tends to mark this student's work more leniently.

- Because a student comes from a family of highly educated, professional parents, a teacher may expect this student to be very motivated and academically successful. The teacher may tend to give this student higher marks, regardless of the student's actual measured aptitude and/or achievement.

- A teacher may have a student who has some learning problems and/or social-emotional difficulties. When the teacher learns that this child comes from a single-parent family, s/he may assume that all the child's school difficulties stem from that fact.

- A student new to Canada speaks English as a second language. This student may be perceived by the teacher as "slow", low-achieving, and unmotivated. The teacher's low expectations and attitude may well form the basis for a self-fulfilling prophecy.

*(Peel, **Book 5**, 1990, p. 49.)*

1. Anecdotal Records

Description

Anecdotal records are brief written notes about what teachers see and hear.

Evaluation Context

The difficulty with anecdotal records is not so much what **can be** assessed as what **should** be assessed with this method since all aspects of a student's behaviour cannot be observed and reported on. Observations should be confined to areas that cannot be assessed by other means.

Using Technique to Best Advantage

These records are especially effective in the Transition Years/Specialization Years when monitoring the progress of a few students in the classroom who are having difficulties academically, socially, or behaviourally.

Guidelines for Use

Teachers should record only what they SEE or HEAR, not their reaction to it, or what they think the student felt or thought. Include verbatim material whenever possible.

Be as objective as possible. Avoid judgmental words like "good", "bad", or "lazy".

Date all entries. Collection instruments include clipboard notes, file folder notes, and large calendars that allow a few comments to be written each day.

Effective Use of Anecdotal Records

- Determine in advance what to observe, but be alert for unusual behaviour.
- Observe and record enough of the situation to make the behaviour meaningful.
- Make a record of the incident as soon after the observation as possible.
- Limit each anecdote to a brief description of a single incident.
- Keep the factual description of the incident and your interpretation of it separate.
- Record both positive and negative behavioural incidents.
- Collect a number of anecdotes on a student before drawing inferences concerning typical behaviour.

(Adapted from Gronlund and Linn, 1990, pp. 381–382.)

Advantages

- gives specific examples of actual spontaneous behaviour in the school setting. It indicates how a student typically behaves in everyday school situations
- if accumulated consistently, anecdotal recordings provide a cumulative picture of the student, showing growth or lack of progress toward important goals
- can provide information on types of outcomes not measured by paper-and-pencil tests
- can often be done on-the-spot in the classroom, bringing detail and relevance to the observational activity

Disadvantages

- monitoring objectively may be a problem
- can be imprecise if specific behaviours or outcomes for observation are not defined
- there is a tendency to emphasize negative incidents/behaviours
- interpretation can be time-consuming

Examples

ANECDOTAL RECORDS IN AN ART CLASS

Student Name: _____

Date or Time Period of Assessment: _____

Activity: _____

1. Attitude   Comments:

Keys:	toward own work
	toward other people
	toward work of others
	materials/techniques
	time frame for completion
	acceptance of criticism

2. Awareness of Visual Art Concepts   Comments:

Keys:	elements/principles of design
	the designed environment
	the natural environment
	own role in an environment

3. Process   Comments:

Keys:	learning experience
	initiative
	self-assessment
	application of learning
	striving for improvement
	imposes a structure for working on self
	develops project into expression of self
	originality/creativity in evidence
	uses elements/principles of design effectively
	brings closure to projects

4. Product   Comments:

Keys:	results in art form of best personal effort
	new learning evident in product
	able to criticize own work constructively
	able to use established work as step to next project/level

(Saskatchewan Education, 1991, p. 70.)

ANECDOTAL RECORDS FOR GROUP PROCESS ACTIVITIES

Students' Names: _____

_____

_____

_____

_____

Date or Time Period of Assessment: _____

Observation Period: _____

Comments Regarding Group Members:

1. Demonstrating balance between talking and listening:

2. Demonstrating respect for others:

3. Demonstrating active participation:

4. Stating own opinion:

    Student(s) who fulfilled the
    role of recorder for group
    information:

    Effectiveness:

    Student(s) who fulfilled the
    role of reporter for the group:

    Effectiveness:

    Student(s) who fulfilled the
    role of participant:

    Effectiveness:

    Student(s) who fulfilled the
    role of time-keeper:

    Effectiveness:

(Saskatchewan Education, 1991, p. 71.)

2. Checklists

Description

A checklist is a list of specific concepts, skills, processes, or attitudes, that are essentially scored as "yes-no" ratings. A check indicates that the characteristic or behaviour was present or absent. Checklists often contain more dimensions than rating scales, but those dimensions are often quite narrow and concrete.

Evaluation Context

The checklist is most appropriately used in situations where teachers want to assess their students' abilities, attitudes, or performance in process areas. This is an important purpose for teachers concerned with the how as well as the what of learning. For example, checklists can be used to assess communication skills, co-operative learning skills, extent of participation, interest in topic, and psychomotor skills.

Using Technique to Best Advantage

If used on a single occasion, the checklist can provide formative evaluation information for the situation in which it is used. For example, to learn how effectively students work in groups, a checklist to observe them in a single session will provide information to guide further instruction. Checklists are most useful when collected over time and used summatively or diagnostically. For best results, use them systematically, not sporadically.

The checklist is normally used during class time. The most efficient way to collect data is to record learning progress on four or five students at the same time. Record the date and the class on every observation checklist you use. Annotate the checklist sheet with any appropriate thoughts.

Example

PROCESS CHECKLIST		
Procedure	**Check if Observed**	**Comments**
Selected approach		
Correct equipment used		
Measurement accurate		
Sought peer help if needed		
Recorded observations		
Cleaned up after experiment		

(Herman, 1992, p. 65.)

Assess for Success

Using the Information for Student Evaluation

For criterion-referenced judgments, refer to the criterion levels established initially.

For self-referenced judgments, all the checklists on one particular student can be studied, providing a measure of progress over a unit or course. This is one of the most powerful uses of the checklist.

Hints

- Where possible, start with an existing checklist and modify it according to needs.
- Choose characteristics that relate directly to the intended outcomes of the unit.
- Choose characteristics that can be observed or reasonably inferred.
- Keep the list of characteristics manageable.
- Keep the description of the characteristics simple and jargon-free. Characteristics should be usable at parent-teacher or student-teacher interviews.

Variants

- Develop checklists that detail a particular series of components. This is particularly useful in minimum competency situations where something has to be done correctly.

Uses

- to record data about personal and social development
- to evaluate skills and procedures
- to encourage student self-evaluation

Advantages

- is focused on the same aspects of performance in all students and has a common scale to record
- is an excellent teaching tool since it can describe to students the type of behaviour required
- is easier to use and interpret than anecdotal
- is useful for peer- and self-evaluation

Disadvantages

- time consuming to construct
- can be influenced by "halo effect"

Sample Checklists

SCIENCE OBSERVATION CHECKLIST

Class:_____

Date: _____

		Names			
	Evaluation Criteria				
Observation	stated an observation				
	accurate (relevant?)				
Discussion Techniques	spoke clearly				
	listened to others				
	waited for turn				
	relevant				
	not repetitious				
	challenged a remark				
	gave reasons for challenging				
'Scientific' Thinking	noticed a discrepant event				
	"I think", "I'm not sure"				
	offered a hypothesis				
	changed opinion on basis of data				
	suggested a model				
	suggested further experiments				
	stated a relationship between facts				
Manipulation of Materials	constructive				
	innovative				
	carried out an experiment				
	devised own experiment				
	made a discovery				
	observed safety rules				

(Saskatchewan Education, 1991, p. 74.)

Assess for Success

CHECKLIST TO ASSESS PROBLEM-SOLVING SKILLS IN MATHEMATICS

Student Name: _____

Date or Time Period of Assessment: _____

Check (√) applicable criteria.

Student is able to decode the words in story problems/
performance tasks/activities.   _____

Student is able to understand the situation or
circumstances described in the story problems/
performance tasks/activities.   _____

Student is able to choose the correct mathematical
operation (addition, subtraction, multiplication,
division).   _____

Student is able to distinguish between relevant and
irrelevant information that is presented in the story
problems/tasks/activities.   _____

The student is able to correctly write down the
necessary computations.   _____

The student demonstrates a facility with number facts.   _____

The student is able to correctly choose the correct
computational algorithm for use in the problem/task/
activity.   _____

> This instrument may be adapted for use as a rating scale.

(Saskatchewan Education, 1991, p. 77.)

CHECKLIST TO ASSESS STUDENT'S
ABILITY TO USE INFORMATION

Student Name: _____

Date or Time Period of Assessment: _____

Check (√) applicable criteria.

1. Student is able to state the purpose for the collection of the information.

2. Student is able to gather information from own recall of past learning.

3. Student is able to identify main elements needed in information.

4. Student is able to organize information into usable units.

5. Student is able to identify related details.

6. Student is able to recognize relationship of information gathered to information remembered.

7. Student is able to clearly state ideas that fit with the topic being addressed.

8. Student is able to give evidence of checking information for accuracy.

This instrument may be adapted for use as a rating scale.

(Saskatchewan Education, 1991, p. 79.)

Assess for Success

CHECKLIST FOR MARKING AN ESSAY

Student Name: _____

Date or Time Period of Assessment: _____

Evaluation Criteria	In Evidence	Not in Evidence
A. General Elements • theme or point of view is evident • theme or point of view is developed in a systematic way • the arguments have a logical consistency • examples or illustrations of the theme or point of view are evident • composition reflects proper essay form • the information included in the essay is compatible with the form in which it is written		

B. Criteria for Confirming a Mark or Grade

Check (√) Applicable Criteria

1. Above Average Answer

   • Clearly stated an overall conclusion based on a synopsis of facts _____

   • Includes information suitable for the main idea or theme _____

   • Presents data to reinforce the particular point of view or idea that is being proved _____

   • If applicable, presents alternate aspects of an issue to demonstrate the superiority of a certain interpretation _____

   • Contains convincing evidence of development of form and clarity of organization and display _____

2. Average Answer

   • Includes sufficient detail to explain the question/topic sufficiently _____

   • Illustrates a perception of the facts implicated in the issues; however, constructs only sufficient connection between the facts and the main idea or point of view _____

   • Undertakes with fair success to validate a point of view and associate proof to that point of view _____

3. Below Average Answer

   • Includes inadequate data to answer the question sufficiently _____

   • Does not adequately support a point of view _____

   • Gives a listing of data rather than structuring them and giving a point of view supported by the data _____

> This instrument may be adapted for use as a rating scale.

(Saskatchewan Education, 1991, p. 78.)

ENGLISH OAC 1: GROUP ESSAY CHECKLIST

A. Introductory Paragraph:				
1. A clearly-stated thesis in the form of a statement. Write it here:			YES	NO
2. Satisfactory lead-in (general to specific) to the thesis.			YES	NO
B. Main Body:				
3. Each paragraph contains an effective topic sentence which directly supports the thesis.		Para 1 Para 2 Para 3	YES YES YES	NO NO NO
4. Each paragraph contains enough specific evidence from both stories to support its case.		Para 1 Para 2 Para 3	YES YES YES	NO NO NO
C. Coherence:				
5. The paragraphs successfully linked together with connecting devices.		Intro/Para 1 Para 1/2 Para 2/3 Para 3/Conc	YES YES YES YES	NO NO NO NO
6a. The paragraphs are all in the same format and compatible with each other.			YES	NO
6b. The paragraphs are in the best possible order.			YES	NO
D. Concluding Paragraph:				
7. The conclusion is satisfactory.			YES	NO
E. Proofreading:				

8. There are no errors in:
  – sentence structure
  – punctuation
  – spelling
			
			YES
			YES
			YES
				
				NO
				NO
				NO

Essay Number: _____ Edited By: _____				

(Frontenac Secondary School, English Department.)

OAC 1: English Argumentative Essay
Rapid-Impression Evaluation Checklist

( ) **EXCEPTIONAL** (Meets and exceeds all thinking and writing objectives) *90–100%*

The quality of the argument and the quality of expression are outstanding. They are integrated and reinforce each other. The essay presents itself as an impressive unity of all six sub-criteria. The thesis shows complexity of thought, the organization is seamless, and the quality of evidence is convincing. The language, syntax, and use of rhetorical devices all reinforce the meaning, and the overall style adds an element of artistry to the effect. (This is no small achievement when a student is working within the time constraints of an examination.)

( ) **SUPERIOR** (Meets the thinking and writing objectives to a high degree) *80–89%*

The quality of the argument and the quality of expression are impressive. Generally, they are integrated and reinforce each other. The essay presents itself as a unity, but there is a sense of lack of strength in one or two of the sub-criteria areas; for example, the thesis might lack sufficient complexity, the supporting evidence might be weak, or mechanical faults might distract the reader at times.

( ) **COMPETENT** (Meets the thinking and writing objectives to a substantial degree) *70–79%*

The quality of the argument and the quality of expression show some complexity but lack the sophistication and integration that mark a superior or outstanding response. The student can take a position, organize his or her thinking, select evidence to support the thesis, and write in such a way that the overall impression is one of control. There are no major weaknesses in any of the sub-criteria that detract seriously from the overall effect.

( ) **ADEQUATE** (Meets the thinking and writing objectives to an adequate degree) *60–69%*

The quality of the argument and the quality of expression are adequate, but the student has not excelled with most of the sub-criteria. The student can sustain and support a straightforward position without obviously contradictory elements and can express it in terms that do not interfere with or detract from the reader's understanding. The structure is likely to adhere closely to a formula (e.g., the five-paragraph essay). Some areas may show weaknesses, but the weaknesses should not interfere with the reader's general understanding.

( ) **MARGINALLY ADEQUATE** (Meets some of the thinking and writing objectives to some degree) *50–59%*

The quality of the argument and/or quality of expression demonstrate serious deficiency in one or more of the sub-criteria areas. Although the reader is able to grasp the writer's basic argument, that argument may be simplistic, poorly organized, and/or poorly supported, or may contain contradictory elements. As well, the response could be seriously weakened by lack of clarity in expression. In fact, if the overall expression is inadequate, this is sufficient to reduce the essay to the unacceptable level. Serious weakness in any one of these areas might be so apparent as to create an overall impression of weakness, and thus reduce the response to the unacceptable level.

( ) **INADEQUATE** (Meets few, if any, of the thinking and writing objectives) *0–49%*

The quality of the argument and/or the quality of expression fail to meet, even minimally, the objectives of the essay component of the OAC 1 English examination. The student is unable either to formulate or to sustain a position and/or cannot write without causing serious reader confusion. Essays that are completely off topic or that deliberately distort the topic also fall into this category.

*(Carleton, **Marking the Examination**, 1992, p. 28.)*

OBSERVATION RECORD
Discussion Checklist

Directions

Answer each of the following questions while observing a small group discussion.

Group Observed: _____   Date: _____

Observed by: _____

	Yes	No
Overall, is the group functioning well?	❏	❏
Are the members listening to each other?	❏	❏
Do the members seem to be comfortable with each other?	❏	❏
Are the members engaged by the task?	❏	❏
Is the group purposeful and directive?	❏	❏
Does the group appear to be sensitive to the needs of its members?	❏	❏
Is the group accomplishing what it has set out to do?	❏	❏
Can the members hear each other easily?	❏	❏
Do you think the group will complete the task in the time allowed?	❏	❏
Is the atmosphere of this group friendly?	❏	❏

Comments and suggestions:

*(**Senior English: OAIP**, "Involving Students in Assessment", 1991, p. 37.)*

Assess for Success

CHECKLIST FOR ORAL DELIVERY

A simple checklist such as the following might be devised to assess the effectiveness of oral delivery.

Students' Names	Voice clear	Good diction	Approp. volume	Speaks with expression	Well paced	Maintains eye contact	Good posture approp. gestures
Sara							
Brent							
Laura							
Allison							
Juan							
etc.							

(Peel, Book 5, 1990, p. 67.)

SPREADSHEET OBSERVATIONAL CHECKLIST
Self-/Peer-Evaluation – Formative

Student Name: _____   Date: _____

Observer/Evaluator: _____

	YES	NO
Operating Tasks		
• Boot spreadsheet program	____	____
• Save file	____	____
• Get file	____	____
• Print file	____	____
Create/Edit Commands		
• Cursor/cell — row and column movement	____	____
• Delete/insert characters	____	____
• Delete/insert columns/rows	____	____
• Create title/headings	____	____
Formatting Commands		
• Set column width	____	____
• Set value format ($. ,)	____	____
• Create windows — horizontal/vertical	____	____
Formula Entry		
• Calculation — 2 cells (+ - * / %)	____	____
• Sum — column/row	____	____
• Copy formula	____	____

*(Metropolitan Toronto, **Accounting**, 1989, p. 75.)*

WORD PROCESSING OBSERVATIONAL CHECKLIST

Peer Evaluation – Formative

Student Name: _____   Date: _____

Observer/Evaluator:

Note to Students: Observe your partner doing the following tasks listed below and indicate with a check mark under YES if completed successfully or a check mark under NO if not completed successfully.

	YES	NO
1. Loaded word processing package without any assistance.		
2. Printed, to the screen, a list of previously stored documents.		
3. Typed a line in solid capital letters.		
4. Deleted a letter, a word, and an entire line.		
5. Inserted a letter, a word, and an entire line.		
6. Adjusted a line — left-justified, right-justified, and centred.		
7. Used spell check.		
8. Set margins — left, right, top, and bottom.		
9. Used emphasizing features — bolding and underscoring.		
10. Move, deleted, and copied a paragraph.		
11. Set and deleted a tab.		
12. Saved a document.		
13. Performed a "quicksave."		
14. Printed a document using single and double spacing.		
15. Removed a document from the disk.		

*(Metropolitan Toronto, **Accounting**, 1989. p. 70.)*

Description

Rating scales are measuring instruments that allow representation of the extent to which specific concepts, skills, processes, or attitudes exist in students and their work. They are used to judge the degree to which the behaviour is present (how much, how well, how often). Rating scales tend to be more subjective than checklists.

Evaluation Context

Rating scales enable the teacher to record student performance on a wide range of skills and attitudes.

Using Technique to Best Advantage

Rating scales are particularly useful in situations where the student performance can be described along a continuum.

Guidelines for Use

Rating scales are normally used during class time. Therefore it must be simple to use.

Decide upon the activity to be rated. Break it up into its constituent parts. Make the parts as specific as possible so as to increase the scale's reliability.

Rating Scale for Observations in Visual Arts

	LOW				HIGH
Incorporates new skills that have been taught	1	2	3	4	5
Respects own work and can discuss it critically and honestly	1	2	3	4	5
Quality is equal to his or he...					

Rating Scale for Group Work	always	often	seldom	never
Stays on Tasks	√			
Encourages Team (no Put Downs)			√	
Listens to Others		√		

*(Waterloo, **Assessment for Learning**, 1992, p. 26.)*

Hints – Principles of Effective Rating

1. Characteristics should be educationally significant.
2. Characteristics should be directly observable.
3. Characteristics and points on the scale should be clearly defined.
4. Between three and seven rating positions should be provided, and raters should be permitted to mark at intermediate points.
5. Raters should be instructed to omit ratings when they feel unqualified to judge.
6. Ratings from several observers should be combined whenever possible.

(Gronlund and Linn, 1990, pp. 391–392.)

Variants

Rating scales have many variants.

Self-evaluation: Rating scales are very useful in allowing students to perform self-evaluation on their own work. The student's ratings can form a useful starting-point for focused teacher-student dialogue.

Holistic Rating Scale: This is a technique that attempts to combine the benefits of global scoring and analytic scoring. It is applicable to written assignments and extended problem-solving exercises.

Advantages

- is focused on the same aspects of performance in all students and has a common scale to record
- is an excellent teaching tool since it can describe to students the type of behaviour required
- is easier to use and interpret than anecdotal
- is useful for peer- and self-evaluations

Disadvantages

- can be time consuming to construct
- is difficult to be consistent in ratings
- can be influenced by "halo effect"

Samples: Rating Scales

RATING SCALE FOR TECHNICAL SKILLS
(Example: Science Laboratory Work)

Student Name: _____

Date or Time Period of Assessment: _____

	unacceptable			excellent
1. Clearly shows an understanding of the problem to be investigated.	1	2	3	4
2. Is able to follow written or oral directions with care.	1	2	3	4
3. Chooses and uses appropriate materials and equipment for the task.	1	2	3	4
4. Is able to use the chosen equipment with efficiency and accuracy.	1	2	3	4
5. Uses the equipment with proper safety procedures.	1	2	3	4
6. Records data in a systematic fashion.	1	2	3	4
7. States conclusions based on data collected.	1	2	3	4
8. Refers to limitations and/or generalizability of the results of the investigation.	1	2	3	4
9. Cleans up work station according to accepted procedure.	1	2	3	4

This instrument may be adapted for use as a checklist.

(Saskatchewan Education, 1991, p. 86.)

RATING SCALE

Activity: *Performance in Debates*

Course: *English*

Date: _____

Activity Component Scale Points		Student Name			
States argument clearly	5 Very logical 4 Logical 3 Average 2 Not very logical 1 Virtually illogical				
Demonstrates background preparation	5 Very well prepared 4 Well prepared 3 Average 2 Not all that well prepared 1 Ill prepared				
Responds to opposition arguments relevantly	5 Very relevant arguments 4 Relevant arguments 3 Average 2 Only some relevance 1 Virtually irrelevant				
Speaks clearly and without hesitations	5 Very clear, no hesitations 4 Clear, few hesitations 3 Average 2 Not always clear 1 Not clear, many hesitations				

(Saskatchewan Education, 1991, p. 84.)

ESSAY ANSWER GUIDE

	ABSENT OR UNACCEPTABLE	POOR	DEVELOPING OR PARTIALLY FORMED	ACCEPTABLE	GOOD TO EXCELLENT	OUTSTANDING
	0	1 2	3 4	5 6	7 8	9 10

1. Focus
   Introduction
   Thesis
   Conclusion
   Clarity of ideas
   Appropriate emphasis						

2. Support of Thesis
   Depth of treatment
   Relevant evidence
   Logical reasoning						

3. Organization
   Plan
   Structure
   Logical order
   Smooth transitions
   Unity of ideas						

4. Style
   Appropriate voice & tone
   Diction
   Sentence structure & variety
   Freshness						

5. Mechanics
   Grammar
   Spelling
   Punctuation
   Correct reference notes
     (if applicable)						

Essay mark out of 50: _____

[ ] Inappropriate response to the topic. It is impossible to apply the above criteria to this piece of writing. See additional comments below.

Additional Comments:

*(Adapted from Carleton, **Exemplar Booklet for OAC 1 English**, 1987, p. 9.)*

BULLETIN BOARD EVALUATION SHEET

Evaluator: _____

	Strongly Agree	Agree	Disagree	Strongly Disagree
Contents: There is plenty to look at The theme of the display is clear It is all on topic It gives us things to think about				
Appearance: It is colourful and attractive It contains variety & is interesting It all looks like one display It's visible from most of classroom				
Presentation: They explained it clearly				
Comments:				

(Frontenac Secondary School, English Department.)

Assess for Success

HOLISTIC RATING SCALE FOR AN ORAL PRESENTATION

Student Name: _____

Date or Time Period of Assessment: _____

Scale: 3 = Words are clear.
Voice has good modulation.
Speed of speech is well-paced.
Pauses or emphases are appropriate.
Voice is loud enough to be heard easily.
Presentation is organized, logical, and interesting.
Large amount of student preparation is evident.
Material in presentation is relevant to topic.
Language used in presentation is appropriate.
Evidence of creativity exists in presentation of topic.
Audience appears 'involved' in the presentation.

2 = Some words are not clear.
Voice has some modulation.
Rate of speech is at times too quick for the listener to catch the full meaning.
Sentences have some inappropriate pauses or run on together, hampering meaning.
Voice dropping in volume at times makes it difficult to get the full import of the presentation.
Presentation shows signs of organization; however, there may be portions that do not tie together.
Presentation has 'down' portions with regard to keeping the audience interested.
There is evidence of a fair amount of student preparation.
Material in presentation is, for the most part, appropriate.
Format of presentation is predictable.
Audience is passive listener.

1 = Many words are not clearly spoken.
Voice is more monotone in presentation.
Rate of speech is either too fast or too slow.
Pauses or emphases for effect are not in evidence.
Voice is low, making hearing of the presentation difficult.
Presentation shows poor organization.
The audience reacts in a disinterested manner.
There is minimal student preparation in evidence.
Material in presentation is inappropriate or does not appear relevant to the topic.
Format of presentation lacks structure.
Audience is not engaged.

Scoring for the presentation is done on the basis of the category that is **most representative**.

(Saskatchewan Education, 1991, p. 92.)

Sample Rubric:
CAP Generalized Rubric for Problem Solving
(California State Department of Education)

RUBRIC FOR PROBLEM SOLVING

Demonstrated Competence

Exemplary Response ... Rating = 6

Gives a complete response with a clear, coherent, unambiguous, and elegant explanation; includes a clear and simplified diagram; communicates effectively to the identified audience; shows understanding of the open-ended problem's ideas and processes; identifies all the important elements of the problem; may include examples and counterexamples; presents strong supporting arguments.

Competent Response ... Rating = 5

Gives a fairly complete response with reasonably clear explanations; may include an appropriate diagram; communicates effectively to the identified audience; shows understanding of the problem's ideas and processes; identifies the most important elements of the problems; presents solid supporting arguments.

Satisfactory Response

Minor Flaws But Satisfactory ... Rating = 4

Completes the problem satisfactorily, but the explanation may be muddled; argumentation may be incomplete; diagram may be inappropriate or unclear; understands the underlying ideas; uses mathematical ideas effectively.

Serious Flaws But Nearly Satisfactory ... Rating = 3

Begins the problem appropriately but may fail to complete or may omit significant parts of the problem; may fail to show full understanding of ideas and processes; may make major errors; may misuse or fail to use terms; response may reflect an inappropriate strategy for solving the problem.

Inadequate Response

Begins, But Fails to Complete Problem ... Rating = 2

Explanation is not understandable; diagram may be unclear; shows no understanding of the problem situation; may make major errors.

Unable to Begin Effectively ... Rating = 1

Words do not reflect the problem; drawings misrepresent the problem situation; copies parts of the problem but without attempting a solution; fails to indicate which information is appropriate to problem.

No Attempt ... Rating = 0

---

*(Waterloo, **Assessment for Learning**, 1993, Appendix A, p. 6.)*

RUNNING TECHNIQUE: RATING SCALE

Runner's Name: _____

A. For the Observer: Circle the number which best describes your partner's running technique.

	rarely			*always*	*Comments*

1. **Head:** is the head steady, looking forward, erect, not falling from side to side? Are facial muscles relaxed?   1 2 3 4 5

2. **Shoulders:** Are shoulders loose and relaxed, not hunched up?   1 2 3 4 5

3. **Arms:** Are arms held at approximately waist level, moving smoothly backwards and forwards, not too high or too low, not crossing over in front of the body?   1 2 3 4 5

4. **Hands:** Are hands loose and relaxed, not clenched tight in a fist?   1 2 3 4 5

5. **Upper Body:** Is the body erect, relaxed, facing forward, not twisting or swaying from side to side, not leaning forward?   1 2 3 4 5

6. **Knees:** Is each knee lifted sufficiently for the foot to swing straight forward?   1 2 3 4 5

7. **Feet:** Is this person light on her/his feet, landing flat-footed, not on toes?   1 2 3 4 5

8. **Stride Length:** Are the steps relatively short, with knees and feet kept under the body?   1 2 3 4 5

9. **Breathing:** Does the breathing look natural, using both the nose and the mouth?   1 2 3 4 5

B. For the Runner:

Review the above rating scale describing your running technique. Note which items are at the extreme ends of the scale — those that are just fine as is and those that need some work.

Ask your partner to demonstrate/explain the areas where you seem to need improvement. Discuss these items together and then practice your improved technique together.

Record the changes you would like to make here:

1.

2.

3.

Switch places with your partner so that you now observe while your partner runs.

C. Discussion:

When both you and your partner have taken turns running and observing, take a few minutes to talk about what you have just done:

1. What idiosyncrasies did you notice in other runners as you were observing your partner?

2. Did you notice any general corrections/hints that might be applicable to most of the people in this group?

*(Scarborough, **Fitness: A Healthy Lifestyle**, 1992, p. 139.)*

STUDIO ART EXPERIENCE AND ART WORK

This form may be used to evaluate any type of studio work.

This rating scale can be used by students and teachers. Students may evaluate their own work as well as that of their peers.

Insert the appropriate ratings in the blank spaces provided.

Learning Objectives	Rating Scale
	Poor Excellent 1 2 3 4 5 6 7 8 9 10
1. Communication/Expression (ideas and feelings obviously portrayed)	_____
2. Confidence/Self-Esteem (a strong visual statement, conviction)	_____
3. Perceptual Development (sensitivity to visual and non visual qualities)	_____
4. Aesthetic Organization (balanced, rhythmical, flowing along, consistent)	_____
5. Knowledge of the Field of Art (style, design, abstraction)	_____
6. Creativity (unique, personal, and uncommon)	_____
7. Skill/Craftsmanship (control of tools and processes)	_____
8. Enjoyment/Satisfaction (obvious involvement with ideas and media)	_____

*(Scarborough, **Visual Arts**, 1987, p. 115.)*

References

Arter, J. and Spandel, V., "Using Portfolios of Student Work in Instruction and Assessment, Educational Measurement, Vol. unknown.

Bennett B., Rolheiser-Bennett, C., Stevahn, L., Co-operative Learning: Where Heart Meets Mind, 1991, Educational Connections, Toronto.

Beyer, Ann, Mathematical Communication — The Writing Connection, workshop materials.

Brandt, Ronald S. (ed.) Performance Assessment, Readings for Educational Leadership, 1992, ASCD, Alexandria, VA.

Burke, Kay, (ed.), Authentic Assessment, A Collection, 1992, IRI/Skylight, Palatine, IL.

Burke, Kay, Authentic Classroom Assessments: Ways to Promote Lifelong Learning, Critical Issues Conference, Battle Creek, Michigan, April 23–25, 1993, IRI/PDK.

Carleton Board of Education, Marking the Examination, 1992.

Cavanaugh and Styles, "Small Group Work and Peer Evaluation Across the Curriculum, Ontario Education, March/April, Vol. 12, No. 2, pp. 18–20, 22–24.

Clarke, Judy, Wideman Ron, Eadie Susan, Together We Learn, 1990, Prentice Hall, Scarborough.

Cornfield et al, Making the Grade, 1987, Prentice Hall, Scarborough.

Covey, Stephen, Principle Centred Leadership, 1992, Simon and Schuster, New York.

Educational Leadership, Authentic Learning, April 1993.

Educational Leadership, The Challenge of Higher Standards, February 1993.

Educational Leadership, The Changing Curriculum, May 1993.

Educational Leadership, Using Performance Assessment, May 1992.

Gronlund, N. and Linn R., Measurement and Evaluation in Teaching, 1990, Macmillan, New York.

Growing Collaboratively, Lincoln County Board of Education, 1993, Prentice Hall, Scarborough.

Herman, J., Aschbacher, P., Winter, L., A Practical Guide to Alternative Assessment, 1992, ASCO.

London Board of Education, Regional Geography — Travel and Tourism, 1992.

McIntosh, Margaret, "No Time For Writing in Your Class", Mathematics Teacher, September 1991, pp. 423–433.

Metropolitan Toronto School Board, Accounting, 1989.

Metropolitan Toronto School Board, Linking Evaluation with Learning in Science, 1989.

North Central Regional Educational Laboratory, Schools that Work, The Research Advantage, An eight program video conference, especially Number 4 Alternatives for Measuring Performance, 1991, Oak Brook, IL.

Northwest Regional Educational Laboratory, Classroom Assessment Based on Observation.

Northwest Regional Educational Laboratory, Paper and Pencil Test Development.

Northwest Regional Educational Laboratory, Using Portfolios Workshop.

Ontario Ministry of Education, Basic English OAIP, Assessment Strategies and Materials, 1991.

Ontario Ministry of Education, Basically Right, 1984.

Ontario Ministry of Education and Training, <u>OAC Evaluation Handbook, Family Studies: Families in Canadian Society</u>, 1993.

Ontario Ministry of Education, <u>Profile: Language Aloud … Allowed</u>, 1987.

Ontario Ministry of Education, <u>Senior English OAIP, Involving Students in Assessment</u>, 1991 draft.

Ontario Ministry of Education <u>Senior English OAIP, Promoting Learning Through Assessment</u>, 1991 draft.

OSSTF, <u>Independent Learning</u>, 1989.

<u>Passages 3</u>, 1992, Addison-Wesley.

Peel Board of Education, <u>Looking at Measurement: More Than Just Marks</u>, 1989, <u>Book 1 Objective Tests, Book 2 Essay Tests, Book 5 Teacher-as-Observer: Beyond the Paper and Pencil Test</u>.

Perrone, Vito (ed.) <u>Expanding Student Assessment</u>, 1991, ASCD, Alexandria, VA.

<u>Phi Delta Kappan</u>, Special Section on Authentic Assessment, February 1993.

Pratt, David, <u>Curriculum Design</u>, 1980.

Pratt, David, <u>Curriculum Planning: A Handbook for Professionals</u>, 1991, David Pratt, Kingston.

Saskatchewan Education, <u>Student Evaluation: A Teacher Handbook</u>, 1991, Saskatchewan Education.

Scarborough Board of Education, <u>A Resource Guide for Senior History/Contemporary Studies, Grades 11 and 12</u>, 1987.

Scarborough Board of Education, <u>Clothing, Family Studies Guideline</u>, 1989.

Scarborough Board of Education, <u>Fitness: A Healthy Lifestyle</u>, 1992.

Scarborough Board of Education, <u>Physical Geography</u>, 1993.

Scarborough Board of Education, <u>Visual Arts</u>, 1987.

Scarborough Board of Education, <u>World Issues OAC</u>, 1988.

Schurr, Sandra, <u>ABC's of Evaluation</u>, 1992, National Middle School Association, Columbus, Ohio.

Sparzo, Frank J., <u>Preparing Better Teacher Made Tests, A Practical Guide</u>, Bloomington, Indiana, Phi Delta Kappan Fastback, Number 311.

Stenmark, Jean K. (ed.), <u>Mathematics Assessment: Myths, Models, Good Questions and Practical Suggestions</u>, 1991, NCTM, Reston, VA.

Ullman, Rebecca, <u>Evaluating for Communication: A Handbook for FSL Teachers</u>, 1990, D.C. Heath, Toronto.

Waterloo County Board of Education, <u>Assessment for Learning in the Transition Years and the Specialization Years</u>, 1993, Waterloo.

Wiggins, Grant, "Creating Tests Worth Taking", <u>Educational Leadership</u>, May 1992, pp. 26–33.

Chapter 6
Subject Specific Applications

Subject Specific Applications

Introduction

King and Peart show in their most recent research, *The Numbers Game*, that teachers use a variety of assessment strategies but this variety tends to be different depending on the subject that is taught. For this chapter, we will look at the current practices as reported by teachers (*The Numbers Game*, Chapter 3) in the various subject areas and then look at ways that teachers can expand their current assessment methodologies to better meet the needs of their students.

> ### A Matter of Style
>
> Student choice, open-ended assignments, and flexible deadlines all support my philosophy of education as a continuum leading to an ideal. A group of students all face a similar objective — to read with more comprehension, to improve writing or speaking skills, to measure a chemical reaction, or to practice with a mathematical equation. In any task, people "come to the table" with different experiences. Sports, music, education — we can do all of these things in groups where we are not all at the same level of competence. Nobody at the family picnic expects Aunt Gertie to hit the softball as well as cousin Ted who plays on his college baseball team, but they can both play and have fun.
>
> In my courses the objectives for the year are a continuum, a line starting at a random point and extending endlessly. My goal is for all students to pinpoint their individual starting points on the line and to be closer to the other end of the continuum by the end of the unit or course.
>
> Students need to be involved in choosing the part or learning style that will help in the trip along the continuum. Designing a poster about a book's setting might serve some students far better than writing an essay on the same topic.
>
> Since my continuum of learning has no end, neither should the assignments that lead to it. A more holistic approach to grading allows students to produce varying amounts of work as they head for their goals.

*(**English Journal**, 1993, p. 82.)*

Part A – Subject Specific Cross Reference

This is a listing of the examples of subject specific assessment techniques included in Chapters 4 and 5. Many of these could be adapted to other subjects. Most of the examples listed under English could be used in any subject where writing is being assessed. There are also many other examples included in these chapters which are not listed here and which are applicable to most subjects taught in secondary schools.

Subject	Page

Part B: Assessment Strategies in Individual Subjects

1. English

In chapter 3 of *The Numbers Game*, King and Peart report that English teachers are in agreement that the English guidelines strongly influence their evaluation practices. In grades nine to twelve, 20–30 percent weighting is prescribed for each of the four components — writing as process, group and oral, work and study habits/independent learning, and summative tests/examination(s). The OAC guideline requires 30% for written work, 30% for summative examination(s), 20% for class work, and 20% for independent study (oral and written).

The most frequently used strategy for evaluation was the in-class assignment involving writing and revision. The essay was used extensively at the advanced level, but only half as frequently in general level courses. Independent study projects formed a major part of evaluation in senior advanced courses. Group work was used far more extensively for evaluation at the advanced level than at the general level.

Student self-evaluation and peer-evaluation were used more frequently in senior grades and OAC courses. Journals were used frequently by about half of the English teachers surveyed. Although a number of English teachers felt that a wide variety of evaluation methods was most effective, different weights were given to three evaluation methods for advanced and general level classes.

If evaluation in English tends to be "soft" (i.e. there is a fair amount of subjectivity called for by the teacher in evaluating group work and oral presentations) as opposed to "hard" (i.e. marks resulting from quizzes, tests and examinations), the expectation then would be that students would be more likely to get high marks. However, King and Peart found that mark distributions in English resembled a "bell curve" with the majority of students grouped in the 70–74 percent range. (By contrast, more students in Mathematics and Science had marks between 90 and 100 percent.) **English teachers appear to be cautious in assigning very high marks to students in English**. King and Peart speculated that English teachers may feel that high marks would not be in keeping with school or department expectations regarding medians or that they may not have thought through their objectives and designed appropriate evaluation activities for the grade and level.

English teachers (partly by virtue of guideline directions and also because of evidence of improved student learning) have already incorporated a variety of assessment methodologies for diagnostic, formative and summative purposes into their programs. There seems to be good understanding that assessment and instruction are inextricably linked and that a range of appropriate assessment methodologies provides not only more, but also, much better and more usable information about student learning. However, English teachers would probably be the first to admit that there are a number of concerns regarding assessment including the issues of "fewer high marks" and "advanced/general weighting".

Suggestions for addressing some of these concerns are predicated upon the English teacher being prepared to move away from the "numbers game" (bell curve/median) mind-set to the "assess for success" (every student achieves essential outcomes) frame of reference.

Specific suggestions include:

- taking more care in thinking through essential outcomes and focusing assessment and evaluation on **achievement** of these outcomes. Greater attention to all students achieving essential outcomes would translate into greater success levels (which would likely be reflected in a greater percentage of higher English marks). Perhaps more importantly emphasis would be shifted away from marks to completion (some, almost all, all) of key learning outcomes at the least. Greater meaning would be attached to the marks.

- incorporating specific assessment practices geared to successful learning. One-third of English teachers already employ incentives for students to be successful: re-writes of essays/tests, second chances for presentation/demonstrations, dropping the lowest mark, and of flexible timelines which contribute to improved understanding and more successful learning.

- relying less on in-class writing assignments and more on demonstrations, collaborative group assessments and self-assessment should lead to higher achievement levels (especially at the general level). Emphasis for grading should be placed on culminating demonstrations/products; other demonstrations should be seen as practice (formative) and should not be averaged into the final grade.

- expanding use of specific criteria that have been teacher and student generated. Involvement of students in the assessment of their learning leads to more successful learning.

- adopting the concept of the student learner profile. This profile, based on portfolios, provides focus on samples of student work collected over time and provides a basis for evaluation by teacher, students and parents. When the significance of this method starts to unfold — when it becomes clear to students and parents (and employers and post-secondary institutions) that it is so rich in meaning in terms of individual achievement — it will sell itself.

- getting to know students well. Ongoing assessment means working with students, providing continual feedback on performance, and working together to achieve program goals. Assessment and evaluation is not what teachers do to students; it is what teachers and students do together.

- using assessment results appropriately. No student (especially general level students) should be disadvantaged by lower expectations, unfair assessment due to unbalanced weighting, de-emphasis of some selected essential outcomes.

- collegial marking to ensure fair application of assessment criteria at all levels.

Student Achievement Profile – English

Student: _____   Class: ENG 1W0

Teacher: _____

GRADE 9 ENGLISH-SPECIFIC OUTCOMES. EXPANDED FROM LEARNING OUTCOMES — ENGLISH YEAR 1 (ENG 1W0).

The Student, _____, is performing:

		B	A	E
Reading	• Response to literature (stories, poems, plays, novels)			
	• Reading between the lines (comprehension)			
	• Application of reading strategies			
	• Reading (at least two books)			
	• Awareness of how various media tell stories			
	• Vocabulary			
Writing	• Writing portfolio			
	• Writing skills (length, quality, precision)			
	• Creation and support of an argument			
	• Organization of ideas and opinions (oral and written)			
Speaking	• Level of confidence in communicating ideas (writing and speaking)			
	• working co-operatively with others (group activities)			
Listening	• ability to listen effectively			
Thinking	• Application of thinking skills/strategies			
	• Ability to work independently			
	• Ability to write an examination			
	• Work habits and management skills			
	• Treatment of others (respect and courtesy)			
	• Perspective on global concerns			

Grade 9 Reading and Writing Tests	Level ___
Attitude ___ Effort ___	
(E) Excellent (G) Good (N) Needs to improve	

B = Below
A = At
E = Exceeding

(Frontenac Secondary School, English Department.)

(Frontenac Secondary School, English Department.)

The Principles of Moderation (Collegial Marking)

The following account describes one possible route towards a program of moderation or collegial marking. Each region or board will want to develop a program congenial to its own needs, structures, and interests. Underlying the account are the following key principles:

1. A program of collegial marking evolves slowly as teachers-learners, curriculum planners, and the wider community interact and learn from each other.

2. The process is inductive, beginning with students' real work (written or oral) as part of their course work, and including teachers' real responses to such work.

3. Folios which include a selection of the students' best oral and written work are the most valid sources of examples of student performance. From these folios, pieces of authentic writing or oral work representing all relevant grades and levels are collected.

4. The goals of moderation include:
   (a) the collection of a set of "exemplars", or pieces of authentic writing or oral work produced by students, which demonstrate the entire range of marks (A's, B's, C's, D's, F's), for each grade and level.
   (b) criteria according to which the grades can be justified.
   (c) a detailed discussion, accompanying each exemplar, of how that piece realizes the different criteria.

*(**Senior English OAIP**, Promoting Learning Through Assessment, 1991, pp. 55–56.)*

2. Mathematics

At the grade 9 and 10 advanced-level, formal examinations are a large part of summative evaluation. At the grade 11 and 12 advanced-levels, exams are to be "the most significant single component". Mathematics teachers use quizzes and tests, homework, and in-class assignments for grades 9 and 10. At the grade 11 and 12 level, they use quizzes, tests, homework, and demonstration of skills. Group work presentations, oral presentations, journal/diaries and peer evaluation are generally not used in mathematics classes. Math teachers tend to believe that group work is not an effective way to learn mathematics skills. At the OAC level, even more reliance is placed on quizzes and tests. King and Peart's research also clearly show that students fail in high numbers in math compared to other subjects but students continue to take math despite these failures because the perception is that they need math for post-secondary institutions.

> "By adding a variety of assessment methodologies to the mathematics classroom, both students and teachers will benefit."
>
> (Jean Stenmark, *Mathematics Assessment: Myths, Good Questions, and Practical Suggestions.*)

Advantages of Assessment Alternatives in Mathematics

Students —

- think more deeply about problems;
- feel free to do their best thinking because their ideas are valued;
- ask deeper and more frequent questions of themselves, their classmates, and their teachers;
- improve their listening skills and gain an appreciation for the role of listening in co-operative work;
- feel responsibility for their thoughts and ownership of their methods;
- observe that there are many right ways to solve a problem;
- experience the value of verbalization as a means of clarifying one's thinking;
- form new insights into mathematical concepts;
- learn ways to identify the places where they need help;
- increase their self-confidence and self-esteem as a result of genuine interest shown by a teacher or classmate;
- feel more tolerance and respect for other people's ideas;
- focus their energy on exploring and communicating ideas about mathematical relationships rather than on finding answers;
- develop strategies for conducting self-interviews while solving problems in other settings;
- find satisfaction and confidence in their ability to solve problems;
- look less to the teacher for clues about the correctness of their methods and focus less on imitating the "right" way.

Teachers—

- gain access to student thinking;
- enhance their ability to use non threatening questions that elicit explanations and reveal misconceptions;
- strengthen their listening skills;

- show respect for their students by being non judgmental;
- use interview results as a source of questions to pose on written assignments for the whole class;
- encourage respect for diversity by modeling appreciation of varied approaches;
- pose questions that encourage students to construct and share their own understandings;
- feel reinforcement for letting go of teaching as "telling".

(Stenmark, 1991, p. 4.)

Alternatives for Mathematics

1. Performance Assessment in Mathematics

A performance assessment in mathematics involves presenting students with a mathematical task, project, or investigation, then observing, interviewing, and looking at their products to assess what they actually know and can do.

A performance task can—
- allow the examination of the process used as well as the answer or finished project;
- be used with groups as well as individuals;
- document, through observation records or student products, accomplishments not revealed by ordinary tests.

Advantages for Students
- There is opportunity to display all their ability, not just speed and accuracy. Many students who can be excellent mathematicians are not fast. The best mathematical thinking is often done slowly.
- Students have more creative problems to work on and more chances to do their own organizing and thinking.
- They understand that mathematics is not "a bunch of rules to memorize and follow" but a process that enables people to solve problems.
- Students work on real tasks that provide engaging contexts and enhance motivation.
- They experience the utility and power of mathematics.

Advantages for Teachers
- Assessment does not interrupt student learning but happens within the instructional program.
- Increased information of higher quality about students' understanding and ability to do mathematics is shown.
- More complete information for instructional decisions about student misconceptions or errors is available.
- There is better assessment of the strengths and weaknesses of the instructional process as well as of students' understanding.
- Performance assessment allows inclusion of investigations, projects, and long-term problems into the curriculum, with integration of content and mathematical modeling.

Advantages for Parents and Administrators

- They see examples of real performance by students.
- Comprehensive evaluation of students' ability to use their understanding of mathematics is available.
- Evaluation of the outcomes of mathematics programs is clear.
- There is evidence that students are learning to think and to use mathematics in new situations.
- The connection between schoolwork and real life is demonstrated.
- Performance assessment presents a broader picture of a rich curriculum.

(Stenmark, 1991, p. 13.)

2. Open-Ended Questions

An open-ended question has many avenues of access and allows students to respond in a variety of ways.

There is a distinction between open- response questions, in which the test writer sets forth a problem or a set of steps leading to a particular answer, and open-ended questions, in which the student may give a variety of successful responses. We may choose to evaluate the diverse paths taken rather than the answers themselves.

The important quality in an open-ended question, as in other forms of assessment presented in this book, is that we are able to see student thinking rather than test-writer thinking.

Creating Open-ended Questions

Curriculum is still being developed to support adapting our classrooms to new assessments, but some changes are fairly simple:

- When students have been using an arithmetic operation, ask them to explain, in writing or with a diagram, what that operation means and how it works.
- To textbook word problems, add "Explain how you arrived at your answer."
- Instead of requesting an answer for an existing problem, substitute a question that prompts additional thinking.
- Monitor the directions and responses given to students, so that whenever possible you can have them explaining to you rather than you explaining to them.
- Look for situations that invite students to formulate hypotheses, write directions, make generalizations, and so on.

Classroom Grading

For a classroom teacher to read all the papers generated by frequent writing in mathematics might seem burdensome. Teachers who have had their students write, however, say that the results are worth it because they learn more about their students' thinking and understanding and about the gaps in their knowledge. Some suggestions to lighten the burden follow:

- Select and review a small sample of papers at one time. This will tell you how the class as a whole is doing.

- Be selective about what is commented on, choosing one or two aspects for evaluation or scoring and detailed feedback.
- Have students review their first drafts with their group, incorporating revisions into the final paper.
- Ask students to underline the ideas they really want you to notice. This will help you see whether they can recognize those important ideas.
- Teach students to assess other students' work. Page 53 describes a process. This is a very powerful communication to students of the requirements for a good paper.
- Anticipate that students' responses will vary a great deal from your expectations.

Evaluation of open-ended questions can be analytical, with points for various aspects of the response, or holistic, with the reader or evaluator looking at the paper as a whole rather than searching for specific details.

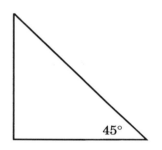

(Stenmark, 1991, p. 20.)

3. List everything you know or can figure out about this triangle:

8 cm

45°

4. With your group, design an activity that will help the class understand how large one million is.

5. Kim doesn't believe that adding a constant (the same number) to every student's test score will simply change the average test score by that same amount. Write an explanation to convince Kim that this is or is not true.

(Stenmark, 1991, p. 20.)

INSIDE A MATHEMATICS PORTFOLIO

A solution to an open-ended question done as homework — not just a neat set of figures, but showing originality and unusual procedures

A mathematical autobiography

Teacher-completed checklists

Work in the student's primary language

Notes from an interview — by the teacher or another student

A report of a group project, with comments about the individual's contribution, for example:

A survey of adult use of mathematics in work

A review of media use of mathematics

Work from another subject area that relates to mathematics, such as an analysis of data collected and presented in a graph for social studies

A problem made up by the student, with or without a solution

Art work done by the student, such as string designs, coordinate pictures, and scale drawings or maps

The focus in student portfolios is on these items:
- Student thinking
- Growth over time (Be sure to date all papers.)
- Mathematical connections
- Student views of themselves as mathematicians
- The problem-solving process

Excerpts from a student's daily journal

A table of contents

Papers that show the student's correction of errors or misconceptions

A letter from the student to the reader of the portfolio, explaining each item

Draft, revised, and final versions of student work on a complex mathematical problem, including writing, diagrams, graphs, charts, or whatever is most appropriate

A photo or sketch made by the student (or teacher) of a student's work with manipulatives or with mathematical models of multidimensional figures

A description by the teacher of a student activity that displayed understanding of a mathematical concept or relation

Standardized Tests – Cautions

- Scores on standardized tests are only one piece of information and should be viewed in context with other information.
- Students' attitudes, behaviours, and oral and written communication skills must be assessed to provide a complete picture. Important data is obtained from student questionnaires or interviews.
- Students' strategies and thought processes must be looked at as well as their answers, e.g. open-response or open-ended items.
- Test items need a balance of content and cognitive process, not overweighing on computation.
- Students must be permitted to use calculators; as the use of these "fast pencils" becomes routine in classrooms, evaluation must keep pace.
- Manipulative usage should be part of the formal evaluation process, e.g. rulers, tangrams, counters, and tiles along with test booklets and answer sheets so that the assessment can be as consistent with instruction as possible.

(Adapted from Stenmark, 1991, p. 9.)

If adaptations are made, then more students should be more successful in mathematics.

3. Science

The curriculum guidelines for science courses call for 15 percent of a grade to reflect student achievement in laboratory skills and reports; and, 50 percent of the term mark is prescribed for each unit of study. At the OAC level, 30 to 40 percent is based on one or more examinations.

The approach to assessment in science is similar to mathematics and involves only a few main strategies. The two main activities science teachers used for assessment were homework and quizzes/tests. Frequently students in all grades (9 to 12) were assigned work to complete in class. Essays, presentations in groups or individually, journals/diaries and students self- and peer-evaluation were infrequently used in science in all grades.

The resulting mark distributions in science are very similar to those in math. Grades 9 and 10 have the highest failure rates with marks rising in senior grades, and particularly OAC.

*(King & Peart, **The Numbers Game**, 1994.)*

In order to increase student success levels in science, movement to a more collaborative, process-oriented approach to assessment (especially in grades 9 and 10) would seem to be worth exploring. Increased opportunities for students to be involved in a wider range of performance assessment activities — group assessment, self- and peer-assessment, response journals — would involve students more directly in the learning process by encouraging reflective practice. The following samples are offered as suggestions to focus what may be for some science teachers alternative assessment activities.

Although the following principles and practices have been taken from the *Junior Division Science Assessment Planning Guide*, they apply directly to assessment and evaluation at the secondary level.

When making decisions about Science programs, several areas should be considered:

1. the philosophy and direction of provincial policy,
2. the needs and interests of the students,
3. the appropriate learning opportunities based upon the abilities of the students,
4. the planning of classroom activities with the students,
5. the unique balance of skills, attitudes, and knowledge necessary to meet the needs of the students,
6. the best combination of whole-class, group, and individual instruction for the program.

The types of assessment and evaluation strategies and the instruments selected must flow from these principles and their underlying philosophy.

These foundation principles include:

1. a child-centred program,
2. direct involvement in hands-on explorations and investigation,
3. enquiry learning,
4. opportunities to develop curiosity about the world and self-confidence to explore it,
5. opportunities to manipulate, invent, build, test, and rebuild things,
6. an atmosphere that encourages questioning.

(*Junior Division Science OAIP*, 1993, p. 4.)

Skills, Attitudes, and Interactions

Active Involvement Indicators

When science teachers design their own student observation sheets, they should select only those indicators most relevant to the learning opportunities being addressed. By observing small groups of different students over a range of activities and using a personally modified observation sheet, a teacher can monitor growth and development over a short period of time. Long-term observations can be used in reporting student progress to parents.

COMMUNICATING

Communicating involves the reception of information from a variety of sources by different means, and the expression of information in a variety of ways.

Indicators for the skill COMMUNICATING		
The student:		
COMM	1	uses a variety of charts, graphs, tables, drawings, computers, interviews, and other sources to gather information.
COMM	2	gathers information using hands-on investigations.
COMM	3	gathers and expresses information using a scientific approach.
COMM	4	evaluates information for its validity and reliability.
COMM	5	reshapes new information.
COMM	6	uses charts, graphs, tables, drawings, computers, interviews, and other resources to express information.
COMM	7	uses a variety of media in the reception and delivery of information.
COMM	8	selects appropriate resources and media for the reception and expression of information.
COMM	9	uses appropriate scientific language correctly.
COMM	10	
COMM	11	
COMM	12	

*(**Junior Division Science OAIP**, 1993, p. 64.)*

INTERPRETING

Interpreting involves the development of conclusions based on the analysis of information that has been gathered.

Indicators for the skill INTERPRETING		
The student:		
INT	1	gives simple explanations for different events.
INT	2	determines whether or not information gathered supports or refutes an explanation or hypothesis.
INT	3	formulates conclusions based on the results of a repeated test or experiment.
INT	4	analyzes observations and draws conclusions from direct experiences (primary sources).
INT	5	analyzes information from secondary sources (e.g., written material, audiovisual material).
INT	6	explains cause-effect relationships based on his or her own investigations (primary source information).
INT	7	recognizes that the validity of the conclusions made depends on the quality of the information gathered.
INT	8	
INT	9	
INT	10	

(Junior Division Science OAIP, 1993, p. 71.)

SAFETY-MINDEDNESS

Safety-mindedness is demonstrated when a learner's actions reflect an internalized sense of safety needs.

Indicators for development in the attitude SAFETY-MINDEDNESS		
The student:		
SAM	1	follows safety procedures consistently.
SAM	2	uses Science equipment safely.
SAM	3	foresees safety hazards and attempts to overcome them.
SAM	4	considers the safety of others when conducting investigations.
SAM	5	uses sources of safety information.
SAM	6	shares safety information with others.
SAM	7	alerts others to possible dangers when necessary.
SAM	8	
SAM	9	
SAM	10	

(Junior Division Science OAIP, 1993, p. 84.)

RISK TAKING

Risk taking is demonstrated when a learner shares or acts upon personal opinions, observations, intuitions, predictions, and questions.

Indicators for development in the attitude RISK TAKING		
The student:		
RIT	1	demonstrates a willingness to take part in Science investigations.
RIT	2	demonstrates a willingness to participate in Science discussions and issues.
RIT	3	suggests alternative ideas and explanations.
RIT	4	subjects personal observations, conclusions, predictions, and hypotheses to the scrutiny of others.
RIT	5	shares personally-created products and performances.
RIT	6	shares predictions and hypotheses.
RIT	7	demonstrates a personal adjustment for change.
RIT	8	
RIT	9	
RIT	10	

(Junior Division Science OAIP, 1993, p. 86.)

LEARNING INDEPENDENTLY

Learning independently involves the development of skills and attitudes required to learn alone.

Indicators for assessing performance while LEARNING INDEPENDENTLY		
The student:		
LEI	1	gathers the necessary resources.
LEI	2	uses time effectively.
LEI	3	stays on task.
LEI	4	seeks help when necessary.
LEI	5	accepts advice and suggestions for improvement of work.
LEI	6	modifies the work to improve the quality.
LEI	7	completes commitments.
LEI	8	takes pride in accomplishments.
LEI	9	
LEI	10	
LEI	11	

(Junior Division Science OAIP, 1993, p. 92.)

LEARNING AS A MEMBER OF A GROUP

Learning as a member of a group involves the development of co-operative skills that enable a group to meet its goals.

Indicators for assessing performance while **LEARNING AS A MEMBER OF A GROUP**		
The student:		
LMG	1	negotiates his or her roles and responsibilities.
LMG	2	contributes ideas and suggestions.
LMG	3	encourages the involvement of each member of the group.
LMG	4	shows a willingness to have his or her suggestions criticized or questioned.
LMG	5	modifies his or her ideas and suggestions when faced with new or better evidence.
LMG	6	listens to the ideas and suggestions of others.
LMG	7	accepts the talents and abilities of each group member.
LMG	8	recognizes the contribution of others and accepts it as an essential part of the group task.
LMG	9	modifies work to improve quality.
LMG	10	completes his or her commitments.
LMG	11	
LMG	12	
LMG	13	

*(**Junior Division Science OAIP**, 1993, p. 93.)*

An Intermediate Science Sample

Act as your village's waste disposal research team. You have a budget of $12 per household to dispose of the glass waste in the village. Make three plans (good, better, best) to recommend to the village council. Provide a budget that is maximally efficient and will leave the village free of glass litter. You will need to consult with village officials and research village data in the library. Be prepared to defend your recommendations and your reasoning. You will submit your plans to the entire class and the class will select the best plan for the village.

Rationale for the Activity

When a teacher ties cooperation and thinking into learning tasks with significant content outcomes, he or she completes the triple agenda. In the "integrating the curriculum" literature, this is known as the nested model. Not only does this model make thinking and cooperating an integral part of every lesson, it also allows for the most logical and simple way to assess and grade student attainment of complex and significant outcomes.

When integrating the three elements of thinking skills, cooperation, and content into a single lesson, it is helpful to follow these guidelines:

1. **KISS**: Keep it simple and structured. The "it" is the process of assessment and evaluation.

2. **START** with a significant outcome. As Sizer (1992) suggests, these are best framed in an "exhibit" framework.

(Costa et al, 1992, pp. 306–307.)

4. Other Subjects

King and Peart's research, *The Numbers Game*, also looks at other subject areas in Chapter 3 (Teachers and Evaluation). Many of the issues already discussed in English are also present in History and Geography while in many ways French is similar to Mathematics in its frequent use of quizzes and tests. Teachers may find it useful to look at the English, Mathematics and Science sections of this chapter for further information and direction.

References

Costa, Bellanca, and Fogarty. If Minds Matter: A Foreword to the Future, Volume Two. Skylight Publishing, Palatine, Illinois, 1992.

King, A. and Peart, M. The Numbers Game. Toronto: OSSTF, 1994.

Ontario Ministry of Education, Basic English OAIP, Handbook. 1990.

Ontario Ministry of Education, Junior Division Science: Assessment Planning (OAIP). 1993.

Ontario Ministry of Education, Senior English OAIP, Promoting Learning Through Assessment. 1991.

Stenmark, Jean Kerr, ed. Mathematics Assessment: Myths, Models, Good Questions and Practical Strategies. Reston, Virginia: The National Council of Teachers of Mathematics, 1991.

Chapter 7
Exceptional Students, ESL and Adult Learners

Exceptional Students, ESL and Adult Learners

> Ask any school administrator to take you through the school and show you some high-quality work in any subject area. ... What is similar about all this work is that none of it could be graded or evaluated by machines — quality never can.
>
> *William Glasser*
>
> **The Quality School**

Assessment and evaluation strategies will need to be modified to meet the special needs of a variety of students. This section will focus on special needs students, English as a Second Language students, and adult learners.

> Assess and evaluate according to individual needs. Take time to teach students about assessment and evaluation. Share with them the criteria to be observed. Show them how the checklists and targets work. Involve them in determining how their progress and achievement will be evaluated. Some students will need to focus on one specific criterion; others may focus on several criteria at a time. Remind students that their individual progress is important.
>
> Provide frequent opportunities for self- and peer-assessment. Encourage students to evaluate the processes of learning as well as the work produced. Use projects, demonstrations, presentations, tests, and examinations for summative evaluation. Make summative evaluation worth no more than 25 per cent. Allow some flexibility by varying the time required if necessary. Think about alternative locations for examinations.

(Basic English OAIP — Handbook, 1990, p. 18.)

Modifying Assessment

Assessment should be modified whenever necessary to allow a student the optimum opportunity to demonstrate learning (acquisition, retention, transfer of concepts and skills) in respect to the desired learning outcomes.

Modification can occur to change slightly/significantly/partially/completely any of the following elements:

- *rate* – the speed at which concepts/skills are presented;
- *volume* – the amount of content in relation to concepts and skills;
- *complexity* – the depth/breadth of concepts and skills presented;

- *presentation* – the way(s) in which concepts and skills are delivered, e.g. verbal, visual, sequential, random, integrated, segmented, etc.;
- *reception* – the way(s) in which concepts and skills are received by the learner: auditory, visual, whole, part, tactile, kinesthetic, etc.;
- *production/performance* – the way(s) in which the student is required to demonstrate the acquisition of concepts and skills: verbal, written, artistic, typed, pictorial, etc.

Modification should result in the student developing:
- *power* – the ability to comprehend and work with concepts and skills related to curriculum expectations and according to individual strengths, weaknesses and needs;
- *momentum* –competence; a sense of day-to-day progress in the acquisition of curriculum expectations;
- *status* – the belief that s/he is a learner capable of acquiring, retaining and transferring concepts and skills according to curriculum expectations.

Modification requires that those responsible for assessment be creative in their attitude and in their actions by demonstrating:
- *fluency:* How many ways can I adapt/alter the form and/or content?
- *flexibility:* How can I develop alternative approaches, channels, attitudes, expectations?
- *originality:* In what unique, unusual way can I modify, adapt, rearrange, combine?
- *elaboration:* How can I make the concepts, skills and/or content clearer/ more explicit?

Modification requires teachers to explore alternatives and consider each of the above elements. In some cases, it may be necessary to modify all elements. It is important to remember that the modification of even one element affects all the others to some degree.

SOME GENERAL SUGGESTIONS FOR MODIFYING YOUR ASSESSMENT PRACTICES INCLUDE:

- ❑ allowing more time for task completion
- ❑ reducing the rate of language
- ❑ simplifying instructional language
- ❑ pairing or grouping students
- ❑ reducing the amount of content to be learned within a given time
- ❑ providing for independent learning activity on a contract basis
- ❑ providing frequent review of concept/skills
- ❑ making frequent positive contacts with students during instructional/ assessment time to clarify tasks and encourage effort
- ❑ allowing the use of a tape recorder as an alternative to a written response
- ❑ promoting the use of computer word processing as an alternative to a hand-written response
- ❑ permitting the student to take an oral test as an alternative to a paper and pencil test
- ❑ permitting the student to use an "open-book" during test situations.

(Waterloo, Windows on Learning, 1993, p. 92–93.)

1. The Exceptional Student

Working with Exceptional Students in the Mainstream Classroom

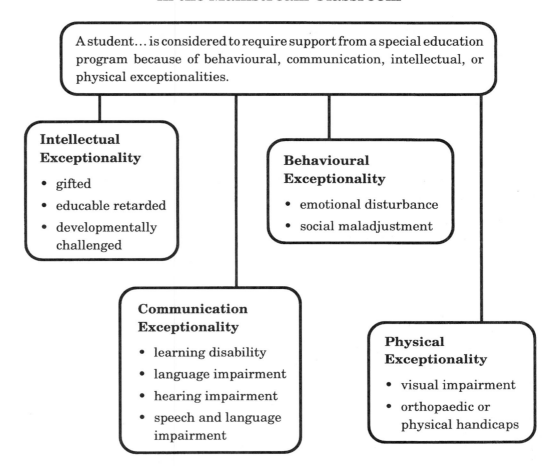

A student… is considered to require support from a special education program because of behavioural, communication, intellectual, or physical exceptionalities.

Intellectual Exceptionality

- gifted
- educable retarded
- developmentally challenged

Behavioural Exceptionality

- emotional disturbance
- social maladjustment

Communication Exceptionality

- learning disability
- language impairment
- hearing impairment
- speech and language impairment

Physical Exceptionality

- visual impairment
- orthopaedic or physical handicaps

*(Peel Special Services, **Program for Exceptional Students**, 1987.)*

Teachers may wish to refer to the following general indicators of learning difficulties to do a quick assessment of a student in the classroom. Learning resource teachers and special education teachers can also provide additional help with initial assessment.

Twenty General Indicators of Learning Difficulties

- may have weakness in short- and/or long-term memory (may experience poor recall);

- may have difficulty in following or creating a sequence;

- may lack organizational skills;

- may lack awareness of time and/or space and shape;

- may have specific gaps in reading, writing, and/or mathematics (e.g., may read well but be unable to write well or may be very weak in spelling);

- may have uneven academic development and progress (e.g., may know a fact or process one week but may not remember or understand it the following week);

- may have difficulty interpreting activities involving auditory, visual, and/or tactile experiences;

- may have difficulty in transferring and applying information from one situation to another;

- may have difficulty with problem-solving tasks in any subject area because of difficulty in applying the known to the unknown;

- may have difficulty learning by observation because he/she cannot analyze the components of an activity or skill;

- may identify and focus on an incidental aspect rather than the central point in a lesson, discussion, or conversation;

- may have a short attention span and be easily distracted, and may be unable to attend to a task long enough to gain adequate knowledge or skill;

- may be able to master content but be unable to produce answers in written form;

- may have difficulty following oral directions; may appear to lack motivation and to be lazy as a result of persistent failure;

- may develop a poor self-concept and may exhibit negative behavioural patterns as a result of his/her lack of success;

- may have difficulty developing and/or sustaining effective social relationships;

- may use personal space inappropriately and may have coordination problems;

- may have the motivation to succeed but be fragmented in personal planning;

- may find it difficult to read non-verbal cues.

*(Peel, **Book 5**, 1990, p. 3.)*

Teachers may wish to check where they are now in terms of modifying current programs. Take the test!

HOW DO I MODIFY?
LET ME COUNT THE WAYS

Use the self-assessment quiz below to reflect on the degree of modification you presently use in your program to assist exceptional students. Rate yourself 1 (low) to 5 (high) for the degree of use.

Be honest with yourself!

I Try To...

1. encourage students to verbalize whenever possible
   - before writing, students discuss topics collaboratively.   1   2   3   4   5
   - when studying, students read material, notes, and directions aloud.   1   2   3   4   5
   - with visual information, students summarize orally.   1   2   3   4   5

2. clarify definitions, terms, and vocabulary in assignments.   1   2   3   4   5

3. tell students the purpose of the assignment and the method/criteria for the evaluation.   1   2   3   4   5

4. ensure that students understand the assignment and lesson material by asking them to retell or paraphrase instructions.   1   2   3   4   5

5. give short, clear instructions and use non-verbal instruction by pointing, holding, touching, tapping, etc.   1   2   3   4   5

6. provide time for students to begin assignments in class in order to assist with preliminary organization and understanding of the assignments as well as time to clarify and review instructions before they leave class.   1   2   3   4   5

7. provide opportunities for peer interaction such as using a peer coach as proofreader, editor, vocalizer, and listener.   1   2   3   4   5

8. prepare a guide or outline to assist students when taking notes; such a guide indicates the specific information which is required from a reading assignment.   1   2   3   4   5

9. record reading materials on tape for disabled readers. (Students in peer tutoring or leadership programs may be able to assist.)   1   2   3   4   5

10. avoid assignments and notes which require extensive copying from the board; instead, I hand out the notes which students require for class and use the time to discuss the key ideas of the lesson.   1   2   3   4   5

11. use drama as a tool to assist students in following directions.   1   2   3   4   5

12. provide opportunities for co-operative learning.   1   2   3   4   5

13. encourage students to pair up and work together.   1   2   3   4   5

14. ensure resources at the appropriate reading level are readily available.   1   2   3   4   5

15. write important phrases on the board as I say them. (Seeing and hearing at the same time act as a reinforcement.)   1   2   3   4   5

16. use individual conferences to guide students and to monitor their understanding of assignments.   1   2   3   4   5

17. give students sufficient time to process instructions before requiring a response.   1   2   3   4   5

18. give all instructions and information both visually and orally.   1   2   3   4   5

CHECK YOUR SCORE!

How do I Modify?
Self -Assessment Quiz — How to Score

To score: add up the circled numbers from your responses.

If your total score was:

70–100	Give yourself a pat on the back! Your special needs students are in good hands.
40–69	Coming along! You're well on the way to a fully modified program.
20–39	Consult the special education teacher in your school. He/she will help you become a 100.
0–19	Gong! Gong!

No matter what your score, this quiz was intended to create an awareness of the many options available to differentiate instruction to meet the individual needs of exceptional students in our classrooms. Remember, exceptional students often possess the ability to understand course material, although their particular disability(ies) may not allow them to translate their thought processes into action. As teachers, we can best assist these students with modifications which bypass their deficits and build on their strengths.

*(Peel, **Book 5**, 1990, pp. 4–5, 32.)*

Hints for working with exceptional students

ARE YOU TEACHING YOUR STUDENTS TO:

1. **Organize?**
   - **Notebook:** Keep a model notebook in the classroom for easy student reference.
   - **Gathering Information:** The computer is a wonderful assistant for all phases of the writing process.
   - **Time Management:** Provide a written outline of class activities at the beginning of a class, or allow time at the end of a class for students to record assignments on a calendar or planner.
   - **Notetaking:** Teach students to use shorthand or abbreviations. Encourage students to develop their own abbreviations.
   - **Outlining:** Acquaint students with a variety of outlining methods such as clustering or mapping. Have students select one process and encourage them to follow this process when approaching written or oral tasks.
   - **Highlighting:** Encourage students to use coloured markers to highlight key words and ideas in notes, texts, tests, and handouts.
   - **Organize Information for Successful Oral Testing:** Have students use an outline method for oral composition and a tape recorder as a scribe.

2. Proofread Their Assignments?

- Allow time between the task of writing and the task of proofreading. When proofreading is done immediately, mistakes are not as evident.
- Suggest that students use peer editing or have a family member go over the work.

3. Use learning tools by providing detailed instruction in the use of

• **Calculators?**	A calculator with printer may assist students to check their work.
• **Spelling Computers?**	A variety exist. Ensure that it has a typewriter keyboard format.
• **Lap-Top Computers?**	
• **Scribes?**	Students should be taught how to use a scribe.
• **Tape Recorders?**	

4. Prepare for Tests?

- Teach and review key words which act as directing words on tests and assignments (i.e., "compare," "contrast").
- Prepare for tests by having students design and answer their own questions.
- Use previous exams or tests as study tools.

*(Peel, **Book 5**, 1990, pp. 6–7.)*

IDEAS TO HELP EXCEPTIONAL STUDENTS GET ORGANIZED:

Sample 1: DAILY WORKING CHART

Date	Pre-Activity	Activity	Materials Needed

Sample 2: Assignments

TIME GUIDELINES FOR PROJECT

_____

_____

Steps Involved in Completing Project	Materials/Resources Required	Date for Completion
1. _____		
2. _____		
3. _____		
4. _____		
5. _____		
6. _____		
7. _____		
8. _____		
9. _____		
10. _____		
11. _____		
12. _____		
13. _____		
14. _____		
15. _____		
16. _____		
17. _____		
18. _____		
19. _____		
20. _____		

Contracted Completion Date: _____

Signature: _____

Teacher: _____

Sample 3: PROJECT LOG

Student _____

Meeting Dates: Date: _____   Purpose: _____

                      Date: _____   Purpose: _____

                      Date: _____   Purpose: _____

                      Date: _____   Purpose: _____

Topic:

Skills required to complete final product:

Description of total final product and/or presentation:

*(Peel, **Book 5**, 1990, pp. 35–37.)*

Try a Math Log ...

MATH LOG

Write number problem

Draw the problem

Explain the problem

---

*(Kay Burke, **Authentic Classroom Assessments**, IRI Group, 1993, p. 31.)*

Modification of Classroom Assignments

ASSIGNMENT FORMAT

- provide a choice of assignment formats
  - written presentation
  - oral presentation
  - hands-on demonstration
  - models or displays
- provide organizational approaches to assist in successful completion
- share or co-develop evaluation criteria when presenting the assignment

TAPED RESPONSE

- allow taped response for written assignment

REDUCED READING

- highlight the most important parts of a chapter
- attempt to provide reading materials at the appropriate reading level

ADJUST HOMEWORK

- reduce the number of questions
- simplify homework questions
- provide choices

SUBSTITUTE RESOURCES AND MATERIALS

- Present information through another medium. Use taped texts, class discussions, film/video, maps, slides, or peer tutors to act as readers. When using taped texts, first determine whether the student learns best with or without the text in front of him/her.
- Change the criteria for task performance (speed and accuracy demands and the amount of work required).
- Vary the level of difficulty in projects.
- Allow sufficient time for individual completion. Periodic monitoring of student progress should occur when additional time is given.
- Encourage the use of graphs, maps, and pictures in project assignments as a replacement for written work.
- Allow the submission of draft assignments so that students can receive constructive feedback from teacher or peers before the final copy is prepared.

*(Peel, **Book 5**, 1990, p. 10.)*

TEACHER SELF TEST

Try Modifying This Assignment

Grade 9 Science Plant Poster Assignment

SNC 1   Plants live in a variety of locations and climates, from the severe conditions of the Canadian Tundra to the constantly warm and moist environment of the Brazilian Rainforest.

Plants are important to humans because they give us many useful products.

In this assignment, you will research ONE kind of PLANT to find out how it has adapted to survive and thrive where it lives. You will also investigate the types of products the plant provides for human use.

The poster you make will be marked on the following criteria:

1. Adaptations
2. Uses
3. * Drawing(s): could be the whole plant, the products, or a close-up on the adaptation, or a combination
4. Neatness and organization
5. Eye appeal, colour.

* If ACTUAL pictures are used, you MUST show your teacher where you are cutting the pictures from BEFORE using them on your poster. Failure to do so will result in a failing grade.

Your poster will be evaluated in three ways:

1. Teacher evaluation using a Rating Scale.
2. Peer evaluation by two of your classmates using a Peer Evaluation Sheet.
3. Self Evaluation using a Self Evaluation Sheet.

Comments:

HOW DID YOU DO? HERE ARE SOME IDEAS.

Modifications of Plant Poster Assignment

Language of Question

- make sure students understand terms (climate, severe, tundra, rainforest, environment, research, adapted, adaptations, survive, thrive, investigate, human use.)
- give concrete examples when explaining terms.
- allow the students to ask clarifying questions even if you feel you already went over it.

Organizers

- show students a variety of exemplary posters which illustrate the criteria you will be marking for:
  - lettering of titles and text;
  - organization of text;
  - pictures, alternatives to drawings;
  - eye appeal, colour.
- have students hand in a sketch showing **title, sub-headings, picture placement, organization of text materials** (students do not have to have the latter written up yet).
- make sure the sketch is included in teacher evaluation.
- the sketch is just to make sure students are getting started.
- provide frequent feedback as the assignment is progressing.

Time

- ensure that library resources are at the appropriate level of difficulty.
- allow at least two library periods for students to complete some basic research.
- allow some class time to get started on the assignment.
- check frequently with the class to see how assignment is coming along.

Evaluation

- hand out the rating scale you will use to evaluate the poster at the same time as you hand out the assignment.
- show the students how the rating scale is connected to the stated criteria.

Learning Tools

- make sure that the student has access and opportunity to use a word processor.
- ensure the computer is equipped with a spell checker and grammatic assister (i.e., Grammatix IV).

*(Peel, **Book 5**, 1990, pp. 13, 34.)*

Testing Exceptional Students — Objective Items

TYPES OF OBJECTIVE ITEMS AND THEIR USE WITH EXCEPTIONAL STUDENTS

Type of Test Item	Skill Required	Advantage	Disadvantage
True/False	Typically emphasizes rote memory.	Easier for poor readers and writers.	Relies on rote memory.
Matching	Relies on memory associations ("recognition memory").	Assists those with word retrieval problems.	Difficult for those with poor recall.
Fill-in the Blank	Measures rote learning.	If an answer box is included, it can assist recall.	Difficult for those with poor recall/word retrieval.
Multiple Choice	Comprehension. Requires good visual tracking (the ability to transfer information from one place to another, i.e., transfer answers to answer sheet).	Easy to modify: the teacher can read the items aloud or pretape the questions.	Difficult for those with visual tracking problems.

*(Peel, **Book 5**, 1990, p. 16.)*

SUGGESTIONS FOR MODIFYING OBJECTIVE TESTS

Question Format

1. Pretape the questions so that a non-reader or poor reader can work from a tape recorder.

2. Present questions in familiar formats which the student has used in class. For example, if Math Operations have been taught with a vertical presentation, do not switch to horizontal format on the test.

3. Alter the reading level of the test by eliminating difficult words; this can be done by rewriting/explaining the difficult words.

    Example:

    (makes)

    The force that *causes* water to run downhill is

4. For fill-in questions, provide the answers on the page. This will help eliminate recall memory difficulties. Students must still be able to understand context and have learned the concepts in order to select and place correct answers.

Option 1: A fill-in question can be adapted by providing a selection of words below each blank.

> *(well known)* *(happened)*
> What *famous* battle *took place* in England in the year 1066?
> _____
> (Hastings, London, York)

Option 2: Answers can be placed in scrambled order in an answer box at the foot of the page.

    (a) If two equal angles add up to 120 degrees, the triangle is called an _____ triangle.

    (b) If two equal angles add up to 135 degrees, the triangle is called an _____ triangle.

> | Obtuse,   Isosceles,   Equilateral |
> | --- |

Instructions for Answering Questions

1. Use simple direct statements in the stem of the question.

    America was named after

        (a) Columbus   (c) Ponce de Leon

        (b) Magellan   (d) Vespucci

2. Familiarize students with the format of the test by reviewing samples from previous tests.

3. Avoid oral directions as the only means of giving instructions on how to complete the test. Place directions at the beginning of each section of a test and where possible illustrate with a completed example.

    Circle the correct answer.

    The most urbanized (high % of population lives in cities) provinces

        (a) Nova Scotia   (c) Ontario

        (b) Quebec   (d) Saskatchewan

Administration of the Test

1. Have another student read the questions aloud to a weak or non-reader.

2. Provide a scribe who can write the answers.

3. Allow extra time for students who are slow in processing or production. However, extended test time is not always appropriate; reduction in the number of questions is sometimes a better strategy.

4. Allow for on-the-spot teacher interpretation of misunderstood test vocabulary.

5. Allow the use of calculators when the objective of the test is understanding concepts, not mechanical accuracy.

6. Provide relevant formulae, key words, and symbols to alleviate recall memory difficulties.

Scoring the Test

1. Students with a writing or memory deficit should NOT be penalized for spelling or grammatical errors.

*(Peel, **Book 5**, 1990, pp. 17–18.)*

CONSIDER THESE ALTERNATIVES TO OBJECTIVE TESTS

Oral Presentation

Allow the student to give an oral presentation of the material learned. This will benefit students who have strength in verbal communication, but a serious deficit in writing.

Concrete Materials

Use concrete application instead of a paper-and-pencil task. This could take the form of a demonstration, project, AV presentation, or graphic display.

Open Book Test

Utilize open-book tests to assist exceptional students with poor recall. A one-page summary sheet may be another alternative.

Jigsaw Puzzle Test

Objective questions can be physically cut up like a jigsaw puzzle. The student can then physically re-organize and align the correct answers. This brings a kinesthetic and spatial response to the test and can greatly assist the exceptional student who has difficulty with abstract organization and/or tracking skills.

*(Peel, **Book 5**, 1990, p. 19.)*

SUGGESTIONS FOR MODIFYING AN ESSAY TEST

Question Format

1. Use simple, direct phrases in the design of your essay questions.
2. Underline the key words in the questions.
   e.g., in one or two paragraphs, *describe* why *teenagers* use drugs and how drugs affect them.
3. Provide alternative key words at the student's independent reading level.
   e.g., in two or three paragraphs, describe (tell) why teenagers use drugs and how drugs affect (change) them.
4. Provide a marking scheme which lists the expectations required in the response.
5. Suggest a number of key points which should be included in the response.
6. Make sure a suggested time frame is given as a guideline.

Instructions

1. Review the question orally with the student to ensure comprehension. You may ask the student to define any terminology in the essay question, or have the student state in his/her own words what needs to be done to complete the task.

2. Provide a proofreading checklist so that students can double check what they have written.

3. Provide the student with an OUTLINE organization sheet. Outlines are useful for students who experience difficulty in the area of written language and organization. Students must be taught how to use and complete a variety of different outlines. You may want to assist the student in developing an outline.

Administration of the Test

1. Allow extended time for students who are slower in processing or production. However, extended test time is not always the most appropriate strategy. Reducing the number of questions or allowing students to complete the test over several sessions may be a better strategy.

2. Provide the opportunity for assistance by allowing the student to write the test in an alternative location with the resource teacher. Another strategy might be to allow a peer to read the essay orally to assist the student in editing.

3. Allow the use of dictionary, thesaurus, spelling computer, or a word processor with a spelling check program.

4. In order to alleviate recall memory difficulties, provide a list of key words or allow students to use the text to refer to content.

5. Allow for teacher interpretation of misunderstood test vocabulary and/or provide feedback during the test.

6. Allow students to use a tape recorder if they have been previously taught how to use one in a test situation.

Scoring

1. Modify the marking scheme to reflect the individual student's strengths and weaknesses:
   - For students with spelling/structural difficulties, the marking scheme should increase points for content and reduce points for style and organization.
   - With respect to content and style, accept responses within the student's level of writing ability. i.e., reduced length of response; grammatical/spelling errors; standard abbreviations.
   - Sample modification:

Content	20	Outline	20
Organization	20	Content	20
Grammatical Precision	10	Organization	5
	50	Grammatical Precision	5
Total	*50*		*50*

2. Provide students with clear evaluation comments related to the original marking scheme.

3. Allow student to review answers orally to extend and elaborate on their written response.

*(Peel, **Book 5**, 1990, pp. 25–26.)*

SAMPLE STRATEGY TO HELP STUDENTS WITH OUTLINING AN ESSAY QUESTION:

Outline
"Hamburger Strategy"

Bun	Topic Sentence
Relish	Individual Ideas
Meat	Facts
Bun	Concluding Sentence

In order to write a good paragraph the writer must first plan it (the ingredients must be collected and prepared), and only then can the paragraph be put together (written). Use the following outline to construct your paragraph.

Topic _____

Topic sentence _____

_____

Ideas and Facts

1. _____

2. _____

3. _____

4. _____

Concluding sentence _____

_____

*(Ontario Ministry of Education, **Handbook for Teachers of Students with Learning Disabilities**, 1986, p. 101.)*

Examples of Modifications to Paper-Pencil Test Items

- tape record the test
- use peers to read questions or scribe responses
- provide relevant formula or descriptions of key words
- give consideration to
    - ◇ use of large print and clear layout
    - ◇ underlining key words or providing alternate key words (e.g. 'tell' rather than 'describe')
    - ◇ providing samples or presenting questions in familiar formats
    - ◇ re-wording the question at the appropriate reading level
    - ◇ indicating suggested time as well as marks
    - ◇ reviewing questions orally prior to the test
- provide students with an organizer for essay questions
- allow access to dictionaries, computer, calculator, thesaurus, word processor and spell checker
- arrange for evaluation to take place in a familiar setting
- prepare the student for the tests by discussing time limits, types of questions and format of tests
- evaluation can recognize improvement

(Saskatchewan Education, 1991, p. 51.)

Alternative Evaluation Techniques for Special Students

Why not consider some of these possibilities?

Oral Tests:	teacher or peer reads questions and/or writes answers
Open Book Test:	use of notes
	if essay questions, teach organization before test
Closed Tests:	without use of notes, short answers, multiple choice, true/false, matching ...
Learning Resource Room:	have student write exams/tests in L.R. room — fewer distractions, easier to extend time, make-up tests
Taped Tests:	student listens and/or responds on tape

Allow use of a dictionary for words other than key content terms

Take-Home Tests

Clarification of Instructions and Questions

Alternative projects rather than written tests

Small Group Tests

Short Quizzes vs. Major Tests

Grading Variations e.g., content vs. spelling

Permit use of a Dictionary

Reduce "language loaded" questions

Spelling concessions for those with severe spelling problems

Use of a Calculator

Partial Marks e.g., right formula chosen with wrong answer

Critique Early Drafts of Papers and encourage follow-up re-writes

Student demonstration or model

Group Presentation

Grade tests on number of items completed rather than total number of items on evaluation

Practical exam

Allow someone to read questions to student

Participation as Part of Evaluation

Practice Exam

Prepare student for Evaluation   e.g., Material covered, Type of evaluation, Expectations, Encouragement

---

For Special Education Students tasks often need to be broken down into small component parts. The student may also need help scheduling him/herself re the time allotted for a particular assignment. For example, an assignment due in four weeks could be broken down into weekly sections to be completed by the student and checked by the teacher. Grading could also be modified to give credit for each part completed.

Evaluation should be a teaching tool — a learning experience.

(Denise Thompson, Workshop notes, London Board of Education.)

2. English as a Second Language Students

> Concern has been expressed ... that young people with certain cultural backgrounds, some indigenous to Canada and some originating in other countries, are being streamed into inappropriate programs before they have time to adjust to the Ontario educational system. It is important ... to review regularly the provisions made for these students to ensure that practices in the schools are consistent with the philosophy of equal educational opportunity.
>
> *(Ministry of Education, "Equal Educational Opportunities for Students", p. 1.)*

Assessment procedures need to be modified for some English as a Second Language/ English Skills Development students. Assessment methods should take into account the cultural and ethnic background and prior experiences of students.

The Ministry of Education and Training in its latest resource document, *Changing Perspectives*, released in July 1993, clearly lists evaluation procedures that should occur:

Evaluation of Student Performance

Evaluation procedures should:

- be clear and purposeful;
- take into consideration problems of adjustment;
- provide for instructions to be given orally when necessary;
- involve a teacher trained in ESL/ESD, FSL or NSL, to ensure that students understand the evaluation process;
- involve clear and constructive reporting;
- distinguish between second-language acquisition needs and content area needs;
- culminate in report cards that are carefully phrased to prevent misinterpretation. Translators should be available to help parents understand what has been written.

---

*(Ministry of Education and Training, **Changing Perspectives**, p. 20.)*

Strategies and materials are needed to challenge the English as a Second Language students while they build on their skills in English.

Evaluation of ESL/ESD Students in Mainstream Classes

Factors Limiting Fair and Informative Assessment and Evaluation:

1. Limited English proficiency hinders student's ability to let you know what he/she knows. His/her cognitive development may be beyond his/her English language skills.

2. Student's lack of experience with some of our methods of teaching and evaluation causes him/her to perform poorly or not at all.

3. Experienced teachers rather accurately predict the learning rate of their students but this does not prepare us for ESL/ESD students whose rates of learning are also affected by irregular and non-predictable speeds of learning English.

To Neutralize These Factors Consider:

- using a **variety** of assessment/evaluation methods. Be sure that students know **what**, **why** and **how** you are assessing.

- **establishing** within a course, the **objectives** that are **Critical**, **Important**, and **Desirable**; then ensuring that more time and weight are given to those deemed Critical and Important than to those labelled Desirable. *(David Pratt)*

- **teaching how** to "do" exams, oral reports, etc. and how to answer specific types of questions. Provide **examples**, **models** and **practice** before actual assessment for grades.

- being **sensitive** and **flexible** re timing of assignments. Let ESL/ESD students see how others perform.

- **modifying** test or exam **procedures** by: *(ESL/ESD Ministry Guideline, 1988)*
  - permitting the use of dictionaries;
  - giving the student extra time;
  - if appropriate, administering part of the test or exam orally, allowing oral responses;
  - permitting the student to write in an ESL/ESD classroom so that the teacher can reword or explain questions.

- **designing** paper and pencil **tests** and exams with:
  - a variety of questions including some that reduce the reading required and some that reduce the writing required, e.g. comparison charts, labelling;
  - a minimum amount of reading required;
  - clearly and succinctly worded instructions and questions;
  - a minimum of idiomatic language;
  - separate marks for content/ideas/arguments and grammar/spelling on essay questions.

- **using the NM** (No Mark) designation if a student is performing well below passing level. Assigning low marks only discourages students. It is preferable to treat them as auditors, until it is clear that they can succeed. *(ESL/ESD Ministry Guideline, 1988)*

- providing meaningful **feedback** to students after evaluation, i.e. designed to provide further learning and a sense of what was learned, through written comments, a test redone on an overhead, etc.

- **weighting** work that the student does near the **end of term** more than that done on his/her first arrival in class.

- weighing **a student's progress** and his/her chances of successfully undertaking a subject at the next grade level against the **possible benefit of repeating** the course. *(Scarborough Secondary Guide, 1990)*

- **acknowledging** student **progress** against benchmarks or standards instead of comparing students, sorting students, or being a gatekeeper.

- **conferring** with a student's ESL/ESD and other teachers when in doubt about a student.

(Mitchell and Posluns, Scarborough, 1993.)

Evaluation of ESL/ESD Students in the Regular Class

Assessment and evaluation of ESL/ESD students is a continuous process which takes into account individual differences in starting points, learning styles, rates of development and experiential and cultural backgrounds.

Assessment and evaluation by the educational team (classroom teacher, ESL/ESD teacher, ISD) will include the use of a variety of methods to provide an ongoing profile for the student's learning to be shared with parents, teachers and administrators.

Individual self-esteem should be the foremost consideration in the evaluation process.

Some Suggested Strategies for Evaluation

- student observation over a period of time
- collection of work done in the classroom
- projects
- presentations
- group work
- informal/intuitive testing
- modified written tests

Other Important Considerations

1. Promoting a non-threatening learning environment will help students relax and become self-confident so that they will learn better and faster.

2. Evaluation should be a collaborative effort in order to achieve an accurate assessment.

3. It takes five to seven years to become language proficient, therefore teachers, students and parents should have realistic expectations in terms of the length of time it takes to learn and fully understand English.

4. Allow ESL/ESD students to progress at their own rate. Some students will learn quickly while others may take a longer time. Being a risk-taker and having self-confidence are influential in how quickly the student will learn a language.

5. The ESL/ESD student's acculturation must be considered when evaluating. If the student is experiencing difficulty with adjustment, they are not working up to their capabilities.

3. Adult Learners

It is important to note that neither Knowles nor Jarvis advocates a specific teaching methodology but rather encourages a humanistic approach which "...may best be summarized by suggesting that both the teacher's role performance and the teaching methods he/she employs should never undermine, but always seek to enhance, the dignity and humanity of the learner: to do less than this is a misuse of the teacher's position, immoral and falls below the high ideals of education".

(Jarvis, 1983, p. 117.)

As many adults return to the classroom to further their education or update existing skills, they bring with them skills, experiences and learning styles that are different from those of adolescents.

- Adults return to the educational environment for many different reasons, but by and large they are **STUDENTS BY CHOICE**. Their goals are very clear and educational choices tend to be made primarily on the basis of what is perceived to be potentially useful to them, usually in the short-term. Returning to school often represents a considerable sacrifice with respect to other priorities. The adult tends to expect this to be reflected in the learning experience.

- Adult learning **NEEDS ARE MORE CONCRETE** than those of children. The theoretical, unless it is a vehicle to practicality, tends to be unsatisfactory.

- Adults have a wealth of **LIFE EXPERIENCE**. This is an advantage to be exploited by the instructor. New information can and should be related to experiences.

- Adults are **MATURE PERSONS**. If not treated as such, their learning experiences will be unsatisfactory.

- Adults are **MORE REALISTIC** than children. Their experiences allow them a greater sense of the possible, the practical, the reasonable. Teaching should be related to previous experience as it facilitates learning, is more meaningful, and more enjoyable.

- Adults **NEED TO EXPERIENCE SUCCESS** — perhaps even more so than do youngsters, at least initially. Typically, the adult is rather unsure about his or her ability as a learner and needs to be "convinced" that this insecurity is ill-founded.

- Adults tend to have relatively **RIGID PATTERNS OF THOUGHT AND BEHAVIOUR**. This tendency needs to be challenged (in a non-threatening manner) so as to facilitate a meaningful learning experience.

- Adults are **LESS TOLERANT** of non-meaningful learning. Objectives are relatively clear for adults and non related experiences will not be successful.

- Adults tend to have a relatively **WELL ESTABLISHED POSITIVE SELF-CONCEPT**. The task is to create a situation which will allow them to translate this rather positive sense of self to the educational setting.

- Adults want to be **SELF-DIRECTED**. This is a developmental phenomenon and is a function of the maturation process. This need must be addressed in many ways, but particularly with respect to strategies and outcomes.

- Adults have **UNIQUE PHYSICAL REQUIREMENTS**. They need more light than do children. Temperature should be constant, and seemingly minor issues such as physical comfort (seats, tables, etc.) need to be carefully considered.

- Adults **NEED MORE TIME** to perform certain tasks. Reaction time can be slower. Physiological efficiency (hearing, sight, etc.) diminishes with age, and the learning "equipment" (memory, etc.) tends to be "rusty".

*(OSSTF, **The Journey**, 1988, p. 7.)*

Adults are not a captive audience, in fact, they will simply leave if their needs are not being met. Due consideration must be given to the following when planning assessments for adults:

life experiences
self-concept
knowledge
specific skills
attitudes
educational background
physical condition
learning style
health
home environment
culture
religion
interests and hobbies

*(OSSTF, **The Journey**, 1988, p. 8.)*

Many of the assessment methodologies that have proven successful with adults are now being used in adolescent classrooms. The methodologies cited in this chapter can be used for adults and adapted where necessary to meet the needs of individual students as you would in any classroom.

Adult Learning Principles

1. Learning is a lifelong process.
2. Adults must feel that they are voluntary learners who have something to offer.
3. Adults come to the learning situation with considerable and varied prior experiences. This prior experience is not only a valuable and reliable resource, but also provides the frame of reference which first screens new information.
4. Adults learn most productively when they are physically, mentally and emotionally well. Where age or disability jeopardizes progress, they must control the modification process.
5. Adults learn best when they are personally involved in the entire learning process. This would include defining their needs, assessing personal competencies, setting goals and objectives, and choosing course content, teaching strategies, evaluation tools and resources. With ownership comes commitment. Generally this is established through discussion and negotiation with the teacher. At this point a relationship of trust and respect must be established.
6. The content of successful adult learning activities reflects current needs and social roles. Learning activities grow out of a need to change circumstances in the immediate present.
7. Adults will learn only what they perceive to be relevant and important to their self-concept.
8. It is important that adults learn how they learn best.
9. Adults are generally well motivated when they initiate a learning activity and respond best to assistance and support.
10. Adults' perception of the success of learning outcomes relates directly to the personal changes experienced as a result of the learning activity. Of lesser import is the evaluation by the teacher, or the standard set by the system.

*(OSSTF, **The Journey**, 1988, p. 23.)*

4. Tutoring Programs

Peer Tutoring (Sir Frederick Banting Secondary School, London) and the Tutoring One-to-One: Reading, Writing, and Relating (Frontenac Secondary School, Kingston) are only two examples of tutoring programs that can assist students either in the classroom or outside of the classroom. Not only will the tutor strengthen his or her skills already mastered but the experience of helping and working with a peer is very beneficial. Tutors assist students with work in subject areas e.g. reading of subject texts, class assignments, and homework). They also act as role models, mentors, and confidants which can only have a positive effect on students' self esteem and overall retention rates.

Further Information

Teachers may wish to refer to other chapters in this resource book for more information on modifying assessment for students.

References

Jarvis, P., <u>Adult and Continuing Education: Theory and Practice</u>, London: Croon Helm, 1983.

Knowles, M.S., "Andragogy, Not Pedagogy!", <u>Adult Leadership</u>, 1968, 16(10), pp. 350–386.

Ministry of Education and Training, <u>Changing Perspectives</u>: A Resource Guide for Antiracist and Ethnocultural – Equity Education, Toronto: Queen's Printer for Ontario, 1992.

Ministry of Education, "Equal Educational Opportunities for Students", Policy/ Program Memorandum No. 84, October 23, 1985.

Ministry of Education, <u>Basic English OAIP — Handbook</u>, Toronto: Ministry of Education, 1990.

Ministry of Education, <u>Handbook for Teachers of Students with Learning Disabilities</u>, Toronto, Ontario: Ministry of Education, 1986.

OSSTF, <u>The Journey: Helping Adults Learn</u>, 1988.

Peel Board of Education, <u>Looking at Measurement, Book 5, (Adapting tests and assignments for exceptional students)</u>, Mississauga, Ontario: Peel Board of Education, 1990.

Saskatchewan Education, <u>Student Evaluation</u>, December 1991.

Waterloo County Board of Education, <u>Assessment for Learning</u>, 1993.

Waterloo County Board of Education, <u>Windows on Learning</u>, 1993.

Chapter 8
Grading and Reporting

Grading and Reporting

> "Grading is the cornerstone of how our educational system operates."
>
> *(Spady, 1991, p. 39.)*

> "Grading — the world of myth, mystery and magic."
>
> *(Stiggins, Workshop presentation, May 1993.)*

> "Reporting — the task is a perplexing one because the evidence of learning and development must be presented on a very brief report form that is understandable to a variety of users."
>
> *(Gronlund and Linn, 1990, p. 427.)*

These quotations summarize the realities of much of educational practice at all levels. Grading and reporting have three main functions: instructional, administrative and communication. The focus of this chapter is how we can adapt our current grading and reporting practices, many of which are effective and efficient, to better serve the goal of successful learning by all students.

With this in mind, it is important to consider how a professional teacher should approach these activities. Pratt, in *Curriculum: Design and Development*, suggests the following:

> The instructor who develops clear and worthwhile objectives, valid and reliable measures of performance, and a sound and relevant grading system; who commits these design variables to paper and has them formally approved; and who can show that the design has been adhered to in arriving at the evaluative decisions made: such an educator is in a position that is both professionally and politically secure.
>
> *(Pratt, 1980, p. 259.)*

Grading and reporting can be very frustrating because there are so many factors to consider; there are no simple answers. Grading and reporting cannot be separated from assessment and evaluation. If learning outcomes are clearly articulated and a variety of assessment methodologies used, then grading and reporting require the summarizing, judging and presenting of information in a form that is understandable to students, parents, teachers, counsellors, administrators, colleges, universities, and the business community.

> The use of the term "outcomes" in this chapter refers to clearly defined demonstrations by students of what they know, are able to do and show what they value. The focus on outcomes is **not** intended as a general reference to Outcomes-Based Education as proposed by Spady and others or the outcomes included in *The Common Curriculum* published by the Ontario Ministry of Education and Training.

The summarizing of assessment and evaluation information and the communicating of this information is an essential part of the process of student learning. In this process "we have to break step with the drive to arrive at single summary statistics for student performance". *(Wolf, Bixby, Glenn and Gardner, Project Zero, Harvard University)* What teachers must seek to do is to provide as clear a picture of student learning as possible while fulfilling the purposes of grading and reporting.

Grading

Perspectives on Grading

WALNUT COVE

© 1993 King Features Syndicate, Inc.

Grading is complicated:	Grades are a shorthand form of communication and unless there is clear understanding of their meaning, they give mixed messages, which depend as much or more, on the receivers' perceptions as on the senders' intentions.
Grading is emotional:	It is important to recognize that teachers, students and parents react differently to grades; grading is value-laden; it is not a dispassionate scientific act.
Grading is required:	Teachers have to respond to Ministry, Board and school policy grading requirements. Although the advocates of transformational outcomes-based education would like to see the elimination of grades, this is not likely to happen in the near future in Ontario or other jurisdictions.
Grading has little research basis:	There has been surprisingly little research and very little teacher training in grading practices. Most teachers rely on their own experience.
Grading cannot be based on a single best practice:	There are parameters or principles (some of which will be described below) which all should follow, but within these parameters teachers have a great deal of flexibility to adapt their grading practices to the needs of each of their classes (students).
Grading, when faulty, can do serious damage to students — and teachers:	Grading which appears to be unfair to students can seriously damage the motivation, self-concept and achievement of students and irreparably harm the relationship between student(s) and teacher(s).

Ingredients in Grades

The main purpose of grades (and reports) as outlined above is to promote learning through high quality communication between teachers and students, parents, employers, and colleges and universities. In order to do this it is vital that only the most appropriate student characteristics be factored in to the report card grade. Typically, report card grades are an amalgam of information on achievement, ability or aptitude, effort and attitude. Some of the arguments for and against each of these ingredients are included in a chart on page 341 . On balance, the negatives outweigh the positives on all the ingredients except achievement. Consider the following statements:

Letter grades are likely to be most meaningful and useful when they represent achievement only. If they are contaminated by such extraneous factors as effort, amount of work completed (rather than quality of the work), personal conduct, and so on, their interpretation will become hopelessly confused. When letter grades combine various aspects of pupil development, not only do they lose their meaningfulness as a measure of achievement, but they also suppress information concerning other important aspects of development. A letter grade of B, for example, may represent average achievement with little effort and some disciplinary infractions. Only by making the letter grade as pure a measure of achievement as possible and reporting on these other aspects separately can we hope to improve our descriptions of pupil learning and development.

(Gronlund and Linn, 1990, p. 45.)

"Of the factors examined, the only one that can be justified as a basis for determining a student's report card grade is academic achievement. Each of the others — aptitude, effort and attitude — carries with it sufficient definitional and procedural measurement problems to cause it to add too much "noise" to our communication system to justify its combination with achievement to determine a report card grade.

Besides, if we measure each factor separately and factor it into the grading equation, it may be receiving more weight than we think. A student's actual achievement is a direct function of that student's effort and attitude. Those who try harder and have a positive attitude probably learn more. So, in effect, each of these factors has influenced the grade if we grade in terms of achievement alone. If we estimate each and factor it in again as a separate contributor when we calculate the grade, have we not considered it twice — given it double the weight?

Let us hasten to add that our position is not that we do not value strong seriousness of purpose and a positive attitude on the part of the student. We value these attributes very much. Teachers should strive to gather the best possible data on these student characteristics and they should strive to provide the clearest possible feedback on them to their students. But decision makers all the way along the student's schooling road need at least relatively pure information on student achievement if they are to act in the student's best interest. In fact, students themselves need that achievement information if they are to see themselves accurately and act in their own best interests."

(Stiggins, 1989, p. 22.)

INGREDIENTS IN STUDENT GRADES

Advantage/Arguments for	Disadvantage/Arguments against
ACADEMIC ACHIEVEMENT	
Represents the primary valued outcome	Some outcomes difficult to measure
Translates into clear target	Many teachers lack assessment experience
Can be measured well	We value more outcomes
Life expects achievement	Few rewards for perennial low achievers
	Differing definitions add noise
APTITUDE/ABILITY	
Can individualize instruction	Definition unclear
Motivates teacher with promise of success with all students	Classroom assessment very difficult
Under achiever is identified for special attention	Achievement/aptitude mix to define over and under achievement unclear
Some reward to low achievers	Can label students unfairly
	Can harm motivation of perennial high achiever
	Different definitions and weights in grade computation add "noise" to the grade meaning signal
EFFORT	
Represents a valued outcome	Definitions differ widely
Provides some reward to low achiever	Difficult to measure well for all
Appears to maximize motivation	Students can manipulate it
Can reward risk taking (innovative training that falls short)	Differing definitions and weights in grade computation add "noise" to the grade meaning signal
	Teacher controls who participates
	Personality traits come into play
ATTITUDE	
Effective tool for classroom management and behaviour control	Nature of valued attitudes often unclear
Provides some reward for perennial low achiever	Difficult to measure well for all
	Students can manipulate it
	Differing definitions and weights in grade computation make the grade meaning unclear
	Behavioural evidence of positive attitude varies

(Adapted from Grading Workshop, Northwest Regional Educational Laboratory, Portland, Oregon.)

If grades are to serve as clear indicators of achievement they must be based on valid measures of achievement; so, there must be alignment between learning outcomes and assessment methodologies (see Chapter 4) and there must be appropriate use of assessment information.

In Ontario, the ingredients to be factored in to students' final marks are often specified or suggested in Ministry guidelines; e.g.

Classwork	20%
Practicum Experiences	15%
Tests	15%
Examination	30%
Independent Study Project	20%
	100%

(Family Studies: Intermediate and Senior Division and OAC, 1987, p. 106.)

(Note: All ingredients in the above table are measurable.)

Where such specific requirements do not exist (e.g. the Transition Years Grades 7–9), teachers should work towards having their report card grades be an accurate summary of student **achievement** of the learning outcomes specified for a course, i.e. what students know, can do and show that they value.

An example of this approach would be to divide the outcomes for a course into

(i)   the critical outcomes which are essential for **all** students,

(ii)   the important outcomes (to be attained by **most** students), and

(iii) the desirable outcomes (to be attained by **some** students).

Activities could then be classified as **foundation** activities — for the critical outcomes — and **extension** activities — for the important and desirable outcomes. Students would be required to **satisfactorily complete** all foundation activities for which they would receive a grade of say 60%. (Satisfactory completion would be clearly defined in a rubric or criteria checklist for each activity.) The student's final grade would be determined by adding the mark (60%) for foundation activities to a mark for extension activities. The mark for extension activities could be obtained by using one of these two options.

Option A

Final Grade

60%:   Satisfactory completion of all foundation activities

70%:   Satisfactory completion of all foundation activities plus satisfactory completion of 25% of extension activities

80%:   Satisfactory completion of all foundation activities plus satisfactory completion of 50% of extension activities

100%: Satisfactory completion of all foundation activities plus satisfactory completion of at least 75% of extension activities

---

or

Option B

> 60%: Satisfactory completion of all foundation activities plus up to 40% for extension activities depending on the number completed and the quality of work.
>
> For the extension activities mark, the following approach could be used: add the percentage marks for all extension activities completed; divide by the total number of extension activities; multiply the resulting percentage by 0.4. This mark out of 40 would then be added to the foundation activity mark to obtain the final grade.
>
> *For example: Student X*
> Course (unit) y   # of extension activities 5
> Marks on extension units completed: 75%, 85%, 65% = 225
> 225% ÷ 5 = 45%; 45% x 0.4 = 18%; 18% + 60% = 78% final grade
>
> \# extension activities   factor for 40% weighting
>
> *(Note: There are many possible variations of this approach.)*

A sample tracking sheet for using this approach for a unit of Grade 9/10 Geography can be found on page 344. This material has been adapted from the work of Fraser Cartwright at Middlefield Collegiate Institute, York Region Board of Education.

Proponents of transformational outcome-based education believe that grades should not be used but they acknowledge that they are required by most jurisdictions. Where an outcomes-based approach is being used and grades must be given, the following approach is recommended:

Culminating Outcomes   60% (all must be done well)
Enabling Outcomes (tests)   30%
Daily Stuff (classwork)   10%

(Adapted from The High Success Network, 1992.)

A significant implication of focusing on outcomes is that students must be given ample time to demonstrate their ability to achieve the specified outcome. This means that teachers must have a very flexible approach to time requirements; examples of this are provided in the two calendars on page 345. It also means:

(i)   judgments should be deferred; marks should be recorded in pencil so that the final demonstration is the one that counts;

(ii)   opportunities for second chance testing/demonstrations must be provided; and

(iii)   marks for second and subsequent attempts should **not** be averaged with the first mark.

TRACKING SHEET

UNIT: HUMAN DIVERSITY	
Foundation Activities Necessary for Critical Outcomes	*Satisfactory Completion*
F1 Human diversity statements	
F2 Pie graph of classroom diversity	
F3 Population distribution terms	
F4 Native peoples cultural changes organizer	
F5 Native issues jigsaw	
F6 Racism — critical words matrix	
F7 Race equity rules	
F8 Immigration policy	
F9 Report on "Portraits of Canadians"	
F10 Wrap up activity — letter, poem, etc.	
FINAL FOUNDATION CHECK *(60%)*	

Extension Activities for Important and Desirable Outcomes	*Satisfactory Completion*	*Mark*
E1 Key elements of human diversity		
E2 Interview: The immigrant experience		
E3 Population distribution — additional graphs		
E4 Personal identity model for culture		
E5 Defining new immigration policy		
	% complete	*% total*
FINAL EXTENSION TOTAL		

Assess for Success

ANY MONTH

SUN	MON	TUE	WED	THU	FRI	SAT
	1 Unit 2 First Opportunity	**2** Start Unit 3	**3**	**4**	**5**	**6**
7	**8**	**9**	**10** Unit 2 Last Opportunity	**11**	**12** End of grading period	**13**
14	**15**	**16**	**17**	**18**	**19**	**20**
21	**22**	**23** Unit 3 First Opportunity	**24**	**25**	**26**	**27**
28	**29**	**30**	**31** Unit 3 Continuing Opportunity			

YEAR END

SUN	MON	TUE	WED	THU	FRI	SAT
				1	**2**	**3**
4	**5**	**6**	**7**	**8**	**9**	**10**
11	**12**	**13**	**14**	**15**	**16**	**17**
18	**19**	**20**	**21**	**22**	**23** *End*	**24**
28	**29**	**30**	**31**			

The Culminating Assessment

N.B. The culminating assessment could be final examinations or demonstrations.

(Adapted from material from The High Success Network.)

Sources of Information

The next issue in the development of a grading system is what source of information should be used to assess student achievement. Current practice usually involves some or all of the following:

- paper-and-pencil tests
- instructional questions
- daily seatwork and homework assignments
- performance assessment and personal communication (i.e. assessment based on observation and judgment) and
- intuitions and feelings about a learner.

Each of these five options is a legitimate way of assessing achievement as long as quality procedures are followed in gathering data. The question that must be addressed here is: "Can each method contribute useful and dependable data to the ongoing achievement record that serves as a basis for determining the individual's report card grade?" *(Stiggins, 1989, p. 24)*

Careful examination of the reasons for and against including each of these options in grades (see page 347), leads to the conclusion that it is appropriate to include information from:

- paper-and-pencil tests (when these have been carefully developed and marked)
- daily assignments (when these assignments are designed for assessment and **not** for practice and when students have had an opportunity to practice before assessment), and
- observation and judgments (when these are based on carefully developed criteria and rubrics).

It is inappropriate to include information from instructional questions and intuitions and feelings. Information from the last two options is valuable and should be used in broad-based reporting but should not be included in report card grades.

SOURCES OF INFORMATION FOR GRADES

Arguments for Inclusion in Grades	Arguments Against Inclusion in Grades
ASSIGNMENTS	
Occur frequently	Assignments are for practice
Closely linked to instruction	Others may do the work
Provides motivation to practice	Can encourage fragmented learning
Controls for anxiety present with tests	Creates paper load for teacher
INSTRUCTIONAL QUESTIONS	
Closely linked to instruction	Performance confounded with personality traits
Help poor test takers demonstrate achievement	Difficult to sample all students
Highly correlated to test performance	Record keeping complex and demanding
Can follow-up to examine thinking	Teachers control opportunities
PAPER-AND-PENCIL TESTS	
Can be objective and efficient	Sometimes are not sufficient
Reflect valued outcomes	Many teachers lack expertise in their development and use
Provide equal opportunity for all	Many text-embedded tests lack quality
Result in a visible, tangible record	Many extraneous factors can influence performance
OBSERVATION AND JUDGMENT, AND PERSONAL COMMUNICATION	
Only valid measure of many valued achievement outcomes	Subjective judgment risks bias
Can measure complex outcomes	Many teachers lack expertise in development and use
Can make students the evaluators	Often criteria are elusive
	Often not as efficient as other options
INTUITIONS AND FEELINGS	
Often based on extensive knowledge of student and thus are correct	Subjective judgment risks bias
Provides rewards to perennial low achiever	Difficult to define vague criteria
	Differing definitions make meaning of grade unclear

*(Adapted from Stiggins, R.J., **Developing Sound Grading Practices**, Classroom Assessment Training, Northwest Regional Educational Laboratory, Portland, Oregon.)*

Information for Grading

1. Grade Distribution:

Grading on a Curve (norm-referenced)

and

Grading on a Preset Standard (criterion-referenced)

Norm-referenced assessment compares students and ranks them, usually on a normal or bell curve.

Criterion-referenced assessment attempts to measure students individually in relation to a set of learning outcomes.

In Chapter 5 of *The Numbers Game*, King and Peart point out that many parents want to know how well their children are doing compared to other students. This desire for comparison with other children the same age is understandable. However, as Pratt points out:

> Relative standing (norm-referenced assessment) is more useful if the standard of comparison is a large group, for example, all people of that age in the school district or the province, rather than merely a specific classroom which may itself be quite atypical.
>
> *(Pratt, 1980, p. 115.)*

Another viewpoint on grade distribution is that

> "there is no pedagogical, psychological or scientific reason to assume in advance that achievement will be distributed in any way — whether normally or skewed in some direction — before instruction begins."
>
> *(Stiggins, Workshop presentation, May 1993.)*

What is important is what students have learned. Criterion-referenced assessment at the classroom and school level provides opportunity for every student to demonstrate learning by attaining the stated outcomes and, consequently, to experience personal success.

Teachers and administrators, parents and students are encouraged to consider carefully the advantages and disadvantages of criterion-referenced assessment and norm-referenced assessment.

(See page 349.)

In *The Numbers Game*, King and Peart refer to the tension that exists between evaluating in a way that will increase learning and evaluating in a way that will maximize the differentiation of students (i.e. the requirements of post-secondary institutions).

GRADE DISTRIBUTION

Grading on a Curve (Norm-Referenced) *and*
Grading on a Preset Standard (Criterion-Referenced)

GRADING ON A CURVE (NORM-REFERENCED)

Advantages

- meaning of the grade is clear
- standard is fixed for all in a single group
- competition is maximized (motivation?)
- "test" difficulty does not effect distribution of grades

Disadvantages

- comparison group (classroom, county, province) is unclear
- percentage of students receiving each grade is arbitrary
- fails to reward improved teaching and learning
- capable students may be penalized
- competition and co-operation are out of balance
- students, however good, are likely to feel unsuccessful
- works against the self-image of low and high achievers
- guarantees that a significant number of students are below average
- norms don't provide a standard — they only sort
- rank is of little value in diagnosing need

GRADING ON A PRESET STANDARD (CRITERION-REFERENCED)

Advantages

- meaning of the grade is clear
- all students can achieve the announced standards
- increases self-esteem as more students are likely to experience success
- students have a clearer picture of what they know and what they can do
- valuable in terms of diagnosing needs
- over time, leads to better teaching and ultimately more success for students
- technically simple to compute

Disadvantages

- cutoff scores are arbitrary
- difficulty of assessment influences student success

(Adapted from Grading Workshop, Classroom Assessment Training, Northwest Regional Educational laboratory, Portland, Oregon.)

2. Record Keeping and Weighting

Any data which is to be included in grade computation must be recorded carefully and accurately.

Grading which follows the principles and practices suggested in this book will require the combining of marks into a composite index of achievement in the form of a weighted average. Using spreadsheets or gradebook software, it is relatively easy to ensure that the major components (e.g., classwork, examinations, tests, independent study, etc.) receive their intended weights, i.e., the weight which reflects the importance of the assessment activity to the learning outcome (or unit or component). However, **within** each of these components it is critical that the marks be recorded on a consistent or **common scale**. The errors that occur when this is not done are illustrated in the table on page 351. The simplest common scale to use is to convert all marks to a percentage mark and then use the weighting factor to create the weighted composite grade. In order to record marks in this way, it would be necessary to have a mark book that looks something like this:

Component	"Tests" or Outcome 1								
Assessment Method	Unit 1 Test			Performance #1			Unit 2 Test		
Weight	2			4			1.5		
Raw scores and weighted scores *Student*	*Marked out of 20*	*Mark as a %*	*Weighted mark out of 200*	*Marked out of 50*	*Mark as a %*	*Weighted mark out of 400*	*Marked out of 80*	*Mark as a %*	*Weighted mark out of 150*
Bill	18	90	180						
Joan	8	40	80						
Sylvia	20	100	200	20	40	160	60	75	112.5
William	10	50	100	50	100	400	40	50	75

In the above example, Sylvia and William have the same raw score total (100) but when the intended weighting is applied to common scale (%) marks, William's total is 575/750 (77%) while Sylvia's total is 472.5/750 (63%). This is what was intended by weighting the performance as being more important than the unit tests.

THE IMPORTANCE OF WEIGHTING GRADES PROPERLY

Unit on "X" – Assessment –
Paper and Pencil Test and Performance Assessment (Speech, project, etc.)

	Betty				**Bill**		
	Test		Performance		Test		Performance
Using Raw Scores							
Marked Out Of	40		20		40		20
Weight	1		2		1		2
Betty's Raw Score	10		20	Bill's Raw Score	40		5
Using Raw Scores	10	50/80	20 (x2)		40	50/80	5 (x2)
Betty's Unit % Mark		62%		Bill's Unit % Mark		62%	
Using Weighted Scores							
Mark Recorded Out Of	40		80		40		80
Betty's Recorded Mark	10	90/120	80	Bill's Recorded Mark	40	60/120	20
Betty's Unit % Mark		75%		Bill's Unit % Mark		50%	
Using Common Scale	25/100	225/300	100/100 (x2)		100/100	150/300	25/100 (x2)
Betty's Unit % Mark		75%		Bill's Unit % Mark		50%	

It can be seen that Betty scores well on the performance and poorly on the test while Bill's scores are the reverse. When the weighting factors are (incorrectly) applied to the raw scores both Betty and Bill receive the same percentage grade. However, when the raw scores are converted to a common scale (%) and the weighting factors applied, Betty's grade is 75% while Bill's is 50%. This is the result that was intended by giving the performance double the weight of the test.

3. How Much Data

Another critical aspect of grading is how much data to include in grades. In general, secondary teachers in Ontario mark everything (or almost everything) that students do in the classroom. This approach has had two major results:

1. a huge (and at times unmanageable) marking load for teachers, and

2. a massive "does this count" syndrome amongst students. Many students have developed this attitude that it is only the mark that counts, not the learning and how it may contribute to their growth.

   It should be recognized that this "mark everything" approach is both unnecessary and undesirable. Any assessment involves a sampling of student performance but the sample assessed has to be only large enough so that a valid generalization can be made about the entire domain that has been sampled. Stiggins, *1989, p. 37*, provides another way of deciding "how much" when he writes

> "you have gathered enough information about the achievement of each student when you can fairly and accurately guess how they would perform given another set of similar exercises to perform".

This means that teachers do not have to "mark" everything that students do. **Almost everything that students do should be assessed in some way, but not all assessment should be for grades.** Assessment of some activities may be diagnostic or formative and may focus on only one aspect of the student activity. This approach to assessment will significantly reduce the marking load on teachers and should reduce the "does this count" syndrome. It is vitally important that students develop an understanding that some activities are for **practice** and that marking their best effort on such activities will assist them greatly in performing at their best on later summative assessments. This approach is clearly consistent with the coaching model.

4. Borderline Grades

When students' grades are near an important borderline (e.g. pass/fail, honours/not honours), teachers often use such characteristics as effort or intuition to raise or lower the grade. Since such practices will not stand up to public scrutiny, teachers should encourage students to hold "in reserve" one or two pieces of work which have not been included in the grade. If reconsideration of a borderline grade is necessary, the work held in reserve can then be marked and the teacher has educationally defensible data on which to base a decision to raise or lower a final grade. Students, parents and administrators must know that this practice is in place for determining borderline grades.

> "Sound grades are our most critical responsibility."
> *(Stiggins, 1989, p. 54.)*

Grades are so important to the lives of our students that it is critical that grading be carried out in a fair and open manner. With this in mind these guidelines adapted from Gronlund and Linn *(1990, p. 443)*, should be followed:

GUIDELINES FOR GRADING

1. Describe grading procedures to students at the beginning of instruction.

2. Make it clear to students that grades will be based on achievement only. (Do **not** lower a grade for lateness, poor effort or misbehaviour.)

3. Explain how other characteristics (effort, participation, attitude, etc.) will be reported.

4. Relate the grading procedure to the intended learning outcomes. (Credit for a course should **not** be granted until a student has achieved, at least, the critical outcomes.)

5. Properly record evidence from quality assessment instruments as the basis for assigning grades.

6. Properly weight the various types of achievement (assessment) included in the grade computation.

7. Use absolute or pre-set standards to distribute grades.

8. Provide second chance assessment opportunities for students.

9. Defer judgment — grade in pencil.

10. Sample student performance — don't mark everything!

Finally, it is important that we not expect too much of grades. Over-reliance on grades as communication vehicles or as motivators will not be beneficial. For effective communication, broad-based reporting with detailed learner profiles is needed. For true motivation, engaging activities which get students involved in the learning process are the keys to success.

Reporting

> "If instructional objectives have been clearly defined in performance terms and relevant tests and other evaluation procedures have been properly used, marking and reporting become a matter of summarizing the results and presenting them in understandable form."
>
> *(Gronlund and Linn, 1990, p. 429.)*

> "There is little doubt that the convenience of the single mark in administrative work has been a major factor in retarding the development of more comprehensive and useful progress reports."
>
> *(Gronlund and Linn, 1990, p. 429.)*

As Gronlund and Linn suggest, the main focus of reporting should be the improvement of student learning. To promote effective learning, a report must;

1. clarify instructional outcomes
2. indicate strengths and weaknesses
3. provide information about personal and social development
4. contribute to motivation

Such a report would have to be much more comprehensive than the typical Ontario secondary school report which provides a numerical mark and one or two computerized comments. This comprehensive report would be much better suited to ensuring the attainment of the three main purposes of reporting — instruction, administration, and communication.

Purposes of Reporting

A. Instructional Use

Effective learning is more likely to take place if students receive feedback from a variety of assessment and evaluation methodologies. Their progress needs to be monitored carefully and focused for them at regular intervals. They need to be told how they are doing in a clear and helpful manner. A well-designed report can fulfill this function by systematically summarizing student progress, identifying strengths and weaknesses in learning, and suggesting remedial or enrichment activities. Reporting that provides specific results in terms of achievement, and is seen as an opportunity to focus on specific activities for growth and development can motivate students to improve and expand their learning. In addition, reporting that provides an opportunity for student self-assessment is desirable because it reinforces the commitment to development of student learning.

B. Administrative and Guidance Uses

Administrative uses include:

- determining promotion and graduation
- awarding honours
- reporting to other schools/prospective employers

Guidance uses include:
- helping students with educational plans
- helping students with career plans
- updating OSR's
- reporting to post-secondary institutions

C. Communication Uses

REPORTING TO PARENTS (GUARDIANS)

Reports should provide parents with a comprehensive learner profile. They should help parents understand how well their son or daughter is achieving the intended learning outcomes of a program and, in particular, identifying strengths, weaknesses and special needs. Purposeful reports enable parents to provide support and encouragement as needed.

There are many important functions served by reporting that point to the need for more elaborate report cards than those currently employed at the secondary level. Marks are useful for administrative functions and are required for post-secondary admissions. However, letter or numerical grades should be supported by the type of information needed to provide effective learning for students and better communication with parents.

REPORTING FORMATS

"Marks plus comments" Format

The letter grade/numerical grade plus computerized comments is the standard reporting format in Ontario secondary schools. Supplementary anecdotal reports are often encouraged. In secondary schools, common reporting practice includes an interim or early report, mid-year or mid-semester report and a final report, as well as opportunities for parent-teacher conferences. This is widely regarded as providing good quality information on student achievement given the many constraints faced by teachers, not the least of which is time. However, if greater attention is to be paid to promoting more effective learning through improved assessment, evaluation and reporting procedures, this format will have to be expanded to include more information.

Expanded Formats

The typical expanded format reporting system retains the use of letter grades or numbers and supplements the marks with checklists or rating scales of outcomes as well as anecdotal comments. Often there are several sections including the learner profile (effort, attitude, personal skills and development), subject achievement, anecdotal comments and self-assessment.

The expanded format makes it possible to report a grade that measures **achievement related to essential subject outcomes only**. Personal characteristics should be assessed separately; this type of reporting provides ample opportunity for detailed information on these characteristics. There appears to be four expanded format reporting systems that are evolving:

(A) a single document which includes subjects with the focus on comments, not the learner profile (pp. 356, 357)
(B) a single document which includes subjects with the focus on the learner profile
(C) a document for each subject with focus on the learner profile (pp. 359, 360)
(D) a document with learning areas to focus the learner profile (pp. 361, 362)

The following report card formats are generalized samples based on actual report cards and experimental report card frameworks developed in Frontenac County, Durham Region and Scarborough.

TYPE A SAMPLE

The Board of Education for the City of _____
Student Progress Report
First Term (Semester) Dec. 18, 1993

School Name _____

Address _____

Home Form _____   Student Number _____

Subject Teacher	Classes Missed		Lates	First	Second	Third	Final
LANGUAGE							
ENG 1W1 01 ENGLISH ENGLISH Gr. 9	2				70–74		75–79
Creative writing assignments are completed with a great deal of enthusiasm. Reading results this term have been outstanding and show particular strength in comprehension. Maintains a high standard of achievement. Knowledge (E) Skills (M) Values (M)							
FSF 1W2 03 FRENCH FRENCH Gr. 9	2				60–64		65–69
This student is a joy to have in class. Knowledge (M) Skills (M) Values (M)							
ARTS							
AMS 1W1 01 ARTS MUSIC–STRINGS Gr. 9	2				75–79		75–79
This student enjoys this form of self expression. Treats equipment with respect and sets a good example for others. A broad general knowledge in Music has been a valuable asset to the achievements made this Term. Knowledge (M) Skills (E) Values (E)							
AMV 1W1 01 ARTS MUSIC–VOCAL Gr. 9	2				85–89		90–95
A most responsible and conscientious student. This student has maintained an exceptionally high standard in all phases of this program. The student demonstrates a creative confident approach to the work. Knowledge (E) Skills (E) Values (E)							
SELF AND SOCIETY							
PHF 1W2 04 PHYS. ED. PHYS. & HEALTH Gr. 9	2				55–59		60–64
More self-discipline is needed to co-operate in group situations. Has proven capable in achieving good results in a strong effort during Track and Field units. Knowledge (M) Skills (M) Values (N)							
MATHEMATICS, SCIENCE AND TECHNOLOGY							
BKI 1W1 01 BUSINESS KEYBOARDING 1 Gr. 9	9				50–54		50–54
Frequent absences have hindered progress. This student is passing; however is capable of achieving a higher standard. We hope to see an improvement in marks next term. Knowledge (M) Skills (M) Values (N)							
MAT 1W2 02 MATHEMATICS MATHEMATICS Gr. 9	2				65–69		65–69
Estimated mark. New student in school. Knowledge (M) Skills (M) Values (N)							
SNC 1W2 02 SCIENCE SCIENCE Gr. 9	2				75–79		75–79
The student's broad knowledge in Science has been a valuable asset in the achievement this term. The student has an inquiring mind and a disciplined approach to all work. A very talented student. Knowledge (E) Skills (E) Values (E)							
Total Absences/Lates	23		5	As at: Dec. 21, 1993			

Each subject class could have up to four teacher comments. Each teacher comment could have up to seventy-five characters. Each school could have up to nine hundred and ninety-nine different teacher comments. Each subject class could also have the "Knowledge, Skills, Values" with the "E", "M", or "N" evaluation for each (see explanation above).

Knowledge: Key ideas, concepts and content outlined in the subject curriculum guideline.

Skills: Abilities related to the performance of mental and/or physical tasks as outlined in the subject curriculum guideline.

Values: Qualities that individuals and groups consider important. Values influence attitudes, decisions and behaviours.

LEGEND

E – Exceeds Expectations
M – Meets Expectations
N – Has Not Yet Met Expectations

This area is reserved for up to four placement comments. Each placement comment could have up to seventy-five characters. Each school could have up to nine hundred and ninety-nine different placement comments.

This area is reserved for up to four general comments. Each general comment could have up to nine hundred and ninety-nine different general comments.

This area for mailing address

For further information about this report please contact Student Services at _____

_____

Principal

SELF EVALUATION

A Strength: _____

A Concern: _____

A Goal for Self Improvement: _____

Student: _____   Teacher: _____

ADDITIONAL STAFF COMMENTS

Staff: _____

TO PARENTS OR GUARDIANS AND STUDENTS

This copy of the report card should be retained for future reference. The original or an exact copy has been placed in the Ontario Student Record (OSR) folder in respect of the student and will be retained for five years after the student retires from school. Every effort has been made to ensure that all entries are a clear indication of the achievement of the student. If you wish to review the information contained in the OSR folder, please contact the principal. Each student and the parent(s) or guardian(s) of a student who is not an adult are entitled to have access to the student's OSR.

ATTENDANCE

Regular attendance is essential to the learning process, and when frequent absences occur, learning experiences are lost and cannot be entirely regained.

Students who habitually miss class will suffer in the evaluation process because their participation and achievement cannot be fully assessed.

Where attendance has been identified as an essential component of a course and where a student, with his/her parents has been appropriately counselled and provided with support and direction to promote regular attendance in the course, and where the student is still unwilling to attend regularly, such a student will normally fail to achieve a pass.

EXPLANATION OF LETTER GRADES WHERE USED

Where Letter Grades are used, the following evaluation code applies

Code Letter	Percentage Attained
A	80–100
B	70–79
C	60–69
D	50–59
E	Less than 50
NM	No Mark Available

Some schools may use A+ to indicate 90–100%; and D– to indicate 50%

Assessment, Evaluation and Reporting for Successful Learning

TYPE B SAMPLE

	Student:		Student Number:				
	Date:		Report Period:				

SUBJECT	English	Geography	French	Mathematics	Science	Technology/ Family Studies	Physical Ed./ Business	Arts
MARK								
ABSENCES								
PARTICIPATION/SOCIAL SKILLS								
Arrives on time								
Prepares for class								
Stays on task								
Participates in class activities								
Co-operates with others								
Completes work								
KNOWLEDGE/LEARNING SKILLS								
Understands basic facts/concepts								
Communicates effectively								
Applies knowledge and skills in familiar situations								
Applies knowledge and skills in new situations								

E: Exceeds expectations   M: Meets expectations   N: Does not meet expectations

PRINCIPAL _____

TYPE C SAMPLE

GRADE NINE LEARNER PROFILE
SUBJECT: MATHEMATICS

School _____
Address _____
Principal: _____

Name: _____
Homeform: _____
Teacher: _____
Date: _____

LEARNING SKILLS PROFILE

Rating Scale: 1 – Always 2 – Usually 3 – Sometimes 4 – Rarely 5 – Never N/A – Not Applicable

	EARLY	MID TERM	FINAL
–comes to class prepared and on time			
–remains on task			
–completes assignments/works on time			
–contributes to class activities			
–follows instructions			
–seeks help when necessary			
–respects rights and needs of others			
–works well independently			

SUBJECT LEARNER PROFILE

Rating Scale: 1 – Always 2 – Usually 3 – Sometimes 4 – Rarely 5 – Never N/A – Not Applicable

	EARLY	MID TERM	FINAL
–skill in dealing with numbers			
–accuracy in calculations			
–understanding of mathematical concepts			
–recollection of facts			
–recognition of reasonable answers			
–ability to solve problems using various strategies			
–demonstration of spatial sense			
–recognition of patterns and use of symbols			
TOTAL ABSENCES TO DATE			
TOTAL LATES TO DATE			

EARLY REPORT COMMENTS: Adapted Program ☐

MID-TERM COMMENTS: Adapted Program ☐

Based on current achievement and the Learner Profile this student would be recommended for _____ level for grade 10 in this subject.

FINAL REPORT COMMENTS: Adapted Program ☐

Student Services Contact Person:

RECOMMENDED LEVEL OF INSTRUCTION IN THIS SUBJECT FOR GRADE 10 _____

NAME _____

SUBJECT _____

ADAPTED PROGRAM ☐

EXPLANATION OF GRADING

Please note that the written explanations of the grading symbols and the rating scales in the report provide more detailed information than grading symbols alone.

ACHIEVEMENT

A+ 90–100	**Exceptional** knowledge and application of the concepts, skills and content.
A 80–89	**Thorough** knowledge and application of the concepts, skills and content.
B 70–79	**Good grasp** of the concepts, skills and content.
C 60–69	**Some improvement** required in knowledge and application of the concepts, skills and content.
NGA	**No Grade Assigned.** Parents are requested to telephone the identified Student Services Contact. (See over).

EFFORT

A+	Exceptional
A	Excellent
B	Good
C	Requires Improvement

Mid-Term for Achievement ☐

Final Grade for Achievement ☐

Mid-Term Grade for Effort ☐

Final Grade for Effort ☐

TYPE D SAMPLE

STUDENT NO. _____

MINISTRY I.D. _____

SCHOOL NAME _____

SCHOOL ADDRESS _____

SCHOOL TELEPHONE _____

STUDENT SURNAME _____

GIVEN NAME(S) _____

HOME FORM _____

DATE _____

SECTION A

	LANGUAGE	ARTS	SELF AND SOCIETY	MATHEMATICS, SCIENCE AND TECHNOLOGY
KNOWLEDGE				
Understands basic facts/concepts				
Applies knowledge in familiar situations				
Applies knowledge in new situations				
SKILLS				
Uses appropriate research techniques				
Uses a planned approach				
Stays on task and completes work				
Communicates effectively				
ATTITUDES/VALUES				
Arrives on time to class				
Comes prepared to class				
Contributes positively to class				
Encourages and supports classmates				

LEGEND   N = OUTCOMES NOT YET ATTAINED   M = MEETS GRADE LEVEL OUTCOMES

E = EXCEEDS GRADE LEVEL OUTCOMES

TYPE D SAMPLE
(Page 2)

MARK RANGE SUMMARY

LANGUAGE

SUBJECT	Classes Missed (ST SCH)		Mark Range
English			
French			
E.S.L.			
Integrated Program #1			
Integrated Program #2			

ARTS

SUBJECT	Classes Missed (ST SCH)		Mark Range
Dance			
Drama			
Music			
Visual Arts			
Integrated Program #1			
Integrated Program #2			

SELF AND SOCIETY

SUBJECT	Classes Missed (ST SCH)		Mark Range
Family Studies			
Geography			
History			
Physical and Health Education			
Business Education			
Integrated Program #1			
Integrated Program #2			

MATHEMATICS, SCIENCE AND TECHNOLOGY

SUBJECT	Classes Missed (ST SCH)		Mark Range
Mathematics			
Science			
Technology			
Integrated Program #1			
Integrated Program #2			

MARK RANGES: <50 50–54 55–59 60–64 65–69 70–74 75–79 80–84 85–89 90–94 95–100

ATTENDANCE LEGEND ST = Student is Responsible for Absence SCH = School Approved Absence

Assess for Success

Anecdotal Reporting

Teacher written comments make it possible to report on the unique strengths, weaknesses, and learning needs of each student and to suggest specific plans for improvement. It should be kept in mind that

(1) comprehensive and thoughtful written reports require a great deal of time and skill,

(2) descriptions of a student's learning weaknesses can be misinterpreted by parents, and

(3) written reports alone do not provide a systematic and cumulative record of student progress.

When **used in connection with a more formal reporting system**, anecdotal reporting can clarify specific points and elaborate upon various aspects of student development. In Chapter Five of *The Numbers Game* King and Peart reported that parents were very critical of the computer-generated comment system used in most Ontario secondary schools. There was a great demand for more constructive, informative and personalized comments. The expanded format report card should include provision for anecdotal reporting.

Student Self-Assessment — Reporting

Many schools encourage students to write their own self-appraisal as a formal part of their school reports. This encourages students to reflect on their own learning and constitutes a valuable source of student comment on school programs.

Student Self-Evaluation
A Strength — _____
A Concern — _____
A Goal — _____

(Scarborough Board of Education.)

Parent-Teacher Conferences

Parent-teacher conferences can help to establish and maintain better communication and co-operation between teachers and parents. Parents receive an informal verbal progress report from the teacher, and have the opportunity to ask questions, raise any issues that concern them, and to make teachers aware of any relevant information of a more personal nature that might be influencing their son or daughter. Collaboration concerning plans for improving a student's learning and development is more likely to occur. Misunderstanding concerning a student's progress is likely to be avoided or overcome. The main limitation to this supplementary form of reporting is that some parents are unwilling or simply unable to attend the conferences. **Ideally**, teachers should telephone the parents of each student (with due consideration to freedom of information issues) at least once in a semester to emphasize the positive aspects of the student's performance. A follow-up telephone call to parents who were unable to attend a parent-teacher conference is an efficient and effective way to personalize reporting practices.

Teachers should prepare for parent conferences by:

- reviewing the student's work

- having examples of the student's work available

- having the student's self-assessment available, if possible

- having the course outline, outcomes, and student's records available

- preparing a tentative plan for remedial strategies or enrichment suggestions (if necessary)

Teachers must show detailed knowledge of student progress. They need to show parents that they care. They must be direct about low achievement, offer suggestions for improvement, and tell parents what they can do to help.

Three-Way Reports (Students, Parents and Teachers)

The three-way reporting process, a relatively new method of conferencing, has developed out of the search for more purposeful reporting systems. Traditionally, reports have been written by the teacher and sent to parents before the parent-teacher conference. Teachers using three-way reports write them **following** the three-way conferences which have included parents, the student and the teacher. Each report provides a written record of the conference discussion including details about learning goals, areas of student strength and/or concern, and a plan as to how the parent and teacher will provide support (see sample conference guides for students and teachers, pages 365–366). The obvious advantage of this approach to reporting is that the emphasis is on collaboration. Student learning profiles and resulting plans of action are terms of agreement; a much stronger sense of working together can be created.

A further refinement of this process is the concept of student-led conferences which are an extension of self-assessment (a key component is the profile of the developing learner). Student-led conferences required students to examine and develop a greater understanding of their own personal learning process and take ownership in their own personal plan for growth. (For detailed ideas see *Davies et al, **Together is Better**, 1992.)

THREE-WAY CONFERENCE GUIDE FOR TEACHERS

Student's Name _____   Date _____

Areas of strength	Areas needing improvement

Notes for the conference	Additional notes

Action Plan

Goal:

Student will …	Teacher will …	Parent will …

Other notes:

(Davies et al, p. 36.)

THREE-WAY CONFERENCE GUIDE FOR STUDENTS

Name _____   Date _____

Two things I need to improve …

Things to show...

My next term goal is...

(Davies et al, p. 37.)

Assess for Success

Teacher Record Book

Teachers are required to keep accurate records of student attendance and assessment of student progress. These records are the teacher's database for reporting. Teachers will develop a method of record-keeping that works best for their particular situation. However, the impact of changes in assessment, evaluation and reporting practices warrants some careful consideration when it comes to teacher record-keeping. Teacher records should reflect fair, consistent, comprehensive and balanced grading practices. Consideration must be given to the following:

- there will be a greater number and variety of assessment and evaluation methods employed
- a more direct linking of assessment and evaluation methods to stated outcomes will need to be displayed
- there will be a need to track and report on each student's learner profile as well as each student's subject achievement profile
- there will be a need for a day-to-day or week-to-week record for ongoing assessment and feedback
- easy access to results of appropriate selected performance assessments will also be required
- compatibility with computer programs may be helpful

On page 368 is a sample tracking sheet for science.

On page 369 is one possible approach to evaluating and recording class activities.

Guidelines for Developing a Reporting System

1. A reporting system should be guided by the functions to be served, and should include the type of information most needed by the report's users.

2. The reporting system should be developed co-operatively by parents, students, and school personnel. Reports are likely to be most useful when all users have some voice in their development.

3. The reporting system should be based on a clear statement of educational outcomes. The same outcomes that have guided instruction and evaluation should serve as a basis for marking and reporting.

4. The reporting system should be based on adequate evaluation. The items included in the final report form should be those on which teachers can obtain reasonably reliable and valid information.

5. The reporting system should be detailed enough to be diagnostic and yet compact enough to be practical. A comprehensive picture of strengths and weaknesses guides student learning and development. This must be balanced by such practical demands as time required to prepare and use the reports, reports that are understandable to all users, and reports that are easily summarized for school records.

6. The reporting system should provide for parent-teacher conferences, as needed. Parent-teacher conferences should supplement a more formal report form, rather than replace it.

(Adapted from Gronlund and Linn, 1990, pp. 435–436.)

SCIENCE TRACKING SHEET

Name of Unit:	1 Activity 1 Completed	2 Activity 2 Completed	3 Activity 3 Completed	4 Activity 4 Completed	5 Activity 5 Completed	6 Skill –	7 Skill –	8 Skill –	9 Attitude – Consideration of Others	10 Attitude	11 Notebook	12 Group Work	
Students													
1.													
2.													
3.													
4.													
5.													
6.													
7.													
8.													
9.													
10.													
11.													
12.													
13.													
14.													
15.													
16.													
17.													
18.													
19.													
20.													
21.													

Notes:

1. Columns 1 to 5 could be completed using a checkmark or a rating scale.
2. Columns 6 to 10: select skills and attitudes appropriate to the unit of study. Holistic scales used as indicator lists to determine students' progress.
3. Column 11 could be completed with a rating scale.
4. Column 12 could be given a rating determined by the students' self-evaluation of group work.
5. Anecdotal comments could be constructed based on information from this chart. A new chart would be needed for each unit.

(*Junior Science Guide*, Scarborough Board of Education, p. 44.)

Using the Teacher Record Book — One Approach
Evaluation of Class Activities: English

Evaluation of CLASS ACTIVITIES (group, oral, general discussion, in-class writing, thinking through writing, participation, listening, viewing)

English courses evaluate the whole range of language activities. Attendance is very important because students are provided with opportunities to write, to think critically, and to practice speaking and listening skills in small and large group situations. The cumulative development of these skills is dependent on continual, sustained practice which is measurable. This practice will lead to improved performance on the final demonstration of the outcome(s). Credit will be given for ACTIVE INVOLVEMENT in (connection with) the course. 20–30% of the course mark will be based on CLASS ACTIVITIES; the criteria on which this 20–30% will be allocated will be clearly stated and will be related to the demonstration of enabling outcomes, i.e. satisfactory participation in/completion of class activities.

CLASS ACTIVITIES MARK (20–30%): to be determined as follows:

Essentially, EVERY CLASS SHOULD PROVIDE MEANINGFUL ACTIVITY. The range of activities in an English course is extensive and teachers should strive to provide variety within a developmental framework. Thus, when a student spends time discussing a topic in a small group, or writing down thoughts on a subject for subsequent discussion, or reading quietly, or viewing a film, or listening to the opinions of others, communication and language skills are being developed.

Several methods may be employed to assign and record class activity marks. The easiest (and perhaps the fairest) would appear to be a regular recording of the main activity or activities, most of which require satisfactory completion only. For example, a student may be asked to prepare a short piece of writing on a topic which is to be used as a basis for group discussion. If the student is absent or very little is completed, an unsatisfactory mark can be recorded when the written notes for the class are handed in. Over the course of a month, several entries would be made and a pattern of completion (or incompletion as the case may be) would emerge. The marks assigned for this section should be based on the satisfactory completion of a range of activities. Credit for simply being in class does not constitute adequate evaluation, but attendance is a prerequisite for involvement, and satisfactory completion of class activities will count. In addition, summative evaluation activities (e.g. projects, essays, tests) will receive marks. If the class activities have been well planned and are challenging, the resulting summative marks will be higher for those who have participated most effectively in the class activities.

Parental Concerns

Parental concerns about the current mark reporting system detailed in Chapter 5 of
The Numbers Game include:

1. More personal comments are needed (computer comments are criticized).
2. Earlier warning about problems is needed.
3. More information is needed on "labour market" shifts (social skills, group work).
4. More details are needed on how the mark is determined.
5. More information is needed on where their son or daughter stands in comparison to other students.

[Note: Parents appear to want this information because the other four "needs" expressed are not being met. If parents were provided with personal comments, earlier warning about problems, more information on "labour market" skills, and more information concerning where a mark comes from, it is likely that the "need" expressed in number five could be avoided. As noted earlier in this chapter, norm-referenced grading carries with it a particular set of problems and disadvantages.]

Expanded format reporting can deal effectively with all of these concerns.

Conclusion

Adjustments to most current grading and reporting practices are needed if the goal of a positive, constructive learning environment for all students is to be achieved. Careful consideration of the issues associated with grading and reporting, and trial implementation of selected strategies for changing practices can lead to improvements and, ultimately, to greater understanding on the part of students, parents and teachers as to what constitutes successful learning.

> "Marks should convey the same message to parents, teachers and students."
>
> (King and Peart, **The Numbers Game**, Chapter 5.)

References

Davies, Ann; Cameron, Caren; Politano, Colleen; Gregory, Kathleen; <u>Together is Better</u>, 1992, Peguis Publishers, Winnipeg.

Gronlund, N. and Linn, R., <u>Measurement and Evaluation in Teaching</u>, 1990, Macmillan: New York.

Northwest Regional Educational Laboratories, <u>Developing Sound Grading Practices Workshop</u>.

Pratt, David, <u>Curriculum Design</u>, 1980.

Pratt, David, <u>Curriculum Planning: A Handbook for Professionals</u>, Kingston, 1991.

Scarborough Board of Education, <u>Junior Science Guide</u>, 1992.

Spady, William, Shifting the Grading Paradigm that Pervades Education, <u>Outcomes</u>, no date available, pp. 39–45.

Stiggins, Richard J., <u>Teacher Handbook: A Practical Guide for Developing Sound Grading Practices</u>, 1989, Northwest Regional Educational Laboratory, Portland, Oregon.

Chapter 9
Standardized Testing

Standardized Testing

Part A: Introduction

"What with the reading readiness tests and the basic skills tests and the I.Q. exams and the sequential tests of educational progress and the mental maturity tests and the minimum competency exams and the grade promotion tests and my prep course for the PSAT, we haven't been learning anything at school."

(The National Center for Fair and Open Testing, n.d., p. 1.)

W is for WARNING:
Standardized Tests Will Dictate Your Curriculum

Beware of the consequences of country-by-country comparisons of standardized test scores. Newspapers across Canada will publish the results; in low-scoring provinces, elected officials will cry out for school reform; pressured to improve scores, school people will begin encouraging teachers (subtly, at first) to teach to the tests. Ultimately, instead of measuring the success of the public education system, standardized tests will dictate what is taught ... the pattern is clear: What is measured becomes a key factor in determining behaviour. So there's every reason to believe the information of country-by-country comparisons of standardized test scores will influence the public's perception of each country's education system. Unfortunately, such comparisons are simplistic and likely to mislead the public into demanding changes that would harm schools. And that's what executive educators must guard against.

*(Weiss, J. G. and Fege, A. F., Warning: Standardized tests will dictate your curriculum, **The Executive Educator**, October, 1988, p. 25.)*

Part B: A Standardized Test Primer

What is a Standardized Test?

> The term STANDARDIZED means that the test has a fixed set of items written by specialists; there are also specific instructions and procedures for administering and scoring the test, which must be followed exactly as given.
>
> The most important characteristic of standardized tests, however, is the provision of NORMS — that is, information on how representative groups of individuals, in different places and at different times, performed on the test. The norms allow us to compare any student's score with the typical scores of peers who took the same test.
>
> The use of standardized tests and their norms is appropriate (and the resulting scores valid) only if the student being tested is fairly similar to norm group students in terms of background and experience, and only if the test content is a reasonable sample of that student's knowledge, skills, and experiences.

*(Peel, **Book 3**, 1989, p. 3.)*

What Standardized Testing Terms Really Mean

Testing is full of terms that are not familiar to many people. Some words don't have the same meaning in testing as they do in regular use.

Achievement Tests:	claim to measure how much a student has learned in a class such as reading, spelling, science or math.
Aptitude Tests:	try to predict a student's ability to do certain types of school work; sometimes called "cognitive abilities" tests; IQ tests may be used for this purpose.
Competency Tests:	are designed to determine whether a student has met a minimum standard of skills and knowledge in a specific subject area.
Criterion-Referenced Tests:	measure how well a student meets certain standards determined by the test-maker.
Cut Score:	is the minimum level a test-taker must attain in order to "pass" a given exam.
Developmental Screening Tests:	are given to identify students who may have problems which need attention from a specialist such as a doctor.
High Stakes Tests:	are tests that are used to make important educational decisions and that educators and students view as important.

IQ (Intelligence Quotient) Tests: supposedly measure a person's native intelligence by assuming a single set of inherited abilities which can be measured by one test.

Items: are test questions or problems.

Measurement Error: is one way by which reliability or lack of reliability of a test is indicated; all tests have measurement error.

Norm-Referenced Tests: are designed so that the scores of all the students who take it fall along a "normal" or "bell-shaped" curve; most of the test-takers will be near the middle, few will be at the ends; half the test-takers will be "below average."

Reliability: estimates how closely a test would produce the same results if it were repeatedly administered to the same student under the same conditions.

Sampling: is a way to get information about a group by examining only some members of the group or by giving all members only small parts of the whole test.

School Readiness Tests: are used to determine whether a child is "prepared" to begin kindergarten or first grade.

True Score: the score a student should get if the test were completely reliable.

Validity: defines how accurately a test really measures what its promoters claim it measures; *predictive validity* measures how well the test predicts future school performance; *content validity* measures how well the test covers the subject content.

(The National Center for Fair and Open Testing, n.d., p. 26.)

What Test Scores Mean

- A *Raw Score* is the total number of questions a child got right on a test. On an exam with 20 items, raw scores could range from 0 to 20. A student's raw score does not tell you much unless you know how many questions there were on the test and how difficult they were.

- A *Percent Correct* score is created by dividing the number of right answers by the total number of questions. For example, a child who gave the wanted answers to 10 out of 20 problems would have 50 percent (50%) correct.

- A *Percentile Score* or *Rank* tells you how a child's test score compares with the students on whom the test was normed. This is not the same as the percent of questions he or she got right. A percentile or rank of 50 means the student's score was better than the scores of half the students in the norming sample.

- A *Standard Score* is designed to report how much a student's score differs from the average score. For example, on an exam with an average score of 100, like most IQ tests, a score of 110 is as much above average as a 90 is below average.

- A *Stanine Score*, short for **sta**ndard **nine**, is one type of standard score. Stanines divide test results into nine groups, with 1 given to the lowest scores and 9 the highest. Scores of 4, 5 and 6 are considered average.

- A *Normal Curve Equivalent* (NCE) is another type of standard score, with an average of 50 and a range of 1 to 99. On any test, each grade has its own NCE. If a child had an NCE of 45 in second grade and 55 in third grade, he or she has made progress according to the test, since his or her scores rose from below average to above average.

- A *Grade Equivalent Score* tries to compare your child's test results to the grade and month of the school year when that score would be average. A student who does as well as the typical test-taker in the fifth month of the second grade would get a grade equivalent score of 2.5. Using this method, half the students who take the test nationally should score below grade level and half above. Grade equivalent scores are misleading for students who do very well or poorly on the test. For example, a student in the fifth month of the second grade who scored a 4.9 is not doing fourth grade work and is almost certainly not able to do fourth grade work. He or she simply is doing very well, as compared with other second graders and as measured by the test.

All tests have **measurement error**. Consider a student who scores a 57 on a typical norm-referenced achievement test with a 0–100 score range and a normal curve. Two-thirds of the time, his or her score would fall between 50 and 64 — the **confidence band** or **score range**. The confidence band is supposed to tell you how much your child's score is likely to change if he or she took the same test again. In fact, the scores can vary even more than the confidence band says is likely. In this example, **one-third of the time, the score would be below 50 or above 64**. When a student takes a test, there is no way to know if, on that day, the score is inside or outside the confidence band.

(The National Center for Fair and Open Testing, n.d., p. 10.)

Common Criticisms of Standardized Tests

1. Standardized achievement tests do not promote student learning.
2. Standardized achievement and aptitude tests are poor predictors of individual students' performance.
3. The content of standardized achievement tests is often mismatched with the content emphasized in a school's curriculum and classrooms.
4. Standardized tests are unsuitable for evaluating school programs or curricula.
5. Standardized tests dictate or restrict what is taught in ways that violate the principle of local control of education.
6. Standardized achievement and aptitude tests categorize and label students in ways that cause damage to individuals.
7. Tests often represent an invasion of privacy for students and their families.
8. Standardized achievement and aptitude measures are racially, culturally, and socially biased.
9. Standardized tests often penalize bright, creative students.
10. Test anxiety accompanying standardized achievement and aptitude testing interferes with student performance and distorts the test results.
11. Standardized achievement and aptitude tests measure only limited and superficial student knowledge and behaviours.
12. Standardized achievement and aptitude tests are not based on sound psychological or educational theory.
13. Standardized achievement tests do not promote quality or foster accountability in our schools.

Critiquing the Criticisms of Testing

1. Standardized tests are strongly supported by many practitioners, parents, and policy makers.
2. Many criticisms of standardized testing assume teachers and other test users are naive and credulous.
3. Most criticisms of standardized tests are really not criticisms of the tests but rather of their misuse or abuse.
    1. Using the wrong tests.
    2. Assuming test scores are infallible.
    3. Using a single test score to make an important decision.
    4. Failing to supplement test scores with other information.
    5. Setting arbitrary minimums for performance on tests.
    6. Assuming tests measure all the content, skills, or behaviours of interest.
    7. Accepting uncritically all claims made by test authors and publishers.
    8. Interpreting test scores inappropriately.
    9. Using test scores to draw inappropriate comparisons among individuals or schools.
    10. Allowing tests to drive the curriculum.
    11. Using poor tests.
    12. Using tests unprofessionally.

(Adapted from Worthen et al, 1993, p. 407–417.)

Issues of Equity and Standardized Testing

> There are constraints on the use of standardized assessment measures with new immigrant students and students with a first language other than English or French.
>
> (Ministry of Education and Training, **Antiracism and Ethnocultural Equity in School Boards**, p. 20.)

> We begin with the conviction that it is desirable that attention be given to questions of equity early in the development of an assessment process rather than as an add-on near the end of such work. ... The task then is to find assessment probes (test items) which measure the same criterion from contexts and perspectives which reflect the life space and values of the learner."
>
> (Edmund Gordon, Yale Professor.)

> "The criterion of equity needs to be applied to any assessment. It is a mistake to assume that shifting from standardized tests to performance-based assessments will eliminate concerns about biases against racial/ethnic minorities or that such a shift will necessarily lead to equality of performance.
>
> (Robert Linn)

Below are some suggestions for modifying and/or selecting alternative testing instruments and approaches for the culturally/language different student.

- Consider the use of tests that are minimally language-based, sometimes called "culture fair" tests. Although it is impossible to produce a test that is universally "fair" to all cultures, many of these measures are useful across a number of cultures. They are good alternatives to measures heavily loaded with verbal items, and can provide insight into a student's non-verbal reasoning ability. The Ravens Progressive Matrices and the Peabody Picture Vocabulary Test are examples of tests that have been specifically designed for populations with poor or minimal language skills. The Non-Verbal and Quantitative batteries of the Canadian Cognitive Abilities Test (CCAT) have been used successfully with some ESL populations; the publishers also note that the instructions for the Non-Verbal battery can be translated directly into other languages.

- Consider using diagnostic tests (such as the Stanford Diagnostic Reading Test) rather than survey-type achievement tests (such as CTBS). Diagnostic tests generally contain a majority of easier items and are geared toward a more in-depth assessment of particular skills.

- If the norms for a particular standardized test provide an inappropriate comparison group for the culturally/language different student, they should not be used. One alternative is to use the students scores as his/her own baseline, against which to compare later test results — that is, to use the test results only as a "yardstick" against which to measure the student's own progress. Or, suggest that the school or Board develop "local" norms for culturally/language different students, with whom your student can be more meaningfully compared.

- Consider "bending the rules" regarding test administration. Remember, however, that once you do this, the test is no longer "standardized" and the norms cannot be used as a reference group for comparison. You might, for example, decide to extend the time limits for the test, or disregard them altogether. Or you might decide to use only selected questions from a test. An easier-to-follow answer sheet might be devised, or else the student might write his/her answers directly on the test booklet. In order to eliminate the need for reading, the test might be administered orally in a one-to-one situation, with the examiner recording the student's answer.

- Find out whether tests are currently available in the student's own language. Some major tests have been translated into other languages and re-normed on those populations, but they may require administration by a native speaker. Don't consider trying to translate existing tests into another language; this does not correct for culture-bound content, nor can one assume that translated items have the same meaning, difficulty, or validity as in the original language.

- Tests should be carefully chosen, keeping each individual student in mind. Examine sample copies and read any available reviews of the test. Determine that the test is appropriate to the student's level of functioning. Sometimes this will mean testing at a level intended for students in a lower grade, but this can provide very useful information on a child's skill levels and will be less likely to be seen as a threatening task.

Finally, two major considerations should be stressed. First, it is important to use many different sources of information in making education decisions about any student. Decisions should never rest on an isolated test score. This is especially critical for the culturally/language different student, where there is a real possibility that standardized test scores may be invalid. Second, initial assessments of these students should be viewed as tentative; plan for regular re-assessments.

*(Peel, **Book 3**, 1989, p. 51–52.)*

Part C: Standards in Ontario

What is meant by "standardized" in a testing situation?

In a standardized test, one finds the following dimensions present:

1. The format is organized or standardized into multiple choice questions.

2. The procedure by which the test is put together is highly standardized in terms of the ways items are written, tried out, analyzed, and revised.

3. The scores are standardized in terms of the norms.

4. All people taking the test do so under uniform or standardized conditions.

(Schurr, 1992, p. 78.)

Ontario uses several approaches to assess student and program achievement that do not follow the traditional standardized test approach, e.g., Provincial Reviews, Standards, Grade 9 Reading and Writing Test. This is a more humane approach than that used in the United States.

Provincial Reviews

Provincial reviews provide a method for public accountability at the school, board, and provincial levels. They are based on Ministry of Education curriculum guidelines and provide a means of gathering information about program implementation and student achievement. Following are the main purposes of provincial reviews:

- to determine the effectiveness of curricula and the level of student achievement at the school, board, and provincial levels;

- to provide Ontario educators with information that may be used to make decisions for modifying and improving programs and improving student achievement;

- to establish baseline data on both program effectiveness and student achievement against which information generated by future reviews can be compared in order to determine progress;

- to provide instruments and procedures that can be used in the future by school boards.

Provincial samples consisting of 100 English-language schools and 100 French-language schools are randomly selected so that all regions of the province are represented. In the Grade 8 Mathematics review, all Grade 8 teachers and students in these schools participated in the review except for students in English as a Second Language programs and students identified as exceptional by an Identification Placement and Review Committee. In addition, 57 school boards opted to have board reviews conducted in English-language schools and 12 school boards opted to have board reviews conducted in French-language schools. School boards had the option of including exceptional students and students in ESL programs.

Date were collected from principals, teachers, and students using the following instruments:

- Principal Questionnaire
- Teacher Questionnaire
- Opportunity-to-Learn Form
- Student Questionnaire
- Student Assessment Booklets
- Calculator Questions
- Mental Computation Questions

These instruments were designed to collect data on the following aspects of the Grade 8 program:

- context within which the program is delivered
- intended curriculum
- implemented curriculum
- achieved curriculum

Standards

Ontario Standards describe Student Outcomes in three columns:

- All students will ...
- Most students will ...
- Some students will ...

In Mathematics for example, in Strand 4: Patterning and Algebra, Grades 7–9, most students will be able to master problems such as the following:

Most Students:

1. Marbles are arranged as follows: (58%)

   If the pattern is continued, how many marbles are used in making the 8th figure?

   A) 28

   B) 36

   C) 45

   D) 55

2. A marathon cyclist travels around a route four times. The total distance travelled is 461.76 km. Let the distance of one lap around the route be d km. (54%)

   The equation that could be used in determining d is:

   A) $d + 461.76 = 4d$

   B) $2d = 461.76$

   C) $d = 4 \times 461.76$

   D) $4d = 461.76$

3. Sixteen added to the product of three and a number is 31. An equation for this statement is: (67%)

   A) $3m - 16 = 31$

   B) $3m \times 16 = 31$

   C) $3m + 16 = 31$

   D) $3(16) + m = 16$

4. The price of tennis balls is as follows: (54%)

1 tennis ball	$ 3.50
2 tennis balls	$ 7.00
3 tennis balls	$10.50

   If n represents the number of tennis balls, which formula can be used to find the cost of any number of tennis balls?

   A) $3.50n$

   B) $3.50 + 3n$

   C) $3.50 + 2n$

   D) $3.50 + n$

Ontario Provincial Standards

The Ministry of Education and Training's recently released document, "Ontario Provincial Standards of Performance for Mathematics — End of Grades 3, 6, and 9" released in September 1993, outlines standards of performance for students at the end of Grades 3, 6, and 9.

Standards of Performance

Descriptions of performance in four categories are provided for each strand at the end of Grade 3, Grade 6 and Grade 9:

Limited Performance	Proficient Performance
Adequate Performance	Superior Performance

Of the four categories described, two are considered to be within the expected standard for student performance in Ontario: Adequate and Proficient. Students whose performance is described as Limited are functioning below the expected standard; students whose performance is described as Superior are functioning beyond the expected standard.

It is unlikely that the performance of any one student would fall exclusively into a single category; rather, a student's performance may vary according to the strand of mathematics. It is important to recognize that the Standards represent descriptions of student performance, not descriptions of students.

The Standards of Performance describe high but reasonable expectations. An effort has been made to blend observations of current performance with desired perform-ances, in order to set Standards that are realistic but future-looking.

Use of the Standards

The Provincial Standards for Mathematics are broad standards for the province against which to assess students' learning. They set worthwhile goals for all, by describing expected provincial levels of performance. Their primary focus is to make a clear statement to teachers, parents and students about expected results.

Teachers may use the Learning Targets as a basis for team planning in divisions. They may use the Standards of Performance, together with the Sample Performance Indicators, to diagnose individual students and to plan for improvement with them. As well, teachers may use the Standards as a reference in reporting student performance to parents.

Parents may use the Standards of Performance to compare their child's performance to provincial expectations. Community groups may use the Standards to compare Ontario expectations with those in other provinces or other countries.

School boards and the Ministry of Education and Training may use the Standards of Performance as a basis for program reviews.

Assessment and Evaluation in the Classroom

To evaluate a student in relation to the Standards of Performance described in this document, it is important that the teacher use a wide range of assessment strategies.

Sample Adequate Performance Descriptor for Students at the End of Grade 6

The student demonstrates understanding of the properties and operations related to whole numbers, decimals and fractions. With prompting, the student readily recognizes and corrects errors. The student continues to develop number sense.

Sample Performance Indicators

The student:

- in a one-step arithmetic problem, identifies the appropriate operation to use.
- understands basic properties of operations on numbers and applies them when prompted [e.g., properties such as $2 + 3 = 3 + 2$; $(6 \times 4) \times 5 = 6 \times (4 \times 5)$].
- demonstrates understanding of the effects of operations on whole numbers (e.g., $65 \div 5$ produces a value less than 65, but 65×5 produces a value greater than 65).
- demonstrates understanding of place value but may require prompting in applying it consistently in reading and writing numbers and in estimation and calculation.
- recalls basic arithmetic facts with some hesitation.
- demonstrates inconsistency in doing pencil/paper procedures involving whole numbers and decimals.
- with the assistance of concrete models, demonstrates an understanding of basic concepts involving fractions, such as representation, magnitude, order and equivalence.
- in school and everyday situations, applies basic skills of mental calculation with inconsistent accuracy.
- in school and everyday situations, applies estimation by rounding with varying degrees of success.
- uses a calculator effectively in applications and problem solving throughout the curriculum and in everyday life.
- uses a calculator to investigate concepts in mathematics.
- chooses the most appropriate calculation method from among mental mathematics, estimation, calculator or paper/pencil procedures.

Ontario Grade 9 Reading and Writing Test

The Minister of Education and Training has announced plans to administer, in the 1993–94 school year, a province-wide test of reading and writing to all Grade 9 students taking English as part of their program.

The test has been designed to be more meaningful to students than traditional external tests. It is essentially a unit of class work which you are asked to treat as an integral part of the curriculum. Having the test built into a unit of work will give students an opportunity to demonstrate their reading and writing abilities in the context of a regular classroom setting. The unit is built around the topic of food and involves the students in group activities as well as individual reading and writing. You will not be expected to teach about food and nutrition.

The unit of work and associated testing will take at least ten class periods of approximately 76 minutes each and you are asked to incorporate it into your program as indicated below:

Semester One:	Last two weeks of October, 1993
Semester Two:	Last two weeks of March, 1994
Non-semestered schools:	First two weeks of February, 1994

Schools with 76 minute periods on alternate days and schools with shorter periods may extend the administration time to three or four weeks as necessary.

During the unit of work the students will do the following: answer a short question-naire, participate in warm-up discussion activities and small-group discussions of five poems, write a personal response to a poem, answer questions (both multiple-choice and open-ended) on a selection of reading passages, engage in a group task, and complete a piece of writing (narrative or supported opinion). In addition, students will be asked to select and submit their best piece of writing completed by the time of the assessment. A flow-chart showing the components of the unit is enclosed.

You will be asked to send both the students' answers to the reading questions and their writing to the Ministry unmarked. The students' work will be assessed by a central committee of teachers and performance levels assigned to each student using six-point scales. Copies of the scales will be made available to you early in the school year. Reading and writing levels for each student will then be returned to you for a more detailed analysis and reporting before the end of the semester and at the end of the school year.

We have found in the testing for both provincial reviews and international assess-ments that students appear not to produce their best effort if the results of the test do not "count" in some way. We are asking you, therefore, to count the various activities in the unit for 10 to 15 per cent of the students' term marks. It is up to you to decide how this percentage is determined for your students. General guidelines will be provided during the training session. The reading and writing levels determined by the ministry, however, are not to be used for placement purposes.

(Ontario Ministry of Education.)

Grade 9 English Test
INTEGRATED ASSESSMENT UNIT

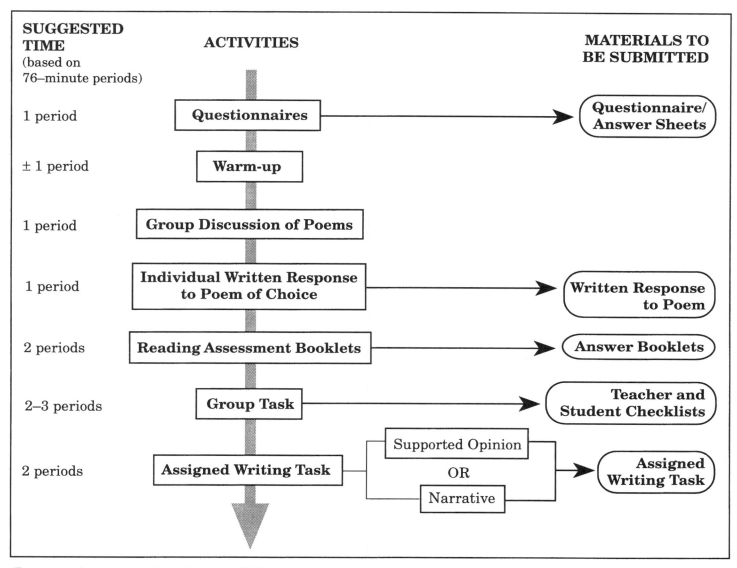

SUGGESTED TIME
(based on 76–minute periods)

ACTIVITIES

MATERIALS TO BE SUBMITTED

1 period	Questionnaires	Questionnaire/ Answer Sheets
± 1 period	Warm-up	
1 period	Group Discussion of Poems	
1 period	Individual Written Response to Poem of Choice	Written Response to Poem
2 periods	Reading Assessment Booklets	Answer Booklets
2–3 periods	Group Task	Teacher and Student Checklists
2 periods	Assigned Writing Task	Supported Opinion OR Narrative → Assigned Writing Task

(*Learning Assessment Branch, June 1993.*)

IS THIS A STANDARDIZED TEST?

In some ways this test is like a standardized test. All students will take it. There are common test booklets and common procedures for administering and marking it.

There the similarities end. Unlike a traditional standardized test, the Grade 9 Reading and Writing Test is based on Ontario's curriculum. Also, the test uses a variety of methods and questions to test a wide range of skills. So it will give a more complete view of students' reading and writing skills.

*(Ministry brochure in the series **About Your Schools** (for parents).)*

IS THIS A STANDARDIZED TEST? — OSSTF

OSSTF recognizes the need for accountability in public education in Ontario. A system that is seen to be accountable will continue to maintain public support and funding. However, OSSTF does not wish to see a public education system that is driven by standardized tests, the one correct answer, that fails to recognize multiple intelligences, creativity and the spirit of inquiry and life-long learning. Further, whatever indicators are developed must be appropriate. It is a common error to develop an indicator for one purpose such as program effectiveness and apply it to another such as a learner's progress. This threatens to be a problem with the Ontario Grade 9 reading and writing test. The test suffers from the significant flaw that it was initially designed to evaluate program and is now being used to evaluate learner progress. The six levels of achievement while reasonable for measuring program quality and areas requiring improvement are unrealistic for measuring mass student achievement. In Ontario, where inclusiveness of public education is viewed as a major plus, setting unrealistically high levels of achievement may lead to results being perceived as "poor" or "failing". Nonetheless, OSSTF is offering guarded support for the test.

(See "Provincial Standards — Grade 9 Reading" and "Provincial Standards — Grade 9 Writing".)

The kinds of uses that will be made of these measurements remains to be seen. The classroom teacher is likely to respond positively to the concept of an integrated unit of work as it represents (potentially) a movement beyond a standardized, norm-referenced, static number to a more authentic external test format.

OSSTF POLICY ON STANDARDIZED TESTS

8.8 Standardized Tests

8.8.1 It is the policy of OSSTF that standardized tests should not be used in the supervision or evaluation of teachers or to compare schools and/or school boards. *(A.93)*

    8.8.1.1 It is the policy of OSSTF that there should be no reintroduction of public, province-wide standardized examinations. *(A.93)*

    8.8.1.2 It is the policy of OSSTF that evaluation/assessment instruments used in Ontario should be developed by the Ministry of Education and/or local school boards in collaboration with the teaching profession through Federation representation during all stages of planning, development, implementation and review. *(A.93)*

8.8.2 It is the policy of OSSTF that if standardized tests are used in Ontario schools, then they should: *(A.93)*

    8.8.2.1 take into account the diversity of the student population n Ontario; *(A.93)*

    8.8.2.2 be based on curriculum objectives; *(A.93)*

    8.8.2.3 be used to make recommendations to improve student achievement; *(A.93)*

    8.8.2.4 be used to make recommendations to improve teaching strategies and/or modify program; *(A.93)*

    8.8.2.5 be free from cultural, racial, and gender bias; *(A.93)*

    8.8.2.6 be reported back to the student and parent by appropriate personnel who have access to pertinent printed information; and *(A.93)*

    8.8.2.7 be accompanied by a booklet giving current information useful in interpreting scores from test programs. *(A.93)*

8.8.3 It is the policy of OSSTF that objective tests should not be used as the sole instrument of evaluation of student achievement. *(A.93)*

8.8.4 It is the policy of OSSTF that there should not be compulsory use of the Ontario Assessment Instrument Pool (OAIP) for testing of students for student evaluation, for comparing schools, for post-secondary admissions or for teacher evaluation/supervision. *(A.93)*

(OSSTF Handbook 1993–94, pp. 60–61.)

Alternatives to Standardized Tests

Frontenac Secondary School: Assessment in Technological Studies

Students at Frontenac Secondary School in Ontario, Canada, spend most of their class hours designing, making, and fixing things: solving practical problems related to auto mechanics, wood-working, machine shop, drafting, and electrical studies. Until recently, however, these skills were assessed only through paper-and-pencil tests, a frustrating contradiction both to students and staff. A new procedure has dramatically improved the ability and usefulness of assessment in the technological studies program.

Procedures. For each course in the technological studies department, half of the final exam is a conventional written test. It stresses knowledge of structural properties of materials, principles of design, mechanical and electrical processes, names of tools and equipment, and safety precautions. But in addition to the written final exam, students are required to demonstrate the ability to use their technical knowledge.

The second half of the exam consists of hands-on performance in the tasks for which the students have been trained. For instance, in electrical studies, the written test covers Olm's law and theories of parallel circuits, among other topics. In the demonstrations, all students in electrical studies are required to create an electrical device, based on a wiring diagram. In a recent exam, the device to be constructed was a type of alarm unit to warn a person that their headlights remain on after the ignition has been turned off.

Within each shop, assessment tasks are standardized, although how assessments are conducted varies from shop to shop depending on the contingencies of the task, class size, and the instructional priorities of the shop teacher. In the example cited above, each student is provided with a workspace, a wiring diagram, and a supply of tools and materials. A two-hour time limit is imposed — realistic in the sense that under actual conditions of employment one is under some pressure to work at a steady pace. How well the alarm unit functions is the main criterion for success, but students are also graded on neatness and precision of work (soldering, wiring, etc.), speed, and safety (putting on safety goggles, unplugging tools after use).

To provide another example, in the auto mechanics shop, a used car is brought in and each student must act as a consultant to the hypothetical buyer. In this capacity, the student must identify mechanical problems and make recommendations. A checklist is used by the instructor to assess the thoroughness and accuracy of the "consultant's" diagnosis and recommendations. The main use of this approach to assessment in the technological studies program is to assign course-end grades. However, this approach has also provided useful feedback to students and teachers alike on the process of teaching and learning these skills.

(Anne Turnbaugh Lockwood, National Center on Effective Secondary Schools, Wisconsin Center for Educational Research, School of Education, University of Wisconsin-Madison, (608) 263–7575.)

References

Fine, J., (January 1988), "Standardized Tests and the Culturally/Language Different Student." Peel Board of Education Research Bulletin, Number 58.

Gronlund, N and Linn, R., Measurement and evaluation in teaching, 6th ed., New York: Macmillan Publishing Company, 1990.

Hills, J.R., (Spring 1983), "Interpreting Grade – Equivalent Scores." Educational Measurement: Issues and Practice, 2, 15, 21.

Hills, J.R., (Fall, 1983), "Interpreting Stanine Scores." Educational Measurement: Issues and Practice, 2, 18, 27.

Lien, A.J., (1976), Measurement and Evaluation of Learning, Third Edition, Dubuque, Iowa: Wm. C. Brown Co.

Lockwood, Anne Turnbaugh, "Frontenac Secondary School: Assessment in Technological Studies." National Center on Effective Schools, University of Wisconsin-Madison.

Ministry of Education and Training, Antiracism and Ethnocultural Equity in School Boards: Guidelines for Policy Development and Implementation, Toronto: Queen's Printer for Ontario, 1993.

Ministry of Education and Training, Ontario Provincial Standards of Performance for Mathematics (Draft), End of Grades 3, 6, and 9. September, 1993.

National Center for Fair and Open Testing, Standardized Tests and Our Children: A Guide to Testing Reform, Cambridge, Mass.: National Center for Fair and Open Testing, n.d.

OSSTF, OSSTF Handbook 1993–94, Toronto, 1993.

Peel Board of Education, Looking at measurement, Book 3., Mississauga, Ontario: Peel Board of Education, 1989.

Sadler, D. Royce, "Specifying and Promulgating Achievement Standards", Oxford Review of Education, Vol. 13, No. 2, 1987.

Schurr, Sandra, The ABC's of Evaluation, Columbus, Ohio: National Middle School Association, 1992.

Weiss, J.G. and Fege, A.F., "Warning: Standardized tests will dictate your curriculum", The Executive Educator, October, 1988.

Worthen, B. et al., Measurement and evaluation in the schools, London: Longman Publishing Company, 1993.

Chapter 10
Future Trends ...

Future Trends ...

Exemplary practices (especially in assessment and evaluation) should become the norm in the near future and into the next century. A "practical vision" for assessment appears to be taking shape. However, the changes demanded are numerous, variable and complex. The demands on individual teachers, students and the system outlined in *The Numbers Game* (King and Peart) are almost overwhelming. Certainly, there are a number of barriers that need to be overcome if the goals of this "practical vision" are to be achieved.

The Numbers Game is an important study for educators. It provides a clear reference point for processing (analysis) of the present (where we are) and provides the opportunity for forming philosophy and strategies for the future (where we should be).

As Jeroski points out:

> Schools have been expected to "produce" students who acquire set content and master specific skills. In this reductionist approach, evaluation is largely a matter of quality control — of mastering the "products" to ensure that they meet standard expectations. ... Now, the emphasis on evaluation is shifting from monitoring (a managerial function) to supporting learning and enhancing development, a learner-focused orientation.
>
> *(Costa et al., 1992, p. 281.)*

The first step would appear to be the need to reassess assessment practices.

> New process-oriented learner-focused goals cannot be measured with established product-oriented assessment techniques ... Changing the focus of assessment **can** be used as an influential tool and significant impetus for restructuring schools — what is inspected is expected; what is tested is what is taught.
>
> *(Costa et al., 1992, p. 273.)*

The classroom teacher can start this process immediately by taking a closer look at assessment practices and by asking students to take a closer look at how they learn. After reassessment, there is the possibility of a **shift to a view of assessment and**

evaluation as an on-going collaborative process for students, teachers and parents.

If we are overwhelmed by the complexity and enormity of the shift, the "practical vision" will not be achieved. ... Most educators realize that new goals for the next century are essential (for survival) in that these need to drive the curriculum.

Such goals include:

- Capacity for continued learning,
- Knowing how to behave when answers to problems are not immediately apparent,
- Co-operativeness and team building,
- Precise communication in a variety of modes,
- Appreciation of disparate value systems,
- Problem-solving that requires creativity and ingenuity,
- Enjoyment of resolving ambiguous, discrepant, or paradoxical situations,
- Organization of an overabundance of technologically produced information,
- Pride in a well-crafted product,
- High self-esteem, and
- Personal commitment to larger organizational and global values.

(Costa et al., 1992, p. 275.)

Perhaps the best approach to the perceived barriers (knowing there are no definitive answers and wanting to move beyond feeling overwhelmed), is to pose a series of questions about the future as it relates to assessment and evaluation, and to attempt to see opportunities in these questions.

Key Questions

1. In the light of the overwhelming complexity of the demands on individual teachers concerning assessment, the key question seems to be: "How to go about it?"

    The simplistic (but realistic) answer would seem to be "one step at a time".

    ### Opportunity — METACOGNITIVE

    > To examine what we are doing, to acknowledge the problems, and to make systematic changes for improved practice is important and challenging. *The Numbers Game* is the most comprehensive study ever done of evaluation practices in Ontario. Information in this document provides a sound reference point for planning.

2. There are so many unclear (mixed) messages from the Ministry. How can clear communication be encouraged, established and maintained?

    ### Opportunity — COLLABORATION

    > The paradigm shift affects the system level the same way it affects the individual. There are valid reasons for the confusion and perhaps

the desire for clear "answers" is wrong-headed. Faced with "open-ended" questions, the need to consult and collaborate increases. This creates the opportunity to stress the need for **more** support and attention to teachers and education as the key to the future.

3. "There is a strong desire for feedback in any human endeavour. We want to know how well we did, if it worked, and we want to know the results. ... With new and more complex goals on the agenda, the question is: **How will we know that these new goals are being achieved?**" *(Costa et al., 1992, p. 273.)*

Opportunity — AUTHENTIC ASSESSMENT

Emphasis on achievement based on multiple, appropriate assessments that co-operatively involve students, teachers, parents and the broader community in the development of comprehensive achievement profiles should present a much clearer and more accurate picture of what individuals can do. Authentic assessment provides more and better information.

4. Won't the demand for greater variety of assessment strategies to assess more complex goals mean more marking?

Opportunity — APPROPRIATE EFFICIENT ASSESSMENT

At first, it is likely that greater time will be spent assessing students as teachers become comfortable with different techniques. Ultimately, with emphasis on assessing for learning, there is less need to "mark everything", so actual "marking loads" should diminish. Most formative assessment is done during class time in connection with the instruction. Marking for the sake of learning (marking appropriately) should lead to improved learning results.

5. We are being asked to challenge students to think, to co-operate, to work on authentic tasks. If we have to summarize and provide grades, how do we do it?

Opportunity — ATTACH MORE MEANING TO GRADES

The expectations of a summary grade is deeply ingrained. Rather than fight the demand, the challenge is to educate students, parents, the community, post-secondary institutions, some teachers and administrators away from this mind-set. Rather than reject grades, the best direction would seem to be to develop and adopt an assessment system that connects feedback to performance on an individual basis. This can be done by attaching more personal meaning to grades by linking them to specific learning outcomes.

If grades are presented in this light and the benefits of alternative assessment, evaluation and reporting methods are demonstrated, the "power" of grades might begin to wane.

6. If we become involved in interdisciplinary (integrated) activities, how do we evaluate them?

Opportunity — THE MOST SIGNIFICANT OUTCOME

"All teaching is for transfer. All learning is for transfer. It's that simple." *(Costa et al., 1992, p. 349.)*

The term transfer seems to be preferable to integration (see note below). Transfer leaves a clear subject base intact and encourages integration. Integration, in the narrow sense, does not leave a clear reference point in place. Transfer of learning — using what is learned in one context in an entirely new context — is perhaps the most important overall learning outcome (for now and for the future). Transfer of learning can be assessed using a continuum of transfer behaviour. (See Situational Dispositions Toward Transfer.)

(*Note:* Integration as it is referred to here is in the commonly misinterpreted narrow sense of a somewhat purposeless mixing of subjects. For the broader view of integration see: Robin Fogarty, *The Mindful School: How to Integrate the Curriculum*, 1990.)

	Situational Dispositions Toward Transfer	
SIMPLE	***Does the learner:***	**NEAR**
	OVERLOOK: Miss appropriate opportunities; persist in former ways?	
	DUPLICATE: Perform the drill exactly as practiced; duplicate with no change; copy?	
	REPLICATE: Tailor, but apply knowledge only in similar situations; produce work that all looks alike?	
	INTEGRATE: Become more aware; integrate; subtly combine knowledge with other ideas and situations; use information with raised consciousness?	
	MAP: Carry a strategy to another content and into life situations; associate?	
COMPLEX	INNOVATE: Invent; take ideas beyond the initial conception; take risks; diverge?	**FAR**

(Costa et al., 1992, p. 350.)

School of 2001

The following chart points to the school of 2001 and emphasizes the difference a decade could make.

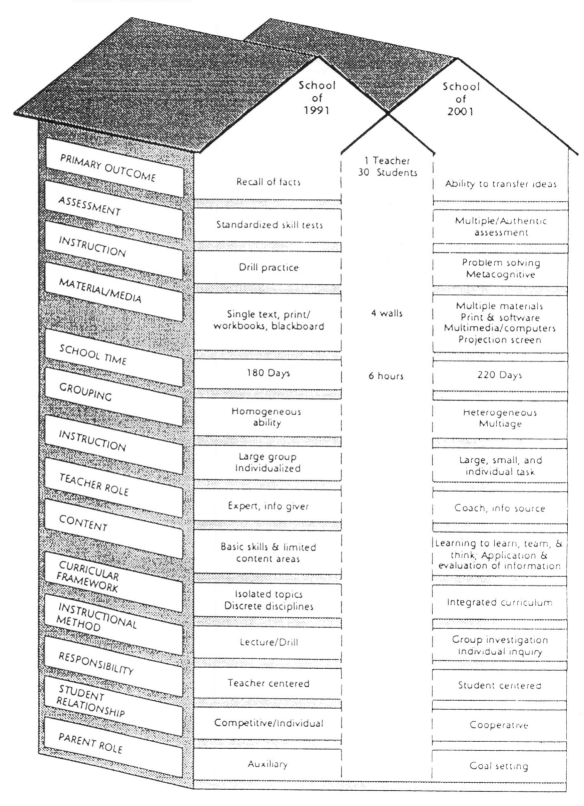

	School of 1991		School of 2001
		1 Teacher 30 Students	
PRIMARY OUTCOME	Recall of facts		Ability to transfer ideas
ASSESSMENT	Standardized skill tests		Multiple/Authentic assessment
INSTRUCTION	Drill practice		Problem solving Metacognitive
MATERIAL/MEDIA	Single text, print/ workbooks, blackboard	4 walls	Multiple materials Print & software Multimedia/computers Projection screen
SCHOOL TIME	180 Days	6 hours	220 Days
GROUPING	Homogeneous ability		Heterogeneous Multiage
INSTRUCTION	Large group Individualized		Large, small, and individual task
TEACHER ROLE	Expert, info giver		Coach, info source
CONTENT	Basic skills & limited content areas		Learning to learn, team, & think; Application & evaluation of information
CURRICULAR FRAMEWORK	Isolated topics Discrete disciplines		Integrated curriculum
INSTRUCTIONAL METHOD	Lecture/Drill		Group investigation Individual inquiry
RESPONSIBILITY	Teacher centered		Student centered
STUDENT RELATIONSHIP	Competitive/Individual		Cooperative
PARENT ROLE	Auxiliary		Goal setting

(Costa et al, 1992, p. 164.)

The Future, Now

Case Example: *(adapted from Costa et al, 192, pp. 161–162)*

> Pat Taylor teaches geometry in a multi-age, heterogeneous secondary classroom in Chesterfield County, Virginia. Unlike her colleagues, who teach a sequence of chapters from the text, Taylor integrates geometry concepts such as "circles" with the thinking skill "estimating," and co-operative learning strategies.
>
> Using manipulatives to help her multi-ability and multi-age students grasp the meanings of radius, circumference, and pi as these relate to estimation of circle size, Taylor guides her students through a variety of hands-on tasks.
>
> At the formal lesson's end, each of Taylor's students return to a computer terminal to demonstrate the ability to solve abstract algorithms and apply the new concepts with a variety of visual and abstract software-generated estimation problems, and assess the quality of their problem-solving.

NOW: The first part of this example describes a real lesson taught in the integrated instructional style the teacher uses throughout the year.

FUTURE: The last part (the last two sequences) presents the desirable direction for the future.

This example emphasizes the fact that the shift to instruction for the next century will require two essential changes:

1. Each classroom will need the electronic tools to extend and simplify both curriculum and instruction.

2. Each classroom will need a teacher trained with the skills to manage integrated instruction and integrated curricula for all students without regard to ability, race, talent, special needs, or motivation.

There are three predictable barriers to these essential changes:

1. Inadequate hardware and software

2. Inadequate staff development (every teacher needs the opportunity to be a life-long learner)

3. A prevailing split view of education (in general terms, basic skills,/ complex thinking — in assessment, evaluation and grading terms, sorting/learning.)

Conclusions

It is very difficult to summarize the mass of information and ideas presented in this book but we feel that it would be helpful to teachers to conclude with a few recommendations on which they can focus as they seek to become reflective practitioners in classroom assessment.

1. Use a variety of assessment methodologies to meet the needs of all students.

2. Match assessment approaches with outcomes/purposes — this will mean more use of performance assessment and less use of paper and pencil "tests".

3. Provide models (or exemplars), feedback, reteaching and second (or multiple) chance assessment.

4. Develop clear criteria (with student involvement) and base grading and reporting on these criteria. This will result in grades with meaning (achievement only) and require expanded format reporting (other valued attributes — e.g. effort, participation, etc.)

5. Emphasize self-assessment — this can be done effectively through the use of portfolios, response journals and student-led parent-teacher conferences.

> What is needed is more appropriate assessment, not more assessment. If the above recommendations are followed we believe that teachers truly can
>
> ## *"Assess for Success"*.

> "The true measure of a school's success is the narrowness of the gap between the highest and lowest achievers."
>
> *(Wiggins, **Educational Leadership**, Feb. 1991.)*

References

Costa, Bellanca, and Fogarty, If Minds Matter: A Foreword to the Future, Volume Two, Skylight Publishing, Palatine, Illinois, 1992.

The following articles contained in this volume are particularly useful.

"Classroom 2001: Evolution, Not Revolution", James Bellanca.

"Reassessing Assessment", Costa and Kallick.

"The Most Significant Outcome", Fogarty.

Annotated References

Detailed reference lists are found at the end of each chapter.

In many ways this resource book is a compilation of material from a wide variety of sources. Listed below are the resources which the authors drew upon most heavily and/or those which they believe will be most helpful to educators who wish to examine the topics of assessment, evaluation and reporting in more depth.

1. Bonstingl, John Jay, <u>Schools of Quality: An Introduction to Total Quality Management in Education</u>, 1992, ASCD, Alexandra VA.

   This book summarizes the most important aspects of Total Quality Management as it relates to education. It also provides a history of the Total Quality Movement in Japan and the United States.

2. Bennett, Barrie, Rolheiser-Bennett, Carol and Stevahn, Laurie; <u>Co-operative Learning: Where Heart Meets Mind</u>, 1991, Educational Connections, Toronto.

   This book provides a wealth of information about the elements of co-operative learning and its implementation. In particular, it has a 71 page chapter on "Evaluating Social and Academic Learning".

3. Brandt, Ronald S., (Ed), <u>Performance Assessment, Readings from Educational Leadership</u>, 1992, ASCD, Alexandria VA.

   This book is a collection of a number of the best articles about assessment which have been published in this influential journal over the last few years.

4. Costa Arthur, Bellanca, James and Fogarty, Robin, (Eds), <u>If Minds Matter: A Foreword to the Future, Volume 2</u>, 1992, Skylight, Palatine, IL.

   A collection of articles focused on the key role of thinking; its contents can be best summarized by listing the three sections of the book: Creating the Thoughtful Classroom, Creating Cooperative Learners and Assessing Significant Outcomes.

5. Davies, Anne, Cameron, Caren, Politano, Colleen and Gregory, Kathleen; <u>Together is Better: Collaborative Assessment, Evaluation and Reporting</u>, 1992, Peguis Publishers, Winnipeg.

   Based on practice in school districts in British Columbia this book describes what the authors call three way reporting. The emphasis is on including the student in assessment, evaluation and reporting in a way which promotes learning. The book contains many blackline masters for teachers to use.

6. Educational Leadership.

    Many issues of this excellent journal have articles on assessment. The May 1992 issue focusses on performance assessment.

7. Gronlund, Norman E. and Linn, Robert L., Measurement and Evaluation in Teaching, 6th Edition, 1990, Macmillan, New York.

    A classic academic textbook which introduces teachers to those elements of measurement and evaluation that are essential to good teaching.

8. Herman, Joan L., Aschbacher, Pamela R. and Winter Lynn; A Practical Guide to Alternative Assessments, 1992, ASCD, Alexandria VA.

    The authors provide clear guidance on the creation and use of alternative measures of student achievement. The model they present links assessment with instruction and is based on contemporary theories of learning.

9. Lincoln County Board of Education, Growing Collaboratively, 1993, Prentice-Hall, Scarborough.

    This book provides an overview of collaborative learning theory and practical guidance on implementing collaborative group learning. It includes one excellent chapter on evaluation.

10. Making the Grade, 1987, Prentice Hall, Scarborough.

    A very influential book that has a great deal of useful information on evaluation techniques (especially paper and pencil techniques) and how they can be modified for special needs and diverse learners.

11. Ministry of Education, Ontario, Junior Division Science: Assessment Planning (OAIP), 1993, Toronto.

    Although this is a junior division resource it has a wealth of material that can be applied practically in Science (and other subjects) throughout the intermediate and senior divisions.

12. National Council of Teachers of Mathematics, Curriculum and Evaluation Standards for School Mathematics, 1989, NCTM, Reston, VA.

    This document contains a set of standards for mathematics curricula (K–12) in North American schools and for evaluating the quality of both the curriculum and student achievement.

13. Peel Board of Education, Looking at Measurement: More Than Just Marks, 1989–90; Book 1 – Objective Tests; Book 2 – Essay Tests; Book 3 – Standardized Tests as Part of an Overall Student Achievement Profile; Book 4 – Adapting Tests and Assignments for Exceptional Students; Book 5 – Teacher as Observer: Beyond the Paper and Pencil Test.

    This excellent series of handbooks are very clearly described by their titles. Each book has a great deal of practical information for teachers to use.

14. Phi Delta Kappan.

    Many issues of this excellent journal have articles on assessment; e.g. the February 1993 issue has a special section on Authentic Assessment.

15. Saskatchewan Education, Student Evaluation: A Teacher Handbook, 1991, Saskatchewan Education, Regina.

    This book is designed as a workbook for teachers to examine and develop their assessment and evaluation strategies. It is very well organized and has many practical suggestions and forms for teachers to use.

16. Schurr, Sandra, The ABC's of Evaluation: 26 Alternative Ways to Assess Student Progress, 1992, National Middle School Association, Columbus, OH.

    Although written for Grades 6 to 8, this book provides belief statements and research about evaluation which form the basis for 26 practical approaches to alternative assessment. Examples from many subjects are included in the book.

17. Spady, William G., "Shifting the Grading Paradigm that Pervades Education", Outcomes, Volume unknown, pp. 39–45.

    The guru of outcomes-based education provides his insightful analysis of how grading affects education and how he believes it should be changed to enhance student learning.

18. Stenmark, Jean Kerr (Ed), Mathematics Assessment, Myths, Models, Good Questions and Practical Suggestions, 1991, NCTM, Reston, VA.

    A refreshing view of how assessment in the most traditional subject can be expanded to improve the understanding of mathematics. Many of the ideas in this book could be applied in other subjects.

19. Waterloo County Board of Education, Assessment for Learning in the Transition Years and the Specialization Years, 1993, Waterloo County Board of Education, Kitchener, ON.

    This is a very practical handbook for teachers. It is very well designed and it has many valuable strategies and forms for teachers to use.

20. Worthen, B. et al, Measurement and Evaluation in the Schools, 1993, Longman, London.

    A new academic text with a very comprehensive treatment of measurement and evaluation.

Glossary

Key Terms

Assessment: the process of gathering information about students or program

Evaluation: the process of integrating information from many sources and using it to make judgments about students or program (Answers the question — "How good?")

Measurement: the process of obtaining a numerical description of some characteristic (Answers the question — "How much?")

Marks (Marking): the number (or letter) "score" given to any student test or performance

Grade (Grading): the number (or letter) reported at the end of a period of time as a summary statement of student performance

Reporting: the process of communicating the results of measurement, assessment and evaluation

---

Criterion-referenced: evaluation in relation to a student's success in meeting stated objectives, outcomes, expectations or criteria

Norm-referenced: evaluation in relation to other students within a class or across classes/schools or a segment of a population

Self-referenced: evaluation in relation to a student's own performance at different points in time

---

Diagnostic: evaluation designed to determine a student's attitude, skills or knowledge in order to identify specific student needs

Formative: evaluation designed to take place during instruction and which is used to provide direction for improvement and adjustment to a program for individual students and for a whole class

Summative: evaluation designed to be used at the end of a unit or prescribed period of time to inform the student and the teacher about the extent of student learning progress (relative to the learning outcomes of the course of instruction)

Additional Terms

achievement: the demonstration of student performance

analytic scoring: scoring based on separate scores for specific components of a "performance"

authentic assessment: gathering information about a task which is genuine and occurs in a real-life context

benchmark: a point of reference which can serve as a standard against which judgments are made

holistic scoring: scoring based upon an overall impression. This type of scoring is usually based on a carefully prepared rating scale

mastery learning: a strategy which permits students to achieve mastery by adjusting learning time for each student based upon individual need

outcome: an observable result as demonstrated by a student's knowledge, skill or values

peer assessment: reflective practise in which students make observations about their peers' performance

process assessment: gathering information which focuses on the process of learning

product assessment: gathering information which focuses on the specific end result of a learning process

rubric: a set of guidelines for giving scores; it should state all the dimensions being assessed with clear performance criteria and a rating scale

self assessment: reflective practice in which a student makes observations about their own performance

standardized tests: a form of measurement that has been normed against a specific population (usually by age or grade level)

Appendices

Appendix 1. Student Essay on Evaluation

> "A grade is an inadequate report on an inaccurate judgment by a biased and variable judge on the extent to which a student has attained an undefined level of mastery of an indefinite amount of material."
>
> *(Anonymous)*

These words entered my life on a single sheet of paper a few weeks ago. On that one little eight and a half by eleven inch page all of my anxieties about grading had been summed up in one sentence. All that the words need now is a little evidence to give them some weight. The value of the grade is an important issue for, sadly, it has been directly equated to intelligence. If the grade does in fact fall under suspicion, then our entire basis for recognizing intelligence is flawed! And if this is so then we should be worried, for the questions of who we have lost, who we may lose in the future, and who is succeeding in society today must be re-examined.

Let us begin with the biased and variable judge, or the teacher. Ideally the teacher's role is to occupy a classroom in which they instruct nearly two hundred students a year in given fields of interest. As the teacher is a specialist in his field he is able to judge each of the two hundred students' aptitudes fairly. This process continues day in and day out for years of the teacher's life. Wouldn't it be nice if the human race was so clear minded that they could make an objective judgment? Unfortunately this is not so. There are numerous other aspects of the student that influence a teacher's judgment. For example, it is a proven fact that students who speak out in class receive a higher grade than those who remain quiet. Then of course there is the Pygmalion effect. Studies show that if a teacher believes that a class is gifted, the students' grades will be higher. The scary thing is that it works the other way as well. I wonder how far this bias goes? I'm sure that leather jackets and heavy metal music do not generally go down well with many teachers. I mean Satan and school do not usually go well together. What about the way a student speaks, or racial reference, why not hair color? Two hundred students a year leave a lot of room for bias.

The grade given by the teacher represents how well that child performed in the system. It is generally accepted, however, that people learn and express themselves in different ways. The grade caters to one way of learning. Surely intelligence should not have to conform to any given structure to prove itself. So then what happens to those who cannot function within the system? They are displaced from learning. They are placed in easier courses when all that they need is to have their intelligence challenged in a different way. Ultimately they get bored because they are denied access to the knowledge that it is their right to have.

The examination is a tool used by the system to measure intelligence. Now there is an interesting concept. I wonder what would happen if someone went to an important business meeting without notes to refer to, and without knowing what was going to be on the agenda. Naturally, the person would lose the account. And yet a student goes through this unnatural process at every exam. The examination does not measure a student's ability to learn in any practical sense of the word, but merely their ability to write examinations. Its only practical purpose is to prepare a student for the continuing artificial world of academics. The examination gives rise to an entirely new set of the three R's: Recalling, Reciting, and Regurgitating. These three learning processes are the basis for the majority of high school education.

A really frightening aspect of grading is the competition that it promotes. Is that the kind of environment we want for learning? The answer is no. Learning should be a cooperative, shared experience where students explore interests and dreams together. Competition should remain in economics, government, and athletics. In learning it is nothing more than a disease.

Albert Einstein was a marvelous man. $E=mc^2$ says it all. It is interesting to consider the fact that he was a high school dropout. It makes you wonder doesn't it. Einstein is an icon of the scientific world. It's just too bad that he's not intelligent. His experience is not an isolated incident either. I have known many "stupid" people who have had fantastic insights into life. It works the other way as well. I've known many "intelligent" people whose interest in life does not stretch beyond what they learned in school. It is sad to think of the Einsteins we've lost. It's scary to think who might be in their place.

I can sense fear in people's eyes as they read these words. They're saying, "If we don't have grades how are we going to know who's best for jobs or who should go to university?" Well in the first place, you cannot deny that mother high school has given birth to a lot of incompetent A's. Success in high school does not always mean that a student is prepared for whatever may lie ahead. I mean look on the simplest level. Universities are crying out that first year students cannot write essays. Now what if students submitted portfolios of their work instead of grades? There's hard core proof of the student's capabilities. I can sense eyes popping again, "Do you know how much work that would be? Universities don't have the time to wade through all those essays." Well all I can say to that is fair is fair. It is a small sacrifice for truth.

I do not claim that extensive educational reform will be easy. Removing the grade is the necessary first step to a number of changes that must take place. The fear is that education cannot change without affecting the rest of the social structure. Such is the nature of a hegemonic society. But if social structure caters to this unfair division of its citizens, then we should not fear the change that must follow. For any change that is based on truth, and obliterates inequality should be embraced.

So what does the grade measure anyway? Does it measure the student's ability to learn? I don't think so. It measures the new three R's, and it measures attendance, good behaviour and proper dress. Overall, I'd say that the grade has nothing to do with a student's intelligence, but merely their ability to conform to, and function within a prescribed structure to achieve an irrelevant goal.

(HUW – Student)

Teacher Response

"Ideally, a <u>grade</u> is an adequate report of an accurate judgment by an unbiased and knowledgeable judge on the extent to which a student has attained a clearly defined level of mastery of clearly outlined learning outcomes."

Appendix 2: OSSTF Principles on Evaluation

OSSTF supports accountability in education.

- Evaluation/assessment are two strategies that can help achieve accountability.

  Definitions:

  - Evaluation is the process of integrating information from many different sources and using it in decision-making about students.
  - Assessment refers to the task of gathering information about students using a variety of tools and techniques.

OSSTF believes:

- that different evaluation systems are needed for individual students, systems and programs;

- that teachers are the prime agents of evaluation for the individual student in their charge;

- that evaluation policies must be developed with input from all partners in learning — students, educators, parents, community;

- that the teaching profession, through Federation representation, must be directly involved at all stages and at all levels of discussion in the planning, development, implementation and reporting aspects of province-wide evaluation/assessment systems.

- that province-wide testing should be directed towards assessment of the system leading to educational changes for improved quality education.

Further:

These principles must serve as the basis for a comprehensive program of professional development on evaluation for Ontario teachers and educators.

Appendix 3: Principles Underlying Assessment and Evaluation

1. **Assessment of student learning is an integral component of Ontario curriculum and effective classroom practice.**

   Assessment must be based on clear statements of expected outcomes. To be effective, assessment and evaluation must be a continuous and ongoing process involving the individual student and his or her peers, teachers, and parents.

Teachers will use the results of the evaluation of student achievement to assess the effectiveness of programs and their classroom practices, and to make modifications in these practices that will enable all students to achieve the intended outcomes. The results of the evaluation of student achievement will also form the basis of reports concerning student progress.

2. Teachers need to employ a wide variety of assessment methods that are consistent with the instructional approaches used and appropriate for describing student achievement.

Teachers need to use both quantitative and qualitative methods of assessment in order to reflect the breadth, depth, and complexity of the learning outcomes of the common curriculum. These methods should encompass all aspects of student learning and should be appropriate for the ages and levels of maturity of the students. The use of a variety of methods and procedures has the added benefit of giving students a range of opportunities for demonstrating their progress.

3. The evaluation and reporting of student achievement is the task of the teacher, who must consider the special requirements of individual students and work in consultation with them and their parents.

Evaluating the effectiveness of students' learning and choosing assessment tools that are appropriate to what is being evaluated require the application of professional judgment. At the same time, it must be recognized that all assessment and evaluation activities have a subjective dimension. For this reason, it is particularly important that teachers tailor their assessment methods to the particular requirements and circumstances of individual students. This means taking into account their cultural, linguistic, and socio-economic backgrounds, as well as their special needs and abilities. The use of a variety of appropriate assessment activities on an ongoing basis will ensure that all these requirements are accommodated, and that a comprehensive record of student progress and achievement is maintained.

It is important that teachers solicit and consider the views of students and parents when making decisions about students' requirements.

4. The evaluation of school programs should effect improvement and should be based on school board and provincial standards.

Teachers and principals will determine the overall effectiveness of programs by evaluating students' results with reference to the performance of all the students in the program within the school, in other schools of the board, and in relation to the standards established in the provincial benchmarks. This process will ensure that achievement of standards is monitored and reported as objectively as possible. The information obtained will be used to improve programs and will have the effect of enhancing student achievement by promoting high standards in all areas of learning and teaching.

Provincial review procedures will provide information on student achievement which can be assessed in relation to provincial benchmark standards in some areas of the curriculum.

*(Ministry of Education and Training, **The Common Curriculum, Grades 1–9**, February 1993, pp. 8–9.)*

Appendix 4: Checklist for Excellence in Assessment

The items below are based on best practices in assessment. The checklist can be used to look at current practices in your school and to jointly set new goals with parents and community groups.

Vision of Learning

❑ Meaningful learning experiences for students and school staff

❑ Students encouraged to make decisions about their learning and to assess their own performance

❑ Restructuring to promote learning in and out of school

❑ High expectations for learning for all students

❑ A community of problem solvers in the classroom and in the school

❑ Teachers and administrators committed to achieving the national education goals

Curriculum and Instruction

❑ Identification of core concepts

❑ Curriculum that calls for a comprehensive repertoire of learning and assessment strategies

❑ Collaborative teaching and learning involving student-generated questioning and sustained dialogue among students and between students and teachers

❑ Teachers assessing to build new information on student strengths

❑ Authentic tasks in the classroom such as solving everyday problems, collecting and analyzing data, investigating patterns, and keeping journals

❑ Opportunities for students to engage in learning and assessment out of school with community members

❑ Homework that is challenging enough to be interesting but not so difficult as to cause failure

❑ Assessments that respect multiple cultures and perspectives

❑ A rich learning environment with places for children to engage in sustained problem solving and self assessment

❑ Instruction that enables children to develop an understanding of the purposes and methods of assessment

❑ Opportunities for children to decide performance criteria and method

Assessment and Grouping

- ❏ Assessment that informs and is integral to instruction
- ❏ Assessment sessions that involve the teacher, student, and parents
- ❏ Performance-based assessment such as portfolios that include drafts, journals, projects, and problem-solving logs
- ❏ Multiple opportunities to be involved in heterogeneous groupings, especially for students at risk
- ❏ Public displays of student work and rewards
- ❏ Methods of assessing group performance
- ❏ Group assessments of teacher, class, and school

Staff Development

- ❏ Opportunities for teachers to attend conferences and meetings on assessment
- ❏ Teachers as researchers, working on research projects
- ❏ Teacher or school partnerships/projects with colleges and universities
- ❏ Opportunities for teachers to observe and coach other teachers
- ❏ Opportunities for teachers to try new practices in a risk-free environment

Involvement of the Community

- ❏ Community members' and parents' participation in assessing performance as experts, aides, guides, or tutors
- ❏ Active involvement of community members on task forces for curriculum, staff development, assessment, and other areas vital to learning
- ❏ Opportunities for teachers and other school staff to visit informally with community members to discuss the life of the school, resources, and greater involvement of the community

Policies for Students at Risk

- ❏ Students at risk integrated into the social and academic life of the school
- ❏ Policies/practices to display respect for multiple cultures and role models
- ❏ A culture of fair assessment practices